Through WIND AND WAVES

Through WIND AND WAVES

On Being a Spiritual Guide

FRANCIS FERNÁNDEZ-CARVAJAL

 Scepter

CONTENTS

"Life is like a voyage on the sea of history, often dark and stormy, a voyage in which we watch for the stars that indicate the route. The true stars of our life are the people who have lived good lives. They are lights of hope. Certainly, Jesus Christ is the true light, the sun that has risen above all the shadows of history. But to reach him we also need lights close by—people who shine with his light and so guide us along our way."

— POPE BENEDICT XVI, *Spe Salvi,* NO. 49

INTRODUCTION

Someone setting out to scale a high mountain first takes care to prepare everything needed to reach the peak: equipment, maps, provisions. . . . And if the peak is especially challenging, a person who knows the best route to the top will be sought out, someone who is familiar with all the dangers and risks. Without the help of such a guide, the climb would often prove impossible. Similarly, someone about to set sail on uncharted waters in a small sailboat—without knowledge of the reefs, the storms, the days without wind—would be in great peril.

We have all been called to scale the highest summit and to set out into the deep: *Duc in altum.* We have been called to the summit of God's love. And no endeavor is more noble than that of striving to climb those heights and helping others to do so—or to reach a safe harbor after many perils. The supernatural life, while always the work of the Holy Spirit, ordinarily requires the cooperation of another person who acts as a guide—a task often called spiritual direction or spiritual accompaniment. This centuries-old practice in the Church "contributes to forming consciences. Today there is a greater need than in the past," Pope Benedict XVI insisted, "for wise and holy 'spiritual teachers.' This important ecclesial service requires an inner vitality that must be implored as a gift from the Holy Spirit in intense and prolonged prayer, and a special training that must be acquired with care."[1]

God, who acts in so many different ways, wanted to guide the Magi through the words of a human being. When the star

---

1. Pope Benedict XVI, Message to the Apostolic Penitentiary, March 12, 2009.

that had guided them from a distant land disappeared and they found themselves in darkness, the Magi did what common sense dictated: they asked someone who should know where the king of the Jews had been born.[2] And Christ Jesus, Lord of all creation, cured the sick in the way he considered best: some he cured from a distance; others, by stages, like the blind man St. John speaks of (see Jn 9:1), while he also cured many people directly, or with the help of the Apostles.

Similarly, in St. Paul's conversion our Lord made use of a disciple: "What shall I do?" Paul asked (Acts 22:10). And Jesus replied: "Rise, and go into Damascus, and there you will be told all that is appointed for you to do." Jesus did not reveal his plans to Paul directly. Rather he chose one of the first Christians, Ananias, asking him to cure the new Apostle's blindness and make known to him the mission he was to carry out. In both the Old and New Testaments we see the great confidence God places in those he entrusts with the mission of guiding others, sometimes asking them to lead souls to very high peaks.[3]

St. Francis de Sales calls the mission of guiding others "the most important of all words of advice."[4] St. Gregory the Great

---

2. "But we Christians have no need to go to Herod nor to the wise men of this world. Christ has given his Church sureness in doctrine and a flow of grace in the sacraments. He has arranged things so that there will always be people to guide and lead us, to remind us constantly of our way" (St. Josemaría Escrivá, *Christ Is Passing By* [New York: Scepter, 1974], no. 34).

3. "The Holy Spirit gives to certain of the faithful the gifts of wisdom, faith, and discernment for the sake of this common good which is prayer (spiritual direction). Men and women so endowed are true servants of the living tradition of prayer. According to St. John of the Cross, the person wishing to advance toward perfection should 'take care into whose hands he entrusts himself, for as the master is, so will the disciple be, and as the father is, so will the son be.' And further: 'In addition to being learned and discreet a director should be experienced. . . . If the spiritual director has no experience of the spiritual life, he will be incapable of leading into it the souls whom God is calling to it, and he will not even understand them'" (*Living Flame of Love*, stanza 3; see CCC, 2690).

4. St. Francis de Sales, *Introduction to the Devout Life*, 1, 4.

says it is "the art of arts" (*ars artium*)[5] that requires a special prudence and spiritual refinement. "It is a well-tried means and has lost none of its value,"[6] Bl. John Paul II insisted. And he called for a rediscovery of this practice, which can do so much good to souls and to the whole Church.[7]

The saints too sought a guides for their interior lives. They never felt safe following their own criteria and asked others for light. St. John of the Cross warned: "He who wants to stand alone without the support of a master and guide will be like the tree that stands alone in a field without a proprietor. No matter how much the tree bears, passersby will pick the fruit before it ripens." In contrast, "a tree that is cultivated and guarded through the care of its owner produces its fruit at the expected time." And the saint concludes: "The virtuous soul that is alone and without a master is like a lone burning coal; it will grow colder rather than hotter."[8] This has been the constant teaching of those who have attained the summit of sanctity. Spiritual

5. St. Gregory the Great, *Pastoral Rules*, 1, 1, 3, PL 77. John Paul II recalled this classic expression of St. Gregory—*ars artium*—in a letter dated July 28, 1990, on the occasion of the 14th Centennial of St. Gregory the Great. Shortly afterwards he repeated it in an address on the teachings of St. Alphonse Liguori.

6. Bl. John Paul II, *Pastores Dabo Vobis*, no. 81, April 7, 1992.

7. "It is necessary," Bl. John Paul II pointed out, "to rediscover the great tradition of personal spiritual guidance which has always brought great and precious fruits to the Church's life" (*Pastores Dabos Vobis*, no. 40). And he goes on to say that although this spiritual practice could, in particular circumstances, be allied to others forms of assistance, it can *never be replaced* (Ibid.). In the same document (no. 81) citing Cardinal Montini, the future Pope Paul VI, he stressed how fruitful this practice has always been in the Church: "Spiritual direction has a wonderful purpose. We could say it is indispensable for the moral and spiritual education of young people who want to find what their vocation in life is and follow it wherever it may lead, with utter loyalty. It retains its beneficial effect at all stages of life, when in the light and affection of a devout and prudent counsel one asks for a check on one's own right intention and for support in the generous fulfillment of one's own duties. It is a very delicate but immensely valuable psychological means. It is an educational and psychological art calling for deep responsibility in the one who practices it. Whereas for the one who receives it, it is a spiritual act of humility and trust."

8. St. John of the Cross, *The Collected Works of St. John of the Cross* (Washington, D.C.: Institute of Carmelite Studies, 1991).

direction has been a practice found in the Church from the first centuries right up to the present. The Second Vatican Council exhorted priests to "have a high regard for spiritual direction."[9]

Those who accompany others on the spiritual path provide advice in many different areas: expanding horizons, helping souls form sound Christian criteria at work, in their family environment, and amid daily difficulties. . . . In moments of discouragement or special challenges, when the path seems steeper, they will provide a word of encouragement or advice that gives strength. They will warn of the obstacles in the interior life, so that souls do not impede the action of grace. They will point out the best path to grow in God's love and prudently correct any possible deviations that may result along the way. They will encourage souls in the interior struggle and help them to be leaven in the midst of the world, right where God has placed them. And, like the Master, those who guide others will never "break a bruised reed or quench a smoldering wick" (Mt 12:20). Rather, they will strengthen the one who is weak and rekindle the one whose fire seems to have died out. And they will never consider anyone as irretrievable.

Pope Benedict XVI, in his June 16, 2009, letter convoking the Year for Priests, pointed to the example of the Curé of Ars, who "dealt with different penitents in different ways. . . . To those who . . . came to him already desirous of and suited to a deeper spiritual life, he flung open the abyss of God's love, explaining the untold beauty of living in union with him and dwelling in his presence: 'Everything in God's sight, everything with God, everything to please God . . . How beautiful it is!' And he taught them to pray: My God, grant me the grace to love you as much as I possibly can."

There also is the possibility that someone who knows himself to be of little value will have to guide others who are far advanced

---

9. Vatican II Decree *Presbyterorum Ordinis,* 18.

on the path of sanctity. But if the necessary spiritual means are employed, there is no need to fear directing those who are more refined in their relationship with God and are already very close to him. The Holy Spirit always grants his light, and the one who guides others can always count on receiving many graces.

Truly to help souls advance, we have to be convinced of God's goodness. He doesn't want anyone to live a mediocre life. He calls all men and women "to a Christian life, to a life of holiness, to a chosen life, to life eternal."[10] Our Lord has created us in such a way that "our spirit and our heart are forever reaching out to the infinite, into eternity. Only in God can we find peace. Our mind strives for boundless knowledge; our heart seeks incessantly for a beloved who will endlessly and completely fulfill its longing. Our short little joys on earth forever aspire to merge in unbounded happiness."[11] And this is true of all souls. St. Teresa of Avila, after stressing that the struggle for holiness is grounded on God's help, and hence the importance of being humble, warns of the danger of a false humility that is short on desire and low in aspirations.

The saint says regarding true humility: "It is necessary that we know what this humility is like. I believe that the devil harms people who practice prayer and prevents them from advancing by causing them to misunderstand humility. He makes it appear to us that it's pride to have great desires and want to imitate the saints and long to be martyrs. Then he tells us or causes us to think that since we are sinners the deeds of the saints are for our admiration, not our imitation."[12] This false humility leads to spiritual mediocrity, so opposed to the true Christian vocation.

Pope Benedict XVI has highlighted the perennial value of this personal spiritual help, which greatly facilitates attaining the

---

10. St. Josemaría Escrivá, *The Forge* (New York: Scepter, 2002), no. 13.
11. Benedict Baur, *In Silence with God* (New York: Scepter, 1997), pp. 15–16.
12. St. Teresa of Avila, *The Book of Her Life* (Washington, D.C.: ICS Publications, p. 124), 13:4.

fullness of life and love for which every human heart longs. "I would like to add that the invitation to have recourse to a good spiritual father who can guide every individual to profound knowledge of himself and lead him to union with the Lord so that his life may be in ever closer conformity with the Gospel still applies for all priests, consecrated persons, and lay people, and especially youth. To go towards the Lord we always need a guide, a dialogue. We cannot do it with our thoughts alone. And this is also the meaning of the ecclesiality of our faith, of finding this guide."[13]

Personal spiritual guidance provides an ever-greater self-knowledge; it helps ensure that the means are proportionate to a person's real possibilities, and it suggests priorities. It would be a great mistake to disdain this help, which opens up to God's light corners of our soul still in darkness.[14]

In concluding these pages of introduction, the author feels the need to express his gratitude to St. Josemaría, whom he remembers with immense affection and who made such a deep impact on his own life. For many of the ideas expressed here, I am indebted to his teachings, which I heard from his lips and meditated on frequently.

FRANCIS F. CARVAJAL
June 11, 2010
Majadahonda, Madrid

---

13. Pope Benedict XVI, General Audience, September 16, 2009. In the *Guidelines for the Ministry and Life of Priests* (January 31, 1994), the Congregation for the Clergy urges priests "to carry out the ministry of spiritual direction. The discovery and spread of this practice, also outside of confession, is a great good for the Church today" (no. 54).

14. "Spiritual direction is a valuable help when trying to discern God's will. A prudent and wise spiritual guide who knows a person well can provide sincere advice with which to check one's own decisions, especially in questions where the general law does not provide enough information to decide among the options it permits. This spiritual guidance never implies letting up in one's own effort to discover God's voice clearly. Rather it humbly assists this effort without ever replacing the judgment, in some sense sacred, of the conscience" (*Diccionario de Teologia*, "Conscience," [Eunsa: Pamplona, 2006], pp. 155–156).

Chapter 1

QUALITIES OF A GOOD GUIDE

AN INSTRUMENT OF THE HOLY SPIRIT

The Holy Spirit acts ceaselessly in the interior life of a Christian who lives in his grace, but normally he also makes use of others to carry out his work. The marvels that a spiritual director may see should lead to the profound conviction of being merely God's instrument, which requires humility and docility. This supernatural conviction will protect against two possible temptations that nourish pride: the vanity of thinking that we can accomplish anything by ourselves and the false humility of viewing the task as totally beyond our ability.

God gives all the help required to those who carry out this work. St. Thomas' teaching is fulfilled to the letter in them: "God prepares those he chooses to carry out a mission in such a way that they are suited to carrying it out."[1] Grace makes them apt for this sensitive task that God entrusts to them.

The humility needed for directing others is shown by having continual recourse to the supernatural means. When our Lord sent his disciples out on an apostolic mission, he told

---

1. St. Thomas Aquinas, *Summa Theologica*, III, q. 27, a. 4.

them: "Take neither purse nor sack" (see Lk 10:4). The apostles well knew that all their effectiveness came from Jesus: the cures, the conversions, the miracles were due not to their own personal qualities, but to the Master's divine power. Years later, St. Paul repeats the same key truth: "Neither he who plants nor he who waters is anything, but only God who gives the growth" (1 Cor 3:7). By ourselves we can do nothing: we are simply servants, unworthy servants (Lk 17:10), incapable of carrying out the mission our Lord has entrusted to us.

Jesus often warned his disciples against trying to build upon anything so frail as their own human capacity. Rather, they were to rely on the strength provided by trusting in him. And during the years they spent accompanying him along the roads of Palestine, he gave the disciples many practical lessons in this regard. He strengthened their conviction that they could do nothing without his help, while showing them that they could accomplish everything by acting in his name and with his power. One day the Master left them alone in the middle of the Lake of Tiberius, in a situation where all their experience and skill at sea was of no use, and they were on the point of perishing. On another occasion, faced with a hungry crowd, they realized they were unable to meet the needs of so many people. When the disciples tried to free a possessed boy from the devil, Jesus allowed them to fail. And he allowed Peter to start sinking into the sea, until he himself stretched out his hand to him. Thus the apostles learned to trust in our Lord, and after passing through the hard trial of Calvary, they became the strong and secure pillars of all who would come afterwards.

The same process of trust and progressive abandonment in God has to be repeated, in one way or another, in all of Christ's followers, but especially in the priest or the person entrusted with the mission of spiritually guiding other faithful. At times, our Lord makes use of our very weaknesses and errors, so that we will have greater recourse to him and grow in humility. St. Augustine advised: "Become valleys [i.e., be humble] to receive the rain; the high places dry out, the low places are filled. Grace is like the rain."[2] The abundant water needed by others will arrive opportunely from heaven, if the one guiding them is humble.

Divine grace strengthens the human talents of the one who provides spiritual counsel and prepares the hearts of those who receive this advice. Therefore, this supernatural help is the first thing we must beseech God for, while also realizing that he does not want to dispense with our human help, just as he did not want to do without the few loaves and fishes available when feeding more than five thousand people.

Certainly, those who guide others spiritually have to be diligent in cultivating their own interior life and make use of the experience they have gained. But we should never lose sight of the fact that the foundation of this *ars artium* is God's constant help and his love for us—his burning "interest" that all men and women may come to share in his divine life. Therefore, because of the greatness of the mission and the continual need for God's help, spiritually guiding others requires a deep humility.

The Humility of Being "Only" an Instrument

When those guiding others set aside all presumption, as well as any false humility or cowardice, putting their talents at the service of others and beseeching God for his grace and light, then they are truly instruments of the Holy Spirit. And they aren't surprised if they feel more deeply from time to time their own deficiencies, as a brush would if it were aware of the great work of art it is helping to carry out. In these circumstances, when we realize we are not only of little worth but of no value at all in the face of what God is asking us to accomplish, we need

---

2. St. Augustine, *Sermon 131.*

to have ever more diligent recourse to the supernatural means: union with our Lord present in the Tabernacle, a more generous mortification. . . . This is especially true when we fail to see clearly the best path to lead a particular soul along, or when it seems that someone is not advancing despite all the advice we give. Then we have to recognize with all simplicity that we are "unsuitable instruments" and trust more in grace, being docile to the Holy Spirit's suggestions in prayer. For God sees further than we do, and he knows the possibilities each person has inside (Jn 2:35). But let us not forget that he also wants to count on us.

The humility of realizing one is *only an instrument* is also shown in the effort to lead others along the path the Holy Spirit wants, for he is the true guide of souls. If the brush is to be useful in the hands of the artist, it has to hold colors well and permit the tracing of broad or fine features, firm or gentler strokes. The brush has to self-effacingly place its own qualities at the disposal of the artist, who is the one creating the work of art. The artist energetically mixes shadows and lights, vivid tones with more subtle ones, until a harmonious and unified painting is produced. Moreover, the brush must be easy for the master's hand to grip; otherwise it will fail to faithfully transmit the impulses it receives, and no work of art will come about. Every good brush must have these qualities.

Therefore, being an instrument in accompanying others spiritually means faithfully transmitting God's spirit and not our own; it means helping the light of the Holy Spirit to reach souls, without personal attachments. Often we will see, with a noonday clarity, how our own capacity has no proportion to the supernatural fruit God is producing. We are truly "the brush in the hands of the artist."[3]

The humility of knowing oneself to be only an instrument leads paradoxically to the special strength that comes when one

---

3. Cf. St. Josemaría Escrivá, *The Way*, no. 612.

is not guided by merely human considerations. This is especially important when the person seeking spiritual help is older than oneself, or has greater experience in the supernatural life, or holds a measure of professional prestige. . . . Humility leads the spiritual counselor to take into account all the grace that God pours into souls, and to realize that one can prescribe the opportune medicine in each case, even in areas of the ascetical struggle that perhaps one has not yet conquered in oneself. Like a good doctor, he or she can cure others even when suffering from the same illness. "Can't a doctor who is sick cure others, even if his illness is chronic? Will his illness prevent him from prescribing proper treatment for other patients? Obviously not. In order to cure others, all he needs is to have the necessary knowledge and to apply it with the same concern as he would in his own case."[4]

However, a doctor would be unable to cure others if his own sickness were to get in the way of treating the patient's malady and prescribing the right remedies—that is, if he were to view as normal, because he himself suffers from it, what is also a grave infection in the one seeking help. In that case, his own sickness would become contagious. The doctor himself would need to "take a break," seek another specialist to heal his own illness, and send his patient to another doctor.

Rejecting Praise

The great "works of art" accomplished by helping others advance on the spiritual path should always be attributed to the Artist alone, and never to the "brush." A practical consequence of this is always rejecting, at least in one's heart, any praise received, immediately directing it to God.[5] Praise for the

---

4. St. Josemaría Escrivá, *Friends of God*, no. 161.
5. "Do we build monuments to an artist's paintbrush? Granted the brush had a part in creating masterpieces, but we give credit only to the painter" (St. Josemaría Escrivá, *Christ Is Passing By*, no. 1).

painting belongs to the painter, while the "brush" has the joy of assisting such a great master, and should never claim the merit for itself. It is not the cistern that the horses seek, but the water contained therein. What souls are seeking, although sometimes without realizing it, is God. At the triumphal entrance into Jerusalem, when the Jews laid down their cloaks and palm branches for the donkey to walk on, it was not the donkey being praised, but Jesus. "When I am paid a compliment," wrote the one who would later become John Paul I, "I must compare myself with the little donkey that carried Christ on Palm Sunday. And I say to myself: If that little creature, hearing the applause of the crowd, had become proud and had begun (jackass that he was) to bow his thanks left and right like a prima donna, how much hilarity he would have aroused! Don't act the same!"[6] If we aren't careful, we too can easily fall into this ridiculous pose.

Therefore the one who wants to be simply a good instrument never feels indispensable. If, for whatever reason, we have to discontinue guiding a particular soul, we should arrange for someone else to continue that work. It would be a bad sign if the person giving advice thought that *only he* knew how to help that person, and that *if he weren't there to do it*, a spiritual catastrophe would ensue.[7]

Anything good that comes from our hands has to be attributed in the first place to God, who "can make use of a wooden stick to draw water from a rock, or a little mud to give sight back to the blind."[8]

---

6. Albino Luciani, *Ilustrisimos Señores*, 2nd ed. (Madrid: BAC, 1978), pp. 59. Our role is to bring souls to Jesus. As St. Josemaría Escrivá says, Christ "makes do with a poor animal for a throne. I don't know about you; but I am not humiliated to acknowledge that in the Lord's eyes I am a beast of burden: 'I am like a donkey in your presence, but I am continually with you. You hold my right hand (Ps 72:23–24), you take me by the bridle'" (St. Josemaría Escrivá, *Christ Is Passing By*, no. 181).

7. A good spiritual director knows that whoever takes his place in that work will carry out that mission as well as he could, and probably better.

8. J. Pecci (Leo XIII), *La practica de la humildad*, (Madrid: Rialp, 1971) p.45.

We have to meditate deeply on our Lord's strong words: He who abides in me, and I in him, he it is that bears much fruit, for apart from me you can do nothing (Jn 15:5). If we strive to remain in him and let him act, we can be confident that we will bear fruit, and even *much fruit*, as our Lord promised. But let us never forget his concluding words: "apart from me you can do nothing."

It can happen that a person we have put a lot of care into helping in spiritual direction may sometimes say, out of gratitude: "How greatly you have helped me!" or "How well you have understood me!" The best reply is to teach that person to direct any gratitude to God alone, although sometimes, if this isn't the right moment, we will simply have to let it pass. As souls advance on the path to God, they will learn not to praise the one who is helping them; and they will come to distinguish gratitude, which is a Christian virtue, from fostering another person's pride.

Humility and High Goals

The humility of being God's instrument brings with it other consequences: the need to be united to our Lord in order to sustain our brothers or sisters; to strive not to fall so that the others don't stumble; to feel as one's own the struggle of those one is trying to bring closer to God; to let oneself be accompanied in one's own spiritual direction. . . . In short, the effort not to deprive others—by neglecting our own formation and failing to struggle to attain sanctity ourselves—of what they have a right to: good doctrine, an encouraging word to continue advancing, the cordial demands that "draw souls upward" and awaken them from a halfhearted and shortsighted struggle. Humility has nothing to do with being happy with "easy goals" in spiritual direction, whether in the guidance one receives or in that given to others.

St. Teresa lamented the possibility that a spiritual director might limit the great desires of souls to fly high. The saint warned against guides "that will teach them to be toads or that will be satisfied in merely showing them how to catch little lizards."[9] God calls all souls to fly very high, each in one's own situation and state in life; therefore the goals set have to be well-suited to each person, but always very high ones, since all men and women are called to intimacy with God amid the tasks of daily life. To do otherwise would be, in the words of the saint from Avila, to teach them "to be toads," to be happy being stuck to the ground, content "with catching little lizards," and never soaring heavenwards: because of little prayer and mortification, little or no Christian leaven brought to the family and to one's work, little effort to draw close to the Most Holy Humanity of our Lord and to the Holy Spirit, a particular examination of conscience[10] that sets very low supernatural goals. . . .

The person providing spiritual counsel has to be convinced that God does not want anyone to lead a mediocre life. He calls all souls "to a Christian life, to a life of holiness, to a chosen life, to life eternal."[11]

Asking for the Gift of Counsel

When we recognize that we are only instruments of the Holy Spirit in trying to help someone advance spiritually, we will be eager to ask for the *gift of counsel* in order to be docile to the Spirit's wishes, give the right advice, and decide quickly and surely. This gift of the Paraclete will give us, as it were, a "divine

---

9. St. Teresa, *Life*, 13, 3 (Carmelite translation, p. 124).

10. By means of the *particular examination of conscience*, one seeks the effective means for a very specific struggle. It is a brief but frequent examination during the day, on a specific and well-defined point. At times the particular examination may involve struggling against one's predominant defect. On other occasions the particular examination will be directed more towards advancing in a particular virtue.

11. St. Josemaría Escrivá, *The Forge*, no. 13.

instinct" to decide on the best path for the person in his or her particular circumstances. The Holy Spirit will inspire in the one giving guidance the right response and prepare the heart of the person being guided to receive it with profit.[12]

This is a gift that corresponds to the beatitude of the merciful, for mercy is required to discreetly discern how to give helpful advice to those who need it—advice which, far from discouraging them, will encourage them strongly yet gently to go forward on the path of sanctity.[13]

An excellent practice is to ask the Paraclete for his help before beginning that conversation of spiritual guidance, as many saints have done.

Personal Sanctity: Care for One's Own Interior Life

Bl. John Paul II insisted: "We need heralds of the Gospel who are experts in humanity, who know in depth the hearts of the men of today, who participate in their joys and hopes, concerns and sorrows, and at the same time are persons in love with God. For this, we need new saints."[14] These words have particular relevance for those who guide others in the Christian life, since they have a special need to be "experts in humanity" and to know "in depth the hearts of the men of today." Therefore, they have to be closely united to God and truly love the souls they are guiding, being men

---

12. A good practice is to invoke the Holy Spirit "especially in difficult cases, praying from one's heart the *Veni Sancte Spiritus* before resolving or deciding a case of importance, and, after having consulted with him, be careful to listen to the interior response with the docility of a child, in order to transmit it to the one you are directing. . . . In this way you will truly be an *instrument of the Holy Spirit*" (Adolphe Tanquerey, *The Spiritual Life: A Treatise on Ascetical and Mystical Theology* [Rockford, IL: TAN, 2001], no. 549).

13. Garrigou-Lagrange, *The Three Ages of the Interior Life*, vol. II (Rockford, IL: TAN, 1989), p. 88.

14. John Paul II, *Address to the Symposium of European Bishops*, October 11, 1985.

and women of prayer and of deep charity. Love for God gives the light needed to advance securely in the spiritual life.

A good priest once went to the Curé of Ars for advice about a complicated matter he could find no solution for.[15] The saint answered with a single word that cast great light on his question. The priest, amazed, asked the pastor of Ars where he had acquired so much knowledge. But St. John Vianney simply pointed to his kneeler, where he had so often gone to our Lord for help.

Bl. John Paul II, writing to priests, stressed the holy Curé of Ars' love for souls with words that are also very relevant for anyone who guides souls spiritually: "John Mary Vianney," recalled the Pontiff, "sanctified himself so as to be more able to sanctify others. Of course, conversion remains the secret of hearts, which are free in their actions, and the secret of God's grace. . . . But the results depend also on the dispositions of those who receive them [the sacraments], and these are greatly assisted by the personal holiness of the priest, by his perceptible witness, as also by the mysterious exchange of merits in the Communion of Saints. St. Paul said: 'In my flesh I complete what is lacking in Christ's afflictions for the sake of his body, that is, the church' (Col 1:24). St. Jean Marie Vianney in a sense wished to force God to grant these graces of conversion, not only by his prayer but also by the sacrifice of his whole life. He wished to love God for those who did not love him, and even to do the penance that they would not do. He was truly a pastor completely at one with his sinful people."[16]

A life of prayer and self-sacrifice is essential if one is to help others. "Since he lacks the light himself," wrote St. Teresa of Jesus about an ineffective guide, "he doesn't know how to enlighten others even though he may want to do so."[17] The

---

15. Procès de l'Ordinaire, p. 1495; cf. Francois Trochu, *The Curé d'Ars*, (Charlotte, NC: TAN, 2007) p. 287.

16. John Paul II, *Letter to Priests for Holy Thursday*, March 16, 1986, no. 11.

17. St. Teresa, *Life*, 13, 17 (Carmelite translation, p. 131).

experience gained by truly striving for sanctity oneself teaches the person guiding others what to say and how to say it. A life of sacrifice moderates one's words, making them both kindly and strong, and purifies one's intention. Any symptom of bitter zeal disappears, and the advice given becomes effective and convincing. Even if the one guiding others is quite young, personal sanctity will bring the special wisdom and maturity, imbued with understanding and strength, needed to help others. The words from the Psalm are then proven true: "I understand more than the aged, for I keep thy precepts" (Ps 119:100).[18] It is not age but rather love for God that is essential. Young people can therefore be very effective guides of souls.

Union with God leads to seeing the best in those we are guiding, since "just as you are, so also do others appear to you,"[19] wrote St. Augustine. When a person is close to our Lord, he or she more easily sees the positive qualities, the great possibilities that people have for sanctity and apostolate, and their capacity to begin again should a fall occur. But if one neglects one's own interior life, it is easy to focus on others' defects and mistakes. And thus it becomes difficult, and even impossible, "to draw souls upward" towards God.[20]

---

18. To be able to offer spiritual help requires maturity and prudence, "the moderation, fortitude, and sense of responsibility that many people acquire only after many years, in their old age." One acquires all this, even if still young, if one tries to live with "the supernatural outlook of a son of God. For he will give you, more than to the old, those qualities you need for your apostle's work" (cf. St. Josemaría Escrivá, *The Forge*, no. 53). Interior life and personal sanctity offset one's lack of experience. One understands then that "youth need not imply thoughtlessness, just as having grey hair does not necessarily mean that a person is prudent and wise" (St. Josemaría Escrivá, *Friends of God*, no. 54).

19. St. Augustine, *Expositions on the Psalms*, 34, 2, 10.

20. The good spiritual guide has a great responsibility to be close to our Lord, to grow continually in intimacy with him: "There are many people around you, and you have no right to be an obstacle to their spiritual good, to their eternal happiness. —You are under an obligation to be a saint. You must not let God down for having chosen you. Neither must you let those around you down: they expect so much from your Christian life" (St. Josemaría Escrivá, *The Forge*, no. 20).

Saints in Order to Sanctify

Caring for our own interior life is the best help we can give others.[21] Moreover, only when we strive to practice the virtues ourselves can we teach them to others effectively and see our words bear fruit. If we are enkindled with God's love, we will be able to enkindle others. Therefore, we need to acquire the "experimental" and practical science that no book contains, the personal sanctity that only the action of the Holy Spirit can bring about. This is what enables us to truly help others.[22] The word of God has to bear fruit first in our own life, the kind of fruit that we hope to see in the lives of others.[23]

To see the interior life grow in those one is helping will be the great spur for the interior struggle of the person guiding them. We must never forget that "whoever has the mission of saying great things, has an equal obligation to practice them."[24] The one guiding others will see with great clarity the need "to be a saint in order to sanctify," to obtain from God the graces others need, to offer sacrifices and make reparation for them. "For their sake I sanctify myself, that they also may be sanctified in truth," our Lord said (Jn 17:19). The spiritual director's own holiness should

---

21. Although in the following quote St. Alphonse Liguori refers to the practice of priests in confession, it is also valid for all who have the task of directing others spiritually: "Those good confessors who occupy themselves in the salvation of sinners will certainly have a great recompense and the assurance of heaven. St. James testifies to this with these words: 'Let him know that whoever brings back a sinner from the error of his way will save his soul from death and will cover a multitude of sins'" (Jas 5:20).

22. "Are you exercising the care of souls?" St. Charles Borromeo once asked in a talk to priests. And he went on to say: "Do not thereby neglect yourself. Do not give yourself to others to such an extent that nothing is left of you for yourself. You should certainly keep in mind the souls whose pastor you are, but without forgetting yourself. . . . Thus we will be able to overcome the difficulties we meet, countless as they are, each day. In any event, this is what is demanded of us by the task entrusted to us. If we act thus, we will find the strength to give birth to Christ in ourselves and in others" (cited in John Paul II, *Pastores Dabo Vobis*, no. 72).

23. Those guiding others are asked "to lead others by their deeds, and show them the path of life, by living it" (St. Gregory the Great, *Pastoral Rules*, 2, 3).

24. Ibid.

be a wall on which others can lean for support. But if the wall is weak, it will provide little support. Hence the responsibility to constantly seek strength from God, and to increase prayer and mortification when a special need arises: when someone is considering a complete self-giving to God, is going through a difficult moment, or finds the path especially steep.

The one guiding souls is like "a city set on a hill" or a lamp placed on a stand that gives light "to all in the house" (Mt 5:14, 15). All the souls entrusted to the spiritual director "live off," so to speak, his own love for God.[25] Being close to God, struggling to be a saint, will lead to a strong supernatural outlook shown in invoking the Holy Spirit frequently and asking for light, especially when beginning a conversation of spiritual direction, convinced that without God's help we would only be a hindrance; in the spirit of service with which one carries out this task; and in one's own self-giving and example, which will win abundant graces from God.

Bringing Souls Frequently to One's Prayer

The people we are guiding should be the frequent theme of our prayer. We need to speak to our Lord about each one, asking for the graces they need to win out in their ascetical struggle and to overcome temptations. And if anyone is slow to correspond to grace, the one guiding that soul will ask God to be patient: "Let it alone, sir, this year also, till I dig about it" (Lk 13:6–9). In front of the tabernacle much will come into focus that would otherwise remain hidden: new possibilities, broader horizons,

---

25. Especially those who guide others in their Christian life have to take these words to heart: "You must inspire others with love of God and zeal for souls, so that they in turn will set on fire many more who are on a third plane and each of these latter spread the flame to their professional companions.

"What a lot of spiritual calories you need! And what a tremendous responsibility if you let yourself grow cold! And—I don't even want to think of it—what a terrible crime if you were to give bad example!" (St. Josemaría Escrivá, *The Way*, no. 944).

obstacles to be overcome. Prayer, without ceasing to be a personal dialogue with our Lord, can also be a good moment to mull over a new particular examination of conscience or a book for spiritual reading. There one can also reflect on the conversations with those we are guiding, their life situation, their difficulties. . . . Only in prayer can we get to know their hearts and the best way to help them. And although it may seem that on a given day one has little light, or one's own soul is especially dry, St. Augustine's words will prove true: "If your heart is filled with charity, you will always have something to give."[26] The Holy Spirit will provide what is needed in abundance.

LOVE AND DETACHMENT

Human affection, true appreciation, is a language that both small children and adults understand. It is also a key to open doors that otherwise would remain definitively shut. In spiritual direction we need to combine affection with fortitude, so as not to fall into two opposing vices equally damaging to souls: being afraid to make demands because one is too "good-hearted," or falling into tyranny and rigidity.

"The work of evangelization presupposes in the evangelizer an ever increasing love for those whom he is evangelizing. . . . What is this love? It is much more than that of a teacher; it is the love of a father; and again, it is the love of a mother. It is this love that the Lord expects from every preacher of the Gospel, from every builder of the Church."[27]

True charity fosters hope and patience;[28] it is the foundation of every spiritual work and of much of its effectiveness. This

---

26. St. Augustine, *Expositions on the Psalms*, 36, 2, 13.

27. Pope Paul VI, *Evangelii Nuntiandi*, no. 79.

28. Patience "moves us to be understanding with others, for we are convinced that souls, like good wine, improve with time" (St. Josemaría Escrivá, *Friends of God*, no. 78).

love leads us to become "all things to all men, that I might by all means save some" (1 Cor 9:22), striving to know and love each person. The saints have experienced with special force the need for true affection if one is to help others. This teaching is important both for our daily dealings with others and for spiritual direction.

St. Gregory the Great advises us: "With a merciful heart we should make our own others' sorrows,"[29] their griefs and problems, whatever weighs most heavily on their hearts. Thus we will imitate the Apostle to the Gentiles. "Being affectionately desirous of you, we were ready to share with you not only the gospel of God but also our own selves, because you had become very dear to us" (1 Thess 2:8), he wrote to those in Thessalonica. Paul's love for God was fused in his heart with his affection for the first Christians who were converting to the faith. It is moving to see his great love for souls, along with his rectitude of intention and detachment.

St. John Chrysostom, putting himself in the place of St. Paul, explained these verses for us: "It is true that I preached the Gospel to you to obey God's command, but I love you with a love so great that I would have wanted to die for you. Such is the perfect model of a sincere and authentic love. A Christian who loves his neighbor should be inspired by these sentiments. He shouldn't wait to be asked to give his life for his brother, but rather should offer it on his own."[30] This is the self-giving asked of all Christians, but this is especially true of the one who acts as a spiritual counselor.

Love with Deeds

Like the apostle Paul, the one who guides others on the path of holiness should be able to say: "I will most gladly spend

---

29. St. Gregory the Great, *Pastoral Rules*, 2, 5.
30. St. John Chrysostom, *Homily on the First Letter to the Thessalonians*, 2, 8.

and be spent for your souls" (2 Cor 12:15). This requires truly loving souls, being available, praying and offering sacrifices for them, and taking the initiative in trying to find ever better ways to help them. In short: it is to feel as our own the sorrows and joys of others: "Who is weak, and I am not weak? Who is made to fall, and I am not indignant?" (2 Cor 11:29). And at times, it means making reparation for them with our own prayer and mortification.

In his letter to priests cited earlier, Bl. John Paul II pointed to the example of the holy Curé of Ars: "He did not wish to get rid of the penitents who came from all parts and to whom he often devoted ten hours a day, sometimes fifteen or more. For him this was undoubtedly the greatest of his mortifications, a form of martyrdom. In the first place it was martyrdom in the physical sense, from the heat, the cold, or the suffocating atmosphere. Secondly in the moral sense, for he himself suffered from the sins confessed and even more from the lack of repentance: 'I weep because you do not weep.'"

And the saint prayed: "O my God, grant me the conversion of my parish: I consent to suffer whatever you wish, for as long as I live."[31]

When giving advice, sincere love for souls will lead us to be understanding with the weaknesses, mistakes, and failings of those we are directing, and to give them practical help to get up immediately if they fall, with the confidence that our Lord is always ready to forgive. Moreover, we need to teach them that their very weaknesses can be a source of greater humility and trust in God. And if anyone is going through a moment of stronger temptations, we must encourage them and remind them that no fall is inevitable. And always, we have to transmit with naturalness the contagious optimism that it is

---

31. John Paul II, *Letter to Priests for Holy Thursday*, March 16, 1986, no. 7ff.

"worth the effort" to follow our Lord and to begin again in any circumstance.

As a Spanish spiritual writer stresses, our appreciation for each person—a participation in Christ's charity—can never be something dry and barren. Rather, it must be clothed in affection and deeds, "because otherwise it would not merit the name of love." And this writer adds: "Under this name of love, many other things are contained, especially these six: to love, to counsel, to assist, to suffer, to forgive, and to edify."[32]

When we truly love people, we can encourage them with words that are both kind and strong to make progress on the path. One who truly feels appreciated easily admits the truth about himself, without "beating around the bush," which can sometimes slow down a soul on its path towards God.

When souls encounter real understanding and interest, expressed by encouraging words that give a strong supernatural focus to their problems, it fosters trust, with the certainty that they are well-liked and that we are truly trying to help them. Then the words of a Father of the Church become a reality: "Friendship that has Christ as its foundation is firm and unbreakable."[33] For charity does not come from us; it is infused into our hearts with God's grace because he loved us first (see 1 Jn 4:10). "You and I are able to lavish affection upon those around us, because we have been born to the faith, through the Father's love for us."[34] We then feel the need to sacrifice ourselves joyfully for each soul in order to bring each one closer to Christ. "I just want to remind you of something you already know: that when you have in your hands the hearts of those you are trying to make better, if you have known how to attract them with Christ's kindness, you have already gone half way

---

32. Luis de Granada, *A Sinner's Guide* (Rockford, IL: TAN, 1985) I, 2, 16.
33. St. John Chrysostom, *Homilies on the Gospel of St. Matthew*, 60, 3.
34. St. Josemaría Escrivá, *Friends of God*, no. 229.

on your apostolic path. When they love and have trust in you, when they are happy, the field is ready for the sowing."[35]

The spiritual director's own soul is refined by this ability to love others truly out of love for Christ. It brings with it a special skill to understand others, and it makes it easier for them to open their hearts so they can be urged to advance on the path. This clean affection that passes through the Heart of Christ shortens distances and fosters sincerity.

When others feel understood and appreciated, they see their possibilities expand and can reach goals that seemed unattainable. Tolstoy relates the tale of a shoemaker who, on his way home one day, sees an unknown person dressed in rags at the door of a church. He brings the beggar home with him, but his wife receives the guest rudely. With each unfriendly gesture from the wife, the guest becomes smaller and smaller. With each harsh word, his face becomes more wrinkled. But when the woman finally shows some compassion and gives him something to eat and offers him new clothes, the stranger begins to grow bigger and more beautiful. As the narrator explains, the guest was an angel who had fallen from heaven and required an atmosphere of goodness and love in order to live. The same happens with us: we grow and improve when we feel appreciated and understood.

True love for souls is very important in spiritual direction, since love and knowledge of a person are closely connected. We get to know someone deeply when we appreciate him or her, and with the help of grace, we can counsel that person more surely. As John Paul I used to ask in his catechetical talks when still Archbishop of Venice: "What is the most important thing needed to teach someone Latin?" And the answer: to love that person. St. Augustine said that to truly know a person, friendship is the first requirement.[36] It is impossible to

---

35. Salvador Canals, *Ascetica Meditada*, pp. 74–75, Rialp, Madrid 2005.
36. See St. Augustine, *Sermon on Various Questions*, 83, 71.

get to know others well and give them sound advice if we do not truly appreciate them.[37]

Fortitude

Along with charity, shown in a kind and cordial understanding for souls, the one who has the mission of counseling others also needs fortitude if he or she is truly to help them. Without this cardinal virtue, charity would not be authentic and spiritual direction would be reduced to a few vague counsels lacking in strength. Fortitude is needed in order not to ask ten from the soul who can and should give twenty, and never to compromise on the Church's doctrine even when circumstances make it difficult to practice, especially in a secularized society that preaches the contrary. This cardinal virtue will also be needed to prevent souls who come for spiritual direction from "unburdening" themselves in a way that does damage to another's reputation or prestige. And one will sometimes have to be strong in order to provoke a reaction of sincerity, if circumstances require it.

Detachment

Our love for those we want to bring to our Lord has to be sincere, *in caritate non ficta* (see 2 Cor 6:6), with a love that is genuine and detached, with austerity of heart,[38] but also deeply human and attentive. The spiritual counselor's only concern

---

37. "Let not those, then, who feed Christ's sheep be lovers of their own selves, lest they feed them as if they were their own, and not His, and wish to make their own gain of them, as lovers of money; or to domineer over them, as boastful; or to glory in the honors which they receive at their hands, as proud . . . All these vices stem from the same root: from men *being lovers of themselves*" (St. Augustine, *Commentary on the Gospel of St. John*, 123, 5, Ibid.).

38. St. Alphonse Liguori gave this advice to confessors, full of common and supernatural sense, in their dealings with women: "Avoid any familiarity. Never accept presents from them and especially do not go to their homes unless you are called in a case of grave illness. And then, when hearing their confession, use great caution; leave the door of the room open, so that those outside can see you . . ." (*Guide for Confessors*, VIII, 4).

should be God's glory, never one's own glory or the desire to win others' appreciation or respect.[39] Everyone should receive the same friendly and fraternal reception, striving to ensure that souls never become attached to oneself, since "souls belong to God."[40] As St. Augustine says, "Those who lead Christ's sheep as if they belonged to themselves and not to Christ show that they love themselves and not our Lord."[41]

When it is a priest who gives spiritual direction, prudence advises an even greater detachment, filled with rectitude, especially when he is caring for women. He needs to practice a charity that treats everyone with human and supernatural affection, but he must also fight against personal likes or dislikes, and always avoid any attachments. In short, he has to be moved by a true zeal for serving those who are seeking Christ the Teacher when they come for spiritual direction.

From a practical point of view, in the many-centuries-old tradition of the Church, it has proved to be quite beneficial that these conversations of spiritual direction with women take place in a confessional. This setting helps make clear, even from a psychological point of view, that the tone and meaning of that conversation is supernatural in nature. Its purpose is to seek spiritual counsel, quite distinct from a friendly conversation

---

39. "The gratitude or ingratitude of souls should not upset one. One has to be serene when they give up spiritual direction or go to someone else. . . . Always respect the freedom of souls; love them solely 'with the affection of Christ Jesus,' as St. Paul said (Phil 1:8). Never accept gifts or presents as human recompense for a work that is entirely divine" (Antonio Royo Marín, *Teologia de la perfeccion Cristiana*, [Madrid: BAC, 2002], p.760).

40. If, through imprudence, "a strong mutual affection should begin to form that is recognized as such by both parties (although it may not yet be gravely dangerous), the best thing would be to counsel the person being directed to seek another director. Not only because of the clear danger that this friendship might degenerate into a sensual and carnal one, but because in such conditions a serious and efficacious spiritual direction seems impossible to carry out, even with the illusory supposition that those dangers are never going to present themselves" (Ibid. p. 796). What should always be something good can easily become evil, perhaps even a great evil.

41. St. Augustine, *Commentary on the Gospel of St. John*, 123.

with someone one likes. This practice also facilitates respectful dealings and discourages inopportune confidences, and it usually makes sincerity easier.

St. Alphonse Liguori, patron of moralists and confessors, advises in chapter eight of his book, *Guide for Confessors*, "Generally with young women, one should try to be austere rather than pleasant." And he concludes: "What is said above holds especially when dealing with women who already have a spiritual life, since the danger of attachment is greater. . . . The devil tries to build mutual attachment between spiritual people by first using the excuse of the other person's virtue; once this attraction is in place, he then tries to ensure that it gravitates from the virtue to the person. Therefore St. Augustine says: with women, have few and austere words. The need to be careful is not less in force because they are holy: the holier they are, the more they attract. And the Angelic Doctor adds: 'Although carnal affection is dangerous for everyone, it is much more so for those who deal with a person who seems spiritual; for although at the beginning the contact may seem pure, later, as mutual contact increases, the main motive will weaken and the purity will become stained. . . . Very soon, these persons will start to deal with each other not like angels, as at the beginning, but as beings of flesh and blood; they exchange glances and their heart is wounded by words that still seem to arise from their former piety. And each begins to desire the presence of the other. *Sicque spiritualis devotio convertitur in carnalem* [A spiritual devotion is converted into a carnal one].' How true it is that many priests, good at first, who give in to these attachments of the spirit, end up losing the spirit and losing God!"

For a priest, this precaution is always prudent and sometimes even necessary, since his good name can be compromised by misunderstandings. In the case of children and young people, the Church has always striven to practice a sacred respect for their dignity and the purity of their souls: "Whoever causes one of these little ones who believe in me to sin, it would be better for him to have a great millstone fastened round his neck and to be drowned in the depth of the sea. . . . For I tell you that in heaven their angels always behold the face of my Father who is in heaven" (Mt 18:6,10). However, nowadays it is indispensable to take the precaution of attending to them spiritually in the confessional or in places clearly visible to everyone.

True love for souls should prevent any sense of "ownership" over them, for as a Spanish author has well said: "One's life and property belong to the king; but one's honor is the soul's birthright, and the soul is God's alone."[42] We have to bring souls to God, just as the apostles brought the fish they caught to Jesus: "'The other disciples followed in the boat (they were not far from land, only some hundred yards away), dragging their catch in their net behind them' (Jn 21:8). They bring in the catch and immediately place it at our Lord's feet, because it is his. This is a lesson for us, so that we may learn that souls belong to God; that no one on earth has that right over souls."[43]

One would be acting as a "proprietor" of souls if one were to forget that spiritual accompaniment is a continuous service to souls. The mission of the one who guides others is that of John the Baptist, who led those who came to him to our Lord. All who give spiritual direction should make their own those words of Jesus' precursor: "He must increase, but I must decrease" (Jn 3:30).

True detachment will prevent the placing of obstacles and sowing of suspicions when someone wants to consult other priests, if the case requires it, or even to change spiritual directors when new circumstances make this advisable.[44]

---

42. Pedro Calderón de la Barca, *El Alcalde de Zalamea*, act. I.
43. St. Josemaría Escrivá, *Friends of God*, no. 257.
44. Ermanno Ancilli, compiler, *Diccionario de espiritualidad, Vol 1* (Barcelona: Herder, 1987), pp. 627–628.

If we love others as our Lord wants, *propter Deum* (out of love for God), their trust and appreciation will never be lacking: "[You] received me as an angel of God, as Christ Jesus," wrote St. Paul in Galatians 4:14.

RESPECT FOR SOULS

The story is told that one day a small child, who lived near the studio where Michelangelo worked, entered the sculptor's studio and saw a huge block of marble lying on the ground. The boy walked out without saying anything. A few months later he went back out of curiosity and found, now almost finished, the imposing sculpture of Moses. Turning to the sculptor, he asked, "How did you know Moses was inside that piece of marble?"

That block really did contain the work of art that today still causes so much admiration and surprise. The skill of Michelangelo was in *being able to see* the figure within the marble, *to believe in* the possibilities hidden inside the shapeless block, despite its external roughness. Without the artist's penetrating look, that marble would have forever remained lacking in grace and beauty.

Something similar happens in spiritual accompaniment. One has to be able "to see" and be firmly convinced of a person's capacity to become a saint: the marvelous work that God wants to carry out in that soul, its possibilities of loving God and of doing apostolate, its potential to attain heroic virtue. And all this despite the fact that at present—like the block of unshaped marble—that soul gives few hints of what it can one day become, and is rough and full of defects. Over time one will have to remove what gets in the way, as Michelangelo did: the bad habits and imperfections that disfigure and mar the image of Christ that the Holy Spirit wants to shape there.

With the eyes of an artist, Michelangelo already saw in the stone the image hidden within, waiting to be liberated and brought into the light. The artist's task, he said, was solely to remove whatever was covering over the image and set it free, not to try to "make" something.

As Joseph Ratzinger said, the same comparison can be found in St. Bonaventure, who uses the example of a sculptor to explain how man becomes authentically human. The sculptor, properly speaking, does not "make" anything. His work is to eliminate, to take away anything that is not authentic. Thus there comes to light the *nobilis forma*—that is, the beautiful image. Similarly, if the image of God is to shine forth in us, we need to first accept the purification that the divine Sculptor uses to free us from all the dross hiding the authentic form of our being. What appears at first to be only a block of rough stone conceals within it the divine image.[45]

Therefore we need to foster in souls docility to the motions of the Holy Spirit, "for if the well is dry, we cannot put water into it."[46] We will also need to foster, little by little, good habits, the virtues, so that the figure of Christ is sculpted with strong features, since all of us have been predestined by our Father God "to be conformed to the image of his Son" (Rom 8:29). St. Francis de Sales went so far as to say that between Christ and the saints the only difference is that of a musical score and its interpretation by different musicians. Each interpretation has its own personal variations; it is the Holy Spirit who guides the different notes, taking into account different ways of being and

---

45. Cardinal Joseph Ratzinger, "Una compañía siempre responsable," in *La belleza de la Iglesia*, (Madrid: Encuentro, 2005), pp. 31–32.

46. And St. Teresa adds: "True, we must not become neglectful; when there is water we should draw it out." (*Life* 11, 18; Carmelite edition, p. 119). Although the saint is referring here to prayer, it can well be applied to the assistance that the spiritual guide provides to the action of grace.

circumstances.[47] One who gives spiritual guidance to others has to ask often: "What is God expecting, today and now, from this soul? How can I help this person to resemble the Master more fully? Where should they focus their struggle? What should their particular examination be? What spiritual book should they be reading?"

God Never Repeats Himself

The goal, the masterpiece of holiness, is identification with Christ. Christian virtues are a reflection of those of the Model, but it's a reflection that takes on different hues in each person. St. Peter reminded the first Christians that Christ assumed human nature and "left you an example, that you should follow in his steps" (1 Pet 2:21). Even more, every Christian should be able to say: "It is no longer I who live, but Christ who lives in me" (Gal 2:20).

Sanctity is the figure of Christ shaped by God in his children. And God doesn't make saints on an assembly line; he never repeats himself. "Each soul is unique. Each has to be handled according to the way God has made it and the way he is leading it," wrote St. Josemaria. *"Omnibus omnia factus sum ut omnes facerem salvos.*[48] We have to become all things to all men. There are no cure-alls. We have to teach people, dedicating to each soul the time it needs, with the patience of a medieval

---

47. Sanctity, while being the same, is always original; it is never a copy of the external attitudes of another person. Therefore, the one who acts as a guide should never put oneself forward as a model. The result would be affected and false. The only model is Christ, and the Holy Spirit is the one who models souls according to his designs and the person's responsiveness. And he chooses—through quite varied circumstances—the guide who seems most suitable. The divisions that St. Paul rebuked the early Christians for at Corinth should never be allowed: "'I belong to Paul,' or 'I belong to Apollos,' or 'I belong to Cephas' . . . Is Christ divided? Was Paul crucified for you? Or were you baptized in the name of Paul?" (1 Cor 1:12–13).
48. 1 Cor 9:22.

monk illuminating a manuscript page by page. We have to help them to mature and to form their conscience, so that each person feels free and therefore responsible."[49] Souls require specific care: "Every person needs specific, personal help."[50] The one who is helping his brothers or sisters needs to care for them "with the humility of a person who knows he is only an instrument, the vehicle of Christ's love. For every soul is a wonderful treasure; every man or woman is unique and irreplaceable. Every single person is worth all the blood of Christ."[51] Hence we can see how much trust our Lord is placing in the one who guides others, and the great effort and solicitude needed to second God's desires.[52]

We have to serve souls, caring for them as Christ would in our place, with the same appreciation and respect, taking into account their age, their special circumstances, their way of being, their health or sickness, the situation in which we find them. We cannot apply the same remedy to each one, "because not all have the same situation in life and because often what is helpful to others would be harmful to some; just as plants that some animals feed on would often cause the death of others."[53]

---

49. Words of St. Josemaria, cited in Federico Suarcz, *El sacerdote y su ministerio,* Sixth ed. (Madrid: Rialp, 2005), p. 94.

50. St. Josemaría Escrivá, *Christ Is Passing By,* no. 80.

51. Ibid.

52. "This is the solicitude of Christ himself, the good Shepherd of all men" (*Redemptor Hominis,* no. 13). A solicitude, the Pope insists, that is directed to each and every person. "We are not dealing with the *abstract* man, but the real, *concrete, historical* man. We are dealing with *each* man, for each one is included in the mystery of the Redemption, and with each one Christ has united himself forever through this mystery. . . . Man as willed by God, as *chosen* by him from eternity and called, destined for grace and glory—this is each man, the very concrete man, the very real man; this is man in all the fullness of the mystery in which he has become a sharer in Jesus Christ, the mystery in which each one of the four thousand million human beings living on our planet has become a sharer from the moment he is conceived beneath the heart of his mother" (Ibid.).

53. St. Gregory the Great, *Pastoral Rules,* III, prol.

Personal Interest for Each One

St. Luke recounts for us the scene of many sick people being brought to Jesus as evening is falling: "And he laid his hands on every one of them and healed them" (Lk 4:40). He placed his hands on each person individually, showing a personal concern for each one. Later, each would recall how our Lord paid special attention to him, as if he were the only one being cared for that day, as if only he counted in those moments. This is what spiritual help has to be: a personal interest, a concern for each person, tailored to each one's needs, knowing that souls are "like a treasure which belongs to God and which he has placed under our care."[54] It is in prayer that we will learn to appreciate souls in all their worth and to rejoice in their diversity.

---

54. St. Gregory of Nyssa, *On Christian Conduct*, PG 46, 297.

Chapter 2

ROLES OF A
SPIRITUAL GUIDE

In a small church high up in the mountains, I once saw two
Gospel texts placed on either side of the vestibule. "Stay with
us" (Lk 24:29), said one of them. The other passage was from
the end of the Gospel of St. Matthew: "Behold, I am with you
always, to the close of the age" (Mt 28:20).

Christ is always present in his Church, above all in her
liturgical actions. He is present in the sacrifice of the Mass,
both in the person of his minister, "the same now offering,
through the ministry of priests, who formerly offered himself
on the cross," and especially in the Eucharistic species.[1] He is
present with his power in the sacraments, so that when anyone
baptizes it is really Christ himself who baptizes. He is present
in his word, since when sacred Scripture is read in the Church
it is Christ who speaks. He is present, finally, when the Church
prays and sings, for he has promised: "Where two or three are
gathered in my name, there am I in the midst of them" (Mt
18:20). He lives in Christians in an intimate and ineffable way
and is always very close to them.

---

1. See Vatican II, *Sacrosanctum Concilium*, no. 7.

Our Lord is also close to Christians in the person who guides us. Therefore, those who spiritually guide souls need a deep humility, since they have to second our Lord's action in souls. Like Christ, they have to carry out the roles of Father, Teacher, Physician, Friend, and Good Shepherd.

A FATHER

In the full sense of the word, we have only one Father, the heavenly Father (see Mt 23:1–12), from whom all fatherhood in heaven and on earth derives (see Eph 3:15). God possesses the fullness of paternity, and our parents and those who have engendered in us the life of faith share in this paternity. St. Paul deeply experienced this reality. He addressed the early Christians at Corinth as "my beloved children. For though you have countless guides in Christ, you do not have many fathers. For I became your father in Christ Jesus through the gospel. I urge you, then, be imitators of me" (1 Cor 4:14–16). The apostle Paul's great love can only be explained by the spiritual paternity—stronger than that of the flesh—which he felt towards his faithful. And those first Christians saw reflected in St. Paul God's loving care for them.

On another occasion he wrote to the first Christians in Galatia with the concern of a parent. Upon hearing news of the trials they were undergoing in their faith and experiencing the powerlessness of not being able to be close to them physically, he wrote: "My little children, with whom I am again in travail until Christ be formed in you!" (Gal 4:19). St. Paul felt in himself the concern of a father for his needy children, and so the word "father" can be used in a real sense not only to describe physical paternity but also a spiritual one.

Every Christian who helps others to encounter Christ in their life—sometimes at the cost of suffering and exhaustion—shares in this spiritual paternity. The greater one's dedication to this task the more fully one shares in this paternity—an important part of the reward God grants in this life to those who serve him.[2]

St. Paul repeatedly shows his anxiety for all the churches (see 2 Cor 11:28) and for those converted to the faith through his preaching. Keeping them on the right path and helping them to make progress is his principal concern; it brings him his deepest joy and sometimes his greatest suffering (see 2 Cor 11:29). Anyone with the mission of helping souls on the path to God can find in Paul a timely model.

Sincere esteem for those we are trying to bring closer to God is not simply friendship. It should be "the same love with which the Incarnate Son loves them . . . the same desire as that of the Son: their sanctification and salvation."[3] It is a love that leads us to love them more, to want them to be saints, and to put great care into whatever can facilitate their sanctity: providing a good example, being available to listen to them, offering prudent suggestions, being punctual in our conversations with them even though we may have to change our personal plans, showing them kindness and encouragement, being cheerful and optimistic. . . .[4] This is especially true of the most effective help we can give them: our daily prayer and mortification. Often the pastoral care of souls will be a spur to strengthen our own fidelity to God and "take the lead" on the path of sanctity, like the Good Shepherd.

On contemplating God's fatherhood, we will learn to have the heart of a father, especially towards those who come to seek

---

2. "He is generous. He returns a hundredfold; and he does so even in children. Many give them up for the sake of his glory, and they have thousands of children of their spirit. Children, as we are children of our Father who is in heaven" (St. Josemaría Escrivá, *The Way*, no. 779).

3. Bonaventure Perquin, *Abba, Father* (NY: Scepter, 2001) p. 229.

4. Some people "need to be shown a special kindness. One has to try to win their trust and obedience with immense kindness and gentleness, while forcefully preserving the principles of spiritual direction" (Antonio Royo Marin, *Teologia de la perfección cristiana*, p. 759).

help when in grave need. What joy to be able to say, "This your brother was dead, and is alive!" (Lk 15:11). If someone has a special need, we have to do everything possible to care for that person and understand him or her. Like the father in the parable, we have to go out in search of the one who has strayed, who did not correspond to God's love, and who perhaps has begun to distance himself from "his Father's house." And if we have to do so with those who have not been completely generous, how should we care for the souls who are faithful to God both in good days and in bad?

The desire to acquire this spiritual paternity should lead us to frequently ask our Lord for a merciful heart that welcomes others and sympathizes with their needs, helping those who have distanced themselves from God to return to him and serve him once again.[5] "Mercy," Bl. John Paul II wrote, "becomes an indispensable element for shaping mutual relationships between people, in a spirit of deepest respect for what is human, and in a spirit of mutual brotherhood. . . . Merciful love also means the cordial tenderness and sensitivity so eloquently spoken of in the parable of the prodigal son, and also in the parables of the lost sheep and the lost coin."[6]

We should never attend to a person in a "formal" or official way, as though fulfilling a strict duty, especially if someone arrives in an unfavorable interior state like the prodigal son. St. Francis de Sales, addressing confessors, wrote: "Although the prodigal son returned ragged, dirty, and smelly after living among pigs, his father nevertheless embraces him, kisses him lovingly, and cries on his shoulder; because he is his father, and

---

5. We should never forget that "mercy is more than simply being compassionate. Mercy is the overflow of charity, which brings with it also an overflow of justice. Mercy means keeping one's heart totally alive, with a life that is both human and divine, with a love that is strong, self-sacrificing, and generous" (St. Josemaría Escrivá, *Friends of God*, 232).

6. Bl. John Paul II, Encyclical *Dives in Misericordia*, no. 14.

the heart of fathers is tender towards the heart of their sons."[7] These are the dispositions that all those with the task of giving guidance to others should foster.[8]

However, it is one thing to have the "heart of a father," and quite another to be "paternalistic." The first does all in his power to ensure that those who come for guidance personally assume and skillfully administer their freedom as they grow in their spiritual life and don't limit themselves to "carrying out mechanically what others tell them."[9] The paternalistic approach, while pretending to have the heart of a father, restricts or suppresses others' legitimate freedom and annuls their personal responsibility. Paternalism leads to the "adult adolescence in which souls, grown up in years, do not mature in their decisions, and do not know how to commit themselves personally." In his homily closing the Pauline Year, Pope Benedict XVI said: "The Apostle, in the fourth chapter of the Letter to the Ephesians, tells us that with Christ we must attain adulthood, a mature faith. We can no longer be 'children, tossed to and fro and carried about with every wind of doctrine' (Eph 4:14). Paul wants Christians to have a 'responsible' and 'adult' faith."

An Adult Faith

Pope Benedict XVI continues: "The words 'adult faith' in recent decades have formed a widespread slogan. It is often meant in

---

7. St. Francis de Sales, *Advice to Confessors*, 2, 3.

8. St. Thomas Aquinas frequently insisted that God's fatherhood and omnipotence are shown in a special way in his mercy (see *Summa Theologica*, I, q.21, a. 4; II–II, q. 30, a. 4): "A person is called merciful because he is affected with sadness for another's plight as though it were his own. He identifies himself with the other, and comes to the rescue; this is the effect of mercy."

"To feel sad about another's misery is not an attribute of God, but to drive it out is supremely his, and by misery here we mean any sort of defect" (Ibid., I, q. 21, a. 3). A spiritual counselor will show a merciful heart by seeking to treat someone as our Lord would have done in the same situation. But this is possible only if one is close to Him oneself.

9. See St. Josemaría Escrivá, *Conversations*, no. 93.

the sense of the attitude of those who no longer listen to the Church and her pastors but autonomously choose what they want to believe and not to believe, and hence a do-it-yourself faith. And it is presented as a 'courageous' form of self-expression against the Magisterium of the Church. In fact, however, no courage is needed for this because one may always be certain of public applause. Rather, courage is needed to adhere to the Church's faith, even if this contradicts the 'logic' of the contemporary world. This is the non-conformism of faith which Paul calls an 'adult faith.' It is the faith that he desires. On the other hand, he describes chasing the winds and trends of the time as infantile.

"Thus, being committed to the inviolability of human life from its first instant, thereby radically opposing the principle of violence also precisely in the defense of the most defenseless human creatures is part of an adult faith. It is part of an adult faith to recognize marriage between a man and a woman for the whole of life as the Creator's ordering, newly re-established by Christ. Adult faith does not let itself be carried about here and there by any trend. It opposes the winds of fashion. It knows that these winds are not the breath of the Holy Spirit; it knows that the Spirit of God is expressed and manifested in communion with Jesus Christ.

"However, here too Paul does not stop at saying 'no,' but rather leads us to the great 'yes.' He describes the mature, truly adult faith positively with the words: 'speaking the truth in love' (see Eph 4:15). The new way of thinking, given to us by faith, is first and foremost a turning towards the truth. The power of evil is falsehood. The power of faith, the power of God, is the truth. The truth about the world and about ourselves becomes visible when we look to God. And God makes himself visible to us in the Face of Jesus Christ. In looking at Christ, we recognize something else: truth and love are inseparable. In God both are inseparably one; it is precisely this that is the essence of God. For Christians, therefore, truth and love go together. Love is the test of truth. We should always measure ourselves anew against this criterion, so that truth may become love and love may make us truthful."[10]

A person who truly loves with the love of God the Father rejoices to see those he is guiding advance spiritually and acquire a great capacity for initiative. Moreover, if he sees that someone "doesn't want" to grow or to take on responsibilities, this same fatherly love leads him to encourage the person, gently but firmly, to grow and mature.

A TEACHER

Giving calm advice grounded on maturity and experience is especially important when striving to strengthen those who are beginning on the path of the interior life, in order to give them the instruction needed to lay the foundations firmly and overcome early obstacles. The apostles soon saw the urgency of strengthening the disciples who were embracing the faith in the midst of a pagan and hostile world. In the Council of Jerusalem they clarified the norms that those who had recently entered the Church needed to live (see Acts 14:21).

The apostles quickly learned that "If good doctrine is planted in the soul when it is still tender, later, when the doctrine takes root, no one will be able to uproot it."[11]

Together with clear teaching, the apostles saw the need the newly baptized had for the warmth of personal contact. The first Christians needed someone who would be beside them, show them understanding, and encourage and strengthen them. Therefore the apostles sent some experienced brethren to teach

---

10. Pope Benedict XVI, Homily at the Closing of the Pauline Year, June 28, 2009.
11. St. John Chrysostom, *On Vainglory*, 20.

the new believers to live the fundamentals of the faith they had received: "We have therefore sent Judas and Silas [two well-formed Christians close to the apostles], who themselves will tell you the same things by word of mouth" (Acts 15:27).

St. Paul showed the same concern. He prayed and mortified himself for the new Christians, traveled from one place to another, and sent trusted disciples when he could not go personally: "When we could bear it no longer, we were willing to be left behind at Athens alone, and we sent Timothy, our brother and God's servant in the gospel of Christ, to establish you in your faith and to exhort you" (1 Thess 3:1–2). This care, shown in a thousand ways, is very important, especially for those who are starting out on the path and therefore weaker and more in need.

Together with a solid human and doctrinal formation, a special wisdom that comes from God is needed to guide others. The one who gives guidance in ascetical questions is a *teacher of interior life*, and will often have to strive to make doctrine accessible and practical, breaking it down into easily understood parts, as our Lord did for those who came to him. When listening to him, the crowds forgot their hunger and cold. Christ's teaching was easy to understand and assimilate: "They were astonished at his teaching, for he taught them as one who had authority, and not as the scribes" (Mk 1:22).

All wisdom, today as well, stems from Christ: "You have only one Teacher, Christ" (see Mt 23:10). Only he can penetrate into each person's heart, seeing the evil that can lurk there and the possibilities for contrition.

"The Gift of Tongues"

If we want to be true guides, we have to strive to be closely united to the Master, who possesses and communicates the divine wisdom we need. "Let us go to Jesus in the Tabernacle where we can get to know him and assimilate his teaching, and then be able to hand out this food to souls."[12] Close to our Lord, we will learn to transmit the treasure of truths that provides nourishment to souls and to help them understand these truths "with the gift of tongues."[13]

To do so, we must strive to acquire a good doctrinal preparation and improve it continually, and we must ask for the gift of knowing how to communicate it so that those we are trying to help might incorporate it into their lives. Often it will be necessary to repeat the same teaching in different ways, as our Lord did. At times this need for repetition comes, not from the doctrine itself, but because the one who is listening is not properly prepared—either because of a lack of formation or an environment where the faith can barely enter. Above all, we need to repeat the sure doctrine passed on by tradition and by the wise experience of the holy souls that have preceded us. These "core ideas" need to become an habitual outlook that leads to viewing events in a Christian way: the sense of divine filiation that imbues all one's daily events; finding the Cross in ordinary life; work that is sanctifying and sanctified; staying close to our Lord every day, regardless of circumstances; unfailing optimism and cheerfulness, etc.[14]

We have to keep going back to what is truly essential, so that this always remains in first place. Good dispositions tend to

---

12. St. Josemaría Escrivá, *The Forge*, no. 938.

13. "I pray every day with all my heart that God may give us the gift of tongues. Such a gift of tongues does not mean knowing a number of languages, but knowing how to adapt oneself to the capacities of one's hearers. . . . It's not a question of 'simplifying the message to get through to the masses,' but of speaking words of wisdom in clear Christian speech that all can understand. . . . This is the gift of tongues that I ask of our Lord and of his Holy Mother for all their children" (St. Josemaría Escrivá, *The Forge*, no. 634).

14. Spiritual authors have always stressed that spiritual guidance should be grounded on the sure doctrine that is the Church's common treasury (see Adolphe Tanquerey, *The Spiritual Life: A Treatise on Ascetical and Mystical Theology*, no. 32 a).

weaken over time, and the truth can become obscured. Putting truth into practice requires setting aside other interests, and it can be lost amid other legitimate but less important concerns. Repeating ideas, however, does not mean becoming tiresome, for "One should reach the hearts of one's listeners with the same doctrine, it's true, but not with the same words,"[15] especially if one's words are monotonous and dry.

In this effort to insist repeatedly on an aspect of the interior life or on a moral truth a person finds especially hard to observe, we will need to be on guard so that our own comfort-seeking or negligence won't hinder us from saying things at the opportune moment. We must be vigilant for any slackening of supernatural outlook in our own life, which can lead to discouragement upon seeing that there is no immediate echo to the advice we give. Or perhaps we may notice a lack of firmness in repeating the same thing when circumstances require it, or a fear of tiring others, or the fear that a new reminder by us will not be well received. When guiding souls on the path of Christian life, we have to teach sound doctrine with loving fortitude, even when few people today may accept it and it involves going against the current. We have a duty of charity, and often of justice, to be firm and rise above these obstacles.[16]

Spiritual Reading

The Christian life requires being very familiar with the Gospels and with the entire New Testament.

"When you open the Holy Gospel, think that what is written there—the words and deeds of Christ—is something that

---

15. St. Gregory the Great, *The Book of Pastoral Rule*, 3 prol.
16. A spiritual guide can never be like those false teachers who "are afraid of getting to the bottom of things. They get uneasy at the very idea, never mind the obligation, of having to use a painful antidote when circumstances require it. You can be quite sure that in such an attitude there is no prudence" (St. Josemaría Escrivá, *Friends of God*, no. 158).

you should not only know, but live. Everything, every point that is told there, has been gathered, detail-by-detail, for you to make it come alive in the individual circumstances of your life.

"God has called us Catholics to follow him closely. In that holy Writing you will find the Life of Jesus, but you should also find your own life there.

"You too, like the Apostle, will learn to ask, full of love, 'Lord, what would you have me do?' And in your soul you will hear the conclusive answer, 'The Will of God!'

"Take up the Gospel every day, then, and read it and live it as a definite rule. This is what the saints have done."[17]

Spiritual reading can be a great help in providing continual formation to others. If it is to be truly effective, one needs carefully to consider the best book for the person's specific circumstances and situation. This practice is especially important in today's world.[18] With so many publications available and the constant bombardment of images that make it hard to find God and can often separate us from him, there is a pressing need for a few moments of study and reflection, which spiritual reading offers. This can sometimes be decisive for a person's life, as it was for the lives of so many saints.[19]

The books that we advise others to read should be truly suited to their situation and provide the nourishment they need. Part of the task of a teacher of interior life is to get to know books that are useful in this regard. Normally, rather than

---

17. St. Josemaría Escrivá, *The Forge*, no. 754.
18. St. John Chrysostom's words lamenting the religious ignorance of many Christians of his day continue to be quite timely. "Sometimes we dedicate all our effort to things that are not only superfluous but even useless or harmful, while setting aside the study of Scripture. Those who are keen fans of horse racing can quickly recite the names, lineage, and trainers of the horses . . . and which horse would win the race if ridden by such and such a jockey. . . . While if we ask them to name the epistles of St. Paul, they would not even be able to say how many there are" (St. John Chrysostom, *Homilies on Passages from the New Testament*, 1, 1).
19. "Don't neglect your spiritual reading. Reading has made many saints" (St. Josemaría Escrivá, *The Way*, no. 116).

works that try to present new "theological problems" (which are probably only of interest for theologians), one needs to look for books that explain clearly the Church's traditional teaching and the content of the faith, help one to discover the riches of the doctrine found in the writings of the Holy Fathers and other holy writers, and contemplate Christ's life. The *Catechism of the Catholic Church* and its *Compendium* are especially useful in this regard, as are other documents from the Magisterium.

For this reading to be of most use, it is good to set a specific amount of time that each person should dedicate to it. It is also very useful to do this reading slowly, with attention and recollection, stopping to reflect on what one has just read, savor the truths, and engrave them deeply on one's heart, so as to love God more. St. Peter of Alcantara gives similar advice: This reading "should not be rushed or hurried, but attentive and peaceful; one should strive not only to understand what one reads, but more importantly to savor it. And when one comes upon an especially devout passage, one should pause to savor it more fully."[20]

Doing this reading with continuity is very helpful, until finishing a specific book. It is good to advise the person to carry the book with them whenever possible (e.g., when leaving for the weekend, going on business trips, etc.). And at times it can be useful to "reread the very good books which have already done us much good. Life is short: we should be content to read and read again whatever bears the mark of God, and not to lose our time on things that are lifeless and of no value."[21]

A Doctor

Like our Lord Jesus Christ, the one who provides spiritual help is also a physician of souls, and needs to know the appropriate

---

20. St. Peter of Alcantara, *Tratado de la oración y meditación*, 1.7.
21. Garrigou-Lagrange, *The Three Ages of the Interior Life*, vol. I, p. 254.

remedies for each illness.[22] But unlike the state of our bodily health, we have to be convinced that there are no incurable diseases in the interior life, and that any difficulty can become a means of interior progress. This optimistic attitude gives great hope to the sick, who perhaps thought their illness had no remedy.

We also know that a doctor can cure someone even when suffering from the same illness. In the spiritual life, the effectiveness of the remedy comes from our Lord and not from our personal qualities. This realization leads to a greater humility, a more determined struggle to overcome our own weaknesses and defects, and a greater trust in God's grace.

Arriving in Time

Just as with bodily maladies, it is much easier to cure souls if one "arrives in time," when the first symptoms appear and the sickness has not yet spread. For example, when one sees that a person begins to be negligent in striving to staying close to our Lord and fails to give importance to small things in fidelity to one's path in life; when work becomes overly absorbing and threatens to take the place owed to family life or to spiritual formation; when there is little desire to struggle, a lack of mortification, scant interest in apostolate, or the beginning of a disordered attachment of the heart. In these situations, charity will require diligently applying

---

22. "Looking on the immense panorama of souls who are awaiting us, and being struck by the wonderful and awesome responsibility before us, you may at times have asked yourself, as I have: 'Can I contribute anything, when the task is so vast? I, who am so puny?'

"It is then we have to open the Gospel and contemplate how Jesus cures the man born blind. He uses mud made from the dust of the earth and saliva. Yet this is the salve that brings light to those blind eyes!

"That is what you and I are. Fully aware of our weaknesses and our worthlessness, but with the grace of God and our good will, we can be salve to give light and provide strength for others as well as for ourselves" (St. Josemaría Escrivá, *The Forge*, no. 370).

the opportune remedy and seeking a thorough cure as quickly as possible. It will mean speaking to these souls in a refined but firm way, possibly suggesting a change of work; helping them to see the importance of what they are doing or failing to do, or the need to break off a specific friendship; or suggesting an appropriate particular examination.

What we can never do is to let the wound become infected and the sickness spread, perhaps thinking that "time cures everything." "It is a great mistake to think that problems can be solved by omissions or procrastination. Prudence demands that the right medicine be used whenever the situation calls for it. Once the wound has been laid bare, the cure should be applied in full and without palliatives. When you see the slightest symptom that something is wrong, be straightforward and truthful about it, irrespective of whether it involves helping someone else or whether it is your own problem. When such help is needed, we must allow the person who, in the name of God, has the qualifications to carry out the cure, to press on the infected wound, first from a distance, and then closer and closer until all the pus is squeezed out and the infection eradicated at its source. We must apply these procedures first to ourselves, and then to those whom, for reasons of justice or charity, we are obliged to help."[23]

So that the remedy will be effective, we must clean out the soul's wound thoroughly by fostering complete sincerity—and, if necessary, contrition—until it is open to the light and cleansed of all ambiguity. What the sick person might find the most painful—sharing the symptoms with all the necessary detail—ends up being a great relief and the beginning of the cure.

If we arrive in time, we can do what a gardener does when a plant begins to dry out: put more care into it, water it, add

---

23. St. Josemaría Escrivá, *Friends of God*, no. 157.

special fertilizer, and if appropriate, move it to a sheltered place away from the rigors of the cold and heat.

When the Illness Is Serious

If a serious illness does develop, we should remember Jesus' consoling words: "Those who are well have no need of a physician, but those who are sick" (Mt 9:12). We will need to stay close to someone in this situation, and be even more patient and charitable.

"Get to the root of problems; don't stay on the surface. Remember that, if we really want to fulfill our obligations as Christians in a holy and manly way, we must anticipate unpleasant moments for others and for ourselves too. Don't forget that it is more comfortable (though it is a mistake) to avoid suffering at any cost, with the excuse of not wanting to hurt others. This inhibition often hides a shameful escape on our part from suffering, since it isn't usually pleasant to correct someone in a serious matter. My children, remember that hell is full of closed mouths."[24]

In these circumstances (serious mistakes or falls, situations that put the soul's health in grave danger, the possibility of not being faithful to one's commitments, etc.), we have to dedicate more attention and perhaps more time to that person, and apply more remedies, even though they may be painful. "The surgeon knows that the cleaning hurts, but he also knows that there will be worse pain later if it is not done. A disinfectant is also applied immediately. Naturally, it stings (or, as they say where I come from, it *prickles*) and hurts the patient. But it's the only way if the wound is not to become infected.

"If it is obvious that such measures must be taken to protect bodily health, although it may only be a relatively minor wound, then when the health of the soul is at stake—the very nerve center of a man's life—how much more necessary it is to wash, to cut away, to scrape, to disinfect, to suffer! Prudence demands

---

24. St. Josemaría Escrivá, *Friends of God*, nos. 160–161.

that we intervene in this way and that we don't flee from duty, because to side-step our obligations here would indicate a great lack of concern for and even a grave offense against the virtues of justice and fortitude."[25]

Our Lord has left in our hands the means to prevent and cure spiritual illnesses and to alleviate suffering. Along with prudence and charity, we should never be afraid to give forceful advice when necessary.

With a Mother's Affection

If we find anyone in these circumstances, we will need to show special affection and understanding, "with the almost infinite tenderness shown by our own mothers, when they were treating the hurts and injuries, big or little, resulting from our childhood games and falls."[26]

We will act as a mother would, without wounding, without causing unnecessary damage—much like a doctor faced with equally effective remedies who chooses the one that is least traumatic for the sick person. But we will also act in time, the sooner the better. "When it is better to wait a few hours, by all means do so. But never wait longer than is strictly necessary. Any other approach would imply cowardice or a desire not to inconvenience ourselves, which is very different from prudence. Everyone, especially those of you who have the job of training others, must put aside the fear of getting at the wound to disinfect it."[27]

The mutual trust that grows stronger from conversation to conversation enables us to give frank advice with naturalness, which is accepted with gratitude. If we act in this way, God will eventually remove obstacles that seemed insurmountable or dispositions that at first were immovable: cutting off at the roots a

---

25. Ibid., no. 161.
26. Ibid., no. 158.
27. Ibid.

particular friendship, or avoiding a proximate occasion of sin, even if it requires extraordinary means.

Ordinarily, the doctor has to speak clearly to the patient, but there are many ways to speak the truth. It may be imprudent at times to say everything in one conversation, and one should never speak in a brusque or ill-tempered way. "Rather than 'pushing' souls, one needs to lead them gently, respecting their freedom."[28] We should always act in a refined way, without wounding or distancing the person we are trying to help. The conversation should be supernatural in tone and should never "pummel" the person we are speaking with. On the contrary, it should be encouraging and hopeful, although at times it may cause someone to suffer. And always, it should be held at the opportune moment, waiting if it is necessary to wait, "because tumors, when lanced too soon, become inflamed and grow worse; while if the remedies are not applied in time, they lose their ability to cure."[29]

Knowing the Symptoms

A good doctor also knows how to discern the signs of true health from those that point to a hidden illness; confusing the symptoms would be disastrous. In the interior life, signs of spiritual health are the struggle to draw closer to God, even when no results may be seen; a lively examination of conscience; docility to advice received; tenacity in mortification and practices of piety, even when one's "feelings" fail to respond. In the apostolate, a sign of vigorous health is prayer for souls and constancy, both when met with apparent failure or abundant fruit.

A physician of souls must put effort and prayer into learning how to discern situations that can disorient souls. One of these is *aridity in the spiritual life*, although here we really should speak about the different types of aridity that have different causes and

---

28. Royo Marin, *Teologia de la perfección cristiana*, p. 748.
29. St. Gregory the Great, *The Book of Pastoral Rule*, 2, 10, 29.

therefore require different treatments (which the spiritual director should be well acquainted with). A common sign of this aridity is a certain inability or reluctance in the spiritual life, more specifically in prayer. This inability can at times be so great that it makes prayer and the struggle to stay close to our Lord very difficult. The most painful form, described by many saints, is when God seems to have abandoned the soul and left it on its own. Therefore, it is important to discern the origin of this aridity and help those suffering from it to respond as God wants.

Spiritual aridity can have a variety of causes. Often aridity is produced by poor health or physical or mental exhaustion; in that case, we will need to help the person recover their equilibrium and offer up that trying situation where responding to grace may be more difficult.

At other times, spiritual aridity can be a healing trial permitted by God, from which the soul, if faithful, emerges purified and strengthened.[30] In this form of aridity, although one "does not feel anything" in one's relationship with God, true devotion remains, although without any sensible consolation or feelings. This is part of the normal path in the ascent towards God.[31] The soul learns that it should seek "the God of all consolation," rather than the "consolation of God." This devotion, which St. Thomas defines as "a firm will to dedicate oneself to everything pertaining

---

30. "Consolations often disappear so that the soul not become attached to them, because the consolations are not God. If the soul becomes attached to them, all of the work of divine grace will be delayed, so to speak" (Joseph Tissot, *La vida interior*, [Barcelona: Herder, 2003], p. 295).

31. "For the person who makes a serious effort there will, however, be moments in which he seems to be wandering in a desert and, in spite of all his efforts, he 'feels' nothing of God. He should know that these trials are not spared anyone who takes prayer seriously. However, he should not immediately see this experience, common to all Christians who pray, as the 'dark night' in the mystical sense. In any case in these moments, his prayer, which he will resolutely strive to keep to, could give him the impression of a certain 'artificiality,' although really it is something totally different: in fact it is at that very moment an expression of his fidelity to God, in whose presence he wishes to remain even when he receives no subjective consolation in return" (Congregation for the Doctrine of the Faith, *On Some Aspects of Christian Meditation*, October 14, 1989, no. 30).

to the service of God"[32]—with consolations or without them—purifies the soul and makes it more docile to the Holy Spirit. One needs to encourage these souls to keep walking firmly on the path, trusting in God, and remind them of the teaching of many saints: "You have a poor idea of your way, if lack of enthusiasm makes you think you have lost it. Can't you see that it is the moment of trial? That is why you have been deprived of sensible consolations."[33] Frequently, this is a good moment to take a big step forward in the interior life: it is the moment to imitate our Lord in the Garden of Olives and on Calvary, and to identify oneself with the co-redemptive sufferings of our Lady.[34]

---

32. St. Thomas Aquinas, *Summa Theologica*, q. 82, a. 1.

33. St. Josemaría Escrivá, *The Way*, no. 996.

34. cf. St. Francis de Sales, *Introduction to the Devout Life: A New Translation* (London: Rivingtons, 1875), pp. 336–337. St. Francis de Sales gives some specific advice for souls who find themselves in this situation: "If, after an honest investigation of our own conduct, we find the cause of our wrongdoing, we must thank God. For an evil is half cured when we have found out its cause. If, on the other hand, we don't find anything particularly that could seem to be the motive of this dryness, don't make a more detailed examination; with the greatest simplicity, without thinking about details, put into practice what I am going to say:

"Humble yourself profoundly before God, acknowledging your nothingness and misery. Alas, what am I when left to myself! no better, Lord, than parched ground, whose cracks and crevices on every side testify its need of the gracious rain of heaven, while, nevertheless, the world's blasts wither it more and more to dust.

"Call upon God, and ask for his gladness.

"Go to your confessor, open your heart thoroughly, let him see every corner of your soul, and take all his advice with the utmost simplicity and humility, for God loves obedience, and he often makes the counsel we take, especially that of the guides of souls, to be more useful than would seem likely; just as He caused the waters of Jordan, commended by Elijah to Naaman, to cure his leprosy in spite of the improbability to human reason (2 Kings 5:14).

"But, after all, nothing is so useful, so fruitful amid this dryness and barrenness, as not to yield to a passionate desire of being delivered from it. I do not say that one may not desire to be set free, but only that one ought not to desire it over-eagerly, but to leave all to the sole Mercy of God's special Providence, in order that, so long as He pleases, He may keep us amid these thorns and longings."

The saint also advises us to be patient and not to become discouraged. We should continue our practices of piety and, if we cannot present our Lord with "sugary preserves, let us offer him dried fruit, because it is all the same as long as the heart which offers them is resolved to remain in his love" (Ibid.).

A person who tries to pray in this situation will often be like someone who draws water from a well, bucket by bucket—with an aspiration, an act of reparation, a short petition. . . . It is hard work, but very effective. God frequently prepares a soul in this way for a greater dedication or a purer love. One needs to give firm and clear guidelines so that this person grows in the theological virtues: a more lively faith, a stronger hope, a greater love grounded not on what one receives or wants to receive from God, but on giving oneself entirely to him. Then, despite the dryness, the soul can say what our Lord said when referring to God the Father: "I always do what is pleasing to him" (Jn 8:29).

Sometimes, however, the dryness experienced in prayer is not a trial sent by God, but the result of a lack of real interest in speaking with him, or a lack of generosity in controlling one's imagination. In short, it is a case of lukewarmness, an infirmity of the will that we will speak about later.[35] This state is radically different from the one just discussed and requires quite different remedies.

A Friend

Jesus is our friend, "the Great Friend who will never fail you."[36] He listens to us, encourages us, and restores lost hope. He is always near and accessible.

Jesus' conversation is kind and friendly, making it pleasant to be in his company. He is the friend of everyone and a personal friend of each one. His love does not lessen when the number of those conversing with him expands. St. Paul's own experience of Christ's friendship led him to exclaim: "[He] loved me and gave himself for me" (Gal 2:20). The Apostle seems to be

---

35. Ibid., see Ch. 5, no. 12.
36. St. Josemaría Escrivá, *The Way*, no. 88.

saying, "For me alone," as though he were the only person in the world. As true friendship demands, our Lord showed himself to be generous and self-sacrificing with those who followed him. At times he had to give up his rest and food to attend to those who were seeking him (see Mk 3:20; 6:31). He called those who followed him closely intimate friends—friends of the bridegroom (see Lk 5:33–39). He wanted to be an example of loyal friendship, drawing everyone with his goodness and affection. St. Jerome compared the power to draw others that emanated from him to an extraordinarily powerful magnet.[37]

Jesus himself said that he "came not to be served but to serve, and to give his life as a ransom for many" (Mt 20:28). He even knelt down to wash the apostles' feet, as though he were a servant (see Jn 13:14–17). He told them, "I have called you friends, for all that I have heard from my Father I have made known to you" (Jn 15:15). Together with his immense affection, Jesus spoke to them clearly and reached their hearts, as he did with Zacchaeus and the Samaritan woman, urging them to improve and truly give themselves. More than once he spoke to the apostles forcefully in order to shake them out of their narrow, earthbound vision. Jesus' friendship spurred their love for the Father and their desire to grow in holiness.

Our Lord is the Model for how we should welcome those who come seeking help. They should always receive a warm and friendly smile from us, with true concern for their problems. We too, if united to God, will be able to say: "All that I have heard from my Father I have made known to you" (see Jn 8:26). A friend gives his friends the best he has. Above all, we need to give our Lord to those who draw close to us.

We should never forget that friendship and charity form a single reality: divine light that gives warmth,[38] that comforts and

---

37. St. Jerome, *Commentary on the Gospel of St. Matthew*, 9, 9.
38. See St. Josemaría Escrivá, *The Forge*, no. 565.

attracts. It is a friendship that leads to God and is grounded in him.[39] When friendship is true, fused with charity, it is easy for others to speak about what is happening in their soul. Trust arises as something normal, and leads to God in a simple and natural way.

Friendship facilitates and makes possible sincerity and trust, especially in moments of difficulty. Trust demands a certain intimacy, and if this intimacy does not exist, it creates it. But it also requires that the person to whom we give our trust truly be able to grasp what we are trying to communicate. Otherwise, that person doesn't understand us, and therefore isn't in a position to give good advice. To truly understand others, an interior climate of being in God's presence is required.

By contemplating Jesus' friendship with people, his always cordial and positive demeanor, we learn to receive attentively those who seek our counsel: to welcome them with a spirit of service, with frank concern for their problems and with human warmth and affection. St. Thomas Aquinas says: "When we are someone's friend, we desire the good for that person as though it were for ourselves and thus consider that friend as another I."[40]

We have to be fully available for others also when personal, family, or professional worries may weigh on our own hearts, or when we find ourselves more tired than usual. We will find it possible to do so if we strive to stay close to our Lord in daily intimate contact with him, for "only in prayer, and through prayer, do we learn to serve others."[41]

---

39. "If the love of God is put into friendships, they are cleansed, reinforced and spiritualized, because all the dross, all the selfish points of view and excessively worldly considerations are burned away. Never forget that the love of God puts our affections in order, and purifies them without diminishing them" (St. Josemaría Escrivá, *Furrow*, no. 828).

"I find I can't love anyone," said Lacordaire, "without Jesus being in the middle. Conversations don't seem intimate to me, if they aren't supernatural" (Henri-Dominique Lacordaire, *Letters* 1:20).

40. St. Thomas Aquinas, *Summa Theologica*, I–II, q. 28, a. 1, c.

41. St. Josemaría Escrivá, *The Forge*, no. 72.

When listening to and assisting someone, our head and heart should be focused on that person's concerns. Everything else is secondary. God always rewards this generous self-forgetfulness, for he himself looks after our own concerns and does so much better than we could. Then each person will have the impression that it is Jesus himself who is listening to and helping him. It is good often to ask ourselves: "How would our Lord care for this person in these specific circumstances? What would he say? How would he encourage this person, gently but firmly, to be more generous, more holy?" If souls feel this genuine concern, they will receive the advice given in that fraternal chat as though coming from Christ himself.

Holy Scripture praises friendship as a great good: "A faithful friend is a sturdy shelter: he that has found one has found a treasure. There is nothing so precious as a faithful friend, and no scales can measure his excellence" (Sir 6:14–15). Those whom we counsel throughout many personal conversations should be able to say the same—that we have been a faithful friend of incalculable value, because our friendship has helped them to make progress in the spiritual life, draw closer to God, and (in many cases) discover and follow their specific path in life. They should be able to say that, after every conversation, they found their love for God strengthened.

The friendship spiritual direction gives rise to facilitates the path to God. There it acquires all its depth and nobility. This supernatural meaning of friendship is shown in not using it for any personal benefit—never accepting gifts or dinner invitations from those we are trying to help. It should never be used to attain any personal goals or seek information on professional matters.

The person receiving guidance can never be seen as a *"longa manus"* of the spiritual director, so as to exert influence over others. Likewise the one giving spiritual guidance should never get involved in any concern not strictly related to the soul and its sanctification. He should never seek to "organize" the family of the person being guided, or assert authority, even if only moral, over other family members. Nor should one give advice on medical or financial matters, even if one is an expert in these fields; instead, one should encourage the person to see a specialist when necessary.

Thus this friendship will keep its proper meaning and be far removed from any "paternalism" or "control" over souls that would deform and debase spiritual direction.

THE GOOD SHEPHERD

Christ Jesus said he was the "Good Shepherd" (see Jn 10:14) who cares for his flock and seeks the lost sheep, in contrast with the bad shepherds who so often had abandoned God's people (see Ezek 34:1–10; Jer 23:1ff). When a sheep is missing from the flock, the good shepherd's concern is so great that he doesn't wait to see if the straying sheep will return to the sheepfold on its own account; he goes out in search of it. "And when he has found it, he lays it on his shoulders, rejoicing" (Lk 15:5). Each soul is of immense value—our Lord will not spare any effort to recover it, and so great is his joy when it returns to his friendship and to his flock that heaven itself rejoices (see Lk 15:10). He is truly the Good Shepherd of whom the prophets spoke.[42]

All those with the mission of leading others along the path of holiness should be seen as the type of good shepherd

---

42. "Jesus presents himself as 'the good shepherd' (Jn 10:11, 14), not only of Israel but of all humanity (cf. Jn 10:16). His whole life is a continual manifestation of his 'pastoral charity,' or rather, a daily enactment of it. He feels compassion for the crowds because they were harassed and helpless, like sheep without a shepherd (cf. Mt 9:35–36). He goes in search of the straying and scattered sheep (cf. Mt 18:12–14) and joyfully celebrates their return. He gathers and protects them. He knows them and calls each one by name (cf. Jn 10:3). He leads them to green pastures and still waters (cf. Ps 22–23) and spreads a table for them, nourishing them with his own life" (*Pastores Dabo Vobis*, no. 22).

described by those words from the Psalm: "The Lord is my shepherd, I shall not want. . . . He leads me in paths of righteousness. . . . Even though I walk through the valley of the shadow of death, I fear no evil" (Ps 23:1–4). The faithful have to feel themselves watched over and protected by the prayer and vigilance of the one who is helping them spiritually, with a concern for each of their specific needs, their way of being, and their defects.[43] And when someone's need is greater, this concern will be shown in redoubling one's prayer and mortification.

The Mercenary

The good shepherd knows his sheep by name, and leads them to safe and abundant pastures.[44] St. Peter said, "Tend the flock of God that is your charge, not by constraint but willingly" (1 Pet 5:2), with the vigilance that comes from love. Bad shepherds, by contrast, are lax in looking after their flock, because their heart is filled with other interests: "The weak you have not strengthened," complains God through the mouth of the prophet Ezekiel, "the sick you have not healed, the crippled you have not bound up, the strayed you have not brought back, the lost you have not sought" (Ezek 34:4). Christ himself said of the false shepherds of his time: "[They] are thieves and robbers . . . The thief comes only to steal and kill and destroy" (Jn 10:8–10). Other shepherds may not be quite as bad, but they still cause many evils for the flock: "He who is a hireling and not a shepherd, whose

---

43. One who counsels others "has the duty of knowing how to harmonize perfectly the impartiality of a father, with the loving intuition of a mother, who treats her unequal children in an unequal manner" (Álvaro del Portillo, *Escritos sobre el sacerdocio*, 6th edition [Madrid: Palabra, 1991], p. 34). The fortitude of a father and the heart of a mother are united in the good shepherd in order to lead souls, one by one, to God.
44. See Pope Benedict XVI, *Jesus of Nazareth* (New York, Doubleday, 2007), p. 280ff.

own the sheep are not, sees the wolf coming and leaves the sheep and flees; and the wolf snatches them and scatters them. He flees because he is a hireling and cares nothing for the sheep" (Jn 10:12–13).

The one who flees like a hireling is, above all, the one who abandons his own interior life, who doesn't pray for the souls our Lord has entrusted to him, who keeps quiet when he should speak, who seeks his own glory instead of God's.[45] This bad shepherd "leads even the healthy sheep towards death,"[46] says St. Augustine. A bad spiritual guide can be disastrous for souls.[47]

Vigilance of the Good Shepherd

Referring specifically to priests, but with words that are applicable to every spiritual director, Bl. John Paul II said that they need to "be capable of loving people with a heart which is new, generous, and pure—with genuine self-detachment, with full, constant and faithful dedication and at the same time with a kind of 'divine jealousy' (cf. 2 Cor 11:2) and even with a kind of maternal tenderness, capable of bearing 'the pangs of birth' until 'Christ be formed' in the faithful (cf. Gal 4:19)."[48]

The good shepherd goes ahead of the flock, opening up the path by his example: faithfully fulfilling his own practices of piety, being docile to the indications he himself receives from his own guide, and demonstating the spirit of service in the many

---

45. See St. Augustine, *Commentary on the Gospel of St. John*, 46, 8.

46. Ibid., *Sermon 46, on shepherds.*

47. "Many false apostles, in spite of themselves, do good to the crowd, to the people, through the very power of the doctrine of Jesus that they preach but do not practice. But this good does not make up the incalculable harm that they do by killing the souls of leaders, of apostles, who turn away in disgust from those who don't practice what they preach. That is why, if such men and women are not willing to live a consistent life, they should never offer themselves as front-line leaders" (St. Josemaría Escrivá, *The Way*, no. 411).

48. Bl. John Paul II, Apostolic Exhortation *Pastores Dabo Vobis*, no. 22.

details of ordinary life. "It is good," says a Father of the Church in this regard, "for those who are leading their brothers to make a greater effort than the others in serving, to be even more submissive than those under them and, like a servant, to spend their life for others, seeing their brothers as truly a treasure that belongs to God and that God has placed under their care."[49]

One who is truly a good shepherd should be filled with joy on hearing the words of the old song by Juan de la Encina:

> Tan buen ganadico, y más en tal valle, placer es guardalle.
>
> Ganado de altura, y mas de tal casta,
>
> Muy presto se gasta en mala pastura,
>
> Y en Buena verdura, y mas en tal valle, placer es guardalle.
>
> Ansi que yo quiero guardar mi ganado,
>
> Por todo este prado de muy buen apero.
>
> Con este tempero, y mas en tal valle, placer es guardalle.
>
> Está muy vicioso y siempre calando,
>
> No anda balando ni es enojoso;
>
> Antes da reposo. en qualquiera valle, placer es guardalle.
>
> Conviene guardalla la cosa preciosa,
>
> Que en ser codiciosa procuran hurtalla.
>
> Ganado sin falla, y más en tal valle, placer es guardalle.
>
> Pastor que se encierra en valle seguro,
>
> Los lobos te juro que no le den guerra
>
> Ganado de sierra traspuesto en tal valle, placer es guardalle.
>
> Pastor de buen grado yo siempre sería,
>
> Pues tanta alegría me da este ganado
>
> Que tengo jurada de nunca dejalle, mas siempre guardalle.[50]

---

49. St. Gregory of Nyssa, *On Christian Conduct*, PG 46, 297.
50. Juan del Encina, *Obras completas*, vol. III, Canción 203.

• • •

Such a good little flock, especially in such a valley, it's a
  pleasure to guard it.
A flock of such quality, especially such a breed,
would quickly waste away in poor pastures.
In good grasslands, especially in such a valley, it's a pleasure
  to guard it.
And so I want to guard my flock
All over this prairie with its very good sheepfolds.
With this prepared soil, and even more in such a valley, it's
  a pleasure to guard it.
It is very numerous and always quiet,
It doesn't go around bleating, nor is it troublesome;
It rather gives repose. In any valley, it's a pleasure to guard it.
It's a good idea to guard it, the precious thing,
Because being covetous, they try to steal it.
The flock without defect, especially in such a valley, it's a
  pleasure to guard it.
The shepherd who is enclosed in a secure valley,
The wolves swear to you that they won't attack you.
Flock of the mountains moved to such a valley, it's a
  pleasure to guard it.
A first class shepherd I will always be,
For this livestock gives me such joy
That I have sworn never to leave it but always to guard it.

St. Thomas of Villanova points to four conditions that a
good shepherd should have: [51]

---

51. See St. Thomas of Villanova, *Obrasa de* . . . BAC, Madrid 1953, "Sermon sobre
el Evangelio del Buen Pastor."

First, *love*. After St. Peter's denials, charity was the only virtue that our Lord demanded of Peter in order to entrust him with the care of his flock. Our Lord continued to trust in him, despite his fall on that momentous night.

Second, *vigilance*. A shepherd must be attentive to the needs of the sheep, in order to be aware when a soul has begun to distance itself from God or when God is asking "more" of it.

Third, *doctrine*. In order to nourish the minds of those one is helping, sound doctrine is required, giving opportune advice so that souls can avoid errors that are widespread today and suggesting sound spiritual reading.

Fourth, *holiness and integrity of life*. This quality is the most important of all, because only thus will one be a good guide who knows the safe paths and the dangers that lie in ambush for the flock. Scripture's promise thus becomes a reality: "I will give you shepherds after my own heart" (Jer 3:15).

Fulfilling the role of good shepherd, besides a refined charity and a tenacious strength, requires a great rectitude of intention,[52] seeking only the glory of God.

In Search of the Lost Sheep

Like the Master, the one who acts as the good shepherd can never consider anyone as lost, as though nothing could be done for that person. Often one cannot wait for the sheep that strays to return on its own, but must go out to seek it with prayer, a special mortification, and greater affection and understanding. "I will go and cure him" (Mt 8:7), he will say when someone has a sickness of the soul. He will then use all the means at his

---

52. As St. Gregory the Great stressed: "The pastor should try to win the love of those he guides so that they will listen to him, but not in order to seek this affection for his own purposes" (*The Book of Pastoral Rule*, 1, 2).

disposal without omitting a single one. One who is counseling others thus imitates our Lord, who said of himself: "I did not come to be served, but to serve" (Mt 20:28). This service to souls is very pleasing to God, and requires watchfulness and true concern for those one is guiding towards holiness: "I want to save the sheep that are outside," said St. Augustine, "but I have greater fear lest those who are inside might come to harm,"[53] those souls entrusted to one's care.

We have to be concerned if someone wavers and provide the opportune remedy in time, going out to seek that soul if necessary. Moreover, we have to make amends before God, not only for our own missteps, but also those of our little flock (see Lk 12:32), the souls our Lord has entrusted to us. For "all good shepherds are truly, as it were, members of the one shepherd and form a single reality with him. When they lead souls to pasture, it is Christ who is leading them."[54] And Christ gave his life for the salvation of everyone. As the liturgy sings: "The Good Shepherd has risen, who laid down his life for his sheep and willingly died for his flock, alleluia."[55]

---

53. St. Augustine, *Sermon 46, on shepherds*, 7, 15.
54. St. Augustine, loc. cit.
55. Communion Antiphon, Fourth Sunday of Easter.

Chapter 3

A FEW GUIDELINES

FORMED IN FREEDOM

Those who decide to follow the path leading to holiness do so because they "feel like it,"[1] because they want to, with a real determination to follow our Lord closely. They seek spiritual direction in order to be helped in the specific circumstances of their lives and to avoid the danger of losing precious time on the path towards God.[2] Hence the two pillars of all spiritual direction: *freedom* and *responsibility*.

Souls are not puppets moved by pulling on strings. Each needs to act with autonomy and free decision. Spiritual guidance "should tend to develop men and women with their own

---

1. St. Josemaría Escrivá liked to use the expression *porque nos da la gana* to stress the importance of deciding to follow our Lord with full freedom: "I opt for God because I want to, freely, without compulsion of any kind. And I undertake to serve, to convert my whole life into a means of serving others, out of love for my Lord Jesus" (*Friends of God*, no. 35). He advised people to "do things as God wants them done, *because we feel like it*, which is the most supernatural of reasons" (*Christ Is Passing By*, no. 17).

2. Thus respecting people's freedom and making strong "demands" upon them are in no way contradictory, since souls come to spiritual direction precisely to receive this help. If they do not find that "demands" are made upon them, they will feel cheated. This is one of the basic principles in the task of guiding others: great respect for personal freedom while constantly spurring them upwards, towards God.

Christian standards. This requires maturity, firm convictions, sufficient doctrinal knowledge, a refined spirit, and an educated will."[3]

Respect for freedom means not trying to use the same mold for every soul, or always taking the same approach in guiding them, even though it's true that the goal of Christian life is always the same: identification with Jesus Christ. Those who guide others must take into account personal diversity and not get tied to rigid schemes. The essential unity of holiness can never become uniformity. "God does not want us all to be the same or to walk alike along exactly the same road."[4]

The aim of spiritual guidance should be forming men and women with sound criteria, who find it easy to confront new experiences in life with a Christian spirit and aren't paralyzed when the unexpected occurs. Such people don't need to ask for advice on how to act every time they confront an unforeseen circumstance, since they themselves know how to seek the right solution. The spiritual life is full of unexpected events, which we all have to face on our own, with the wisdom that comes from the desire to do God's will in everything.[5]

Spiritual direction should seek to remove any fear of exercising personal freedom. It should encourage souls to use their freedom well in making binding decisions, in taking the initiative in their interior life, in sanctifying family life, in the apostolate, and in carrying out their work.[6] It is precisely this responsible, committed freedom that forges virtue and leads to

---

3. *Conversations*, no. 93, 3.

4. St. Josemaría Escrivá, *Furrow*, no. 401.

5. The docility required of those who seek spiritual guidance is therefore not that of a person without free will, but of someone who freely wants to strive for holiness. A consequence of this docility is the effort to put into practice the advice received, trying to be faithful to these counsels and apply them to new situations.

6. The more one does what is good, the freer one becomes. There is no true freedom except in the service of what is truly good and just (see CCC, 1733).

the maturity proper to adults who desire to live in accord with God's will. "Human freedom is a force for growth and maturity in truth and goodness; it attains its perfection when directed toward God, our beatitude."[7]

With this free and responsible effort, the guidelines one receives are seen not as obligations, but as advice and suggestions that never take away spontaneity and freedom or weaken personal initiative. These counsels are like the road signs that help travelers to reach their destination safely. Rather than feeling "coerced" by these indicators, they are grateful for the help in reaching the goal they themselves have freely chosen. Those who seek spiritual guidance have freely committed themselves to following our Lord closely "because they feel like it." And they want to test their own initiatives on the one who guides them, seeking help and suggestions. Thus, freely, they make their own the indications and advice received, and they struggle more resolutely and effectively.

This advice often helps channel what they themselves have seen in their own prayer: the need to strengthen family life, to put more intensity into work, to be more charitable with others or more daring in the apostolate. There is much room for initiative on the path to sanctity.

In the realm of professional work, the spiritual director should help people to form their consciences correctly, to sanctity their work by offering it to God, and to be concerned about others' needs (reminding them when suitable of the Church's social doctrine and the ethical obligations every profession brings with it). Those receiving direction, in turn, need to find specific ways to put these suggestions into practice—in an intelligent way and not as inert instruments. And

---

7. Ibid., 1731.

the spiritual director will of course never try to solve technical problems that arise in the course of someone's work.[8]

Free and Responsible

Besides freedom, spiritual direction rests on a second firm pillar: taking responsibility for one's own holiness. No one can act as a substitute for another in that individual's commitment to God.[9] People must travel their own individual path, getting up if they fall, and taking responsibility for their decisions.[10] Therefore, the spiritual guide has been compared to the Magi's star, which pointed out the way to them but didn't spare them the arduous effort of following it. Similarly, St. John the Baptist pointed out to his disciples the One they should follow, but they themselves had to decide to seek out our Lord. Another image used by some ancient authors is that of a lighthouse and a boat. The lighthouse indicates where the harbor is, but the sailors still have to row vigorously or set the sails to take advantage of the wind and keep firm control of the rudder. Therefore, spiritual direction, far from suppressing the soul's own response, should

---

8. The spiritual guide should "illuminate and help within the sphere of Christian virtues. The spiritual director should not intervene in the organization of the family, nor get involved in professional problems. His help is doctrinal; it affects the Christian formation of the interior dispositions from which the decisions should come" (Gustave Thils, *Santidad cristiana*, pp. 475–476).

9. "The advice of another Christian and especially a priest's advice, in questions of faith or morals, is a powerful help for knowing what God wants of us in our particular circumstances. Advice, however, does not eliminate personal responsibility. In the end, it is we ourselves, each one of us on our own, who have to decide for ourselves and personally to account to God for our decisions" (St. Josemaría Escrivá, *Conversations*, no. 93).

10. "A child learning to walk at first finds it hard to do so, but he would never learn if he didn't make an effort on his own. A confessor or—since the case is the same—a spiritual director is a guide, not a wheelchair for invalids or a support for those lacking will power" (Federico Suarez, *El sacerdote y su ministerio*, p. 93). The person giving counsel can indicate the way, point out the obstacles, give a word of encouragement in moments of discouragement. . . . But it is the one being directed who has to travel the path of sanctity, hence the importance of always fostering the desire to seek God.

foster personal initiative and responsibility in making headway towards God in every circumstance.

Teaching others to be responsible for their own sanctity also entails pointing out the false reasons a soul might hide behind to abandon the high goals once embraced. Those who truly want to follow our Lord closely have to be careful not to lessen the level of sanctity they aspire to due to factors at work, in the family, or in their health. They could thereby fall into the trap of finding excuses for not making progress precisely in the situations that should lead one more rapidly towards sanctity. "Because I am sick, I can't set a high goal to truly try to improve." "Since I have a sick child and a lot of worries, I can't struggle to love God more." "Since I'm in the middle of exams and have a lot of work. . . ." On the contrary, it is precisely these adverse circumstances that should strengthen a person's virtues; they are a marvelous opportunity to seek our Lord with greater rectitude of intention and find meaning in the Cross.[11]

The suggestions received should be seen as signs of the divine will, which the soul makes its own. Responsibility comes down to being faithful to God's will: doing what pleases God and in the way that he wants. *One is truly free and responsible when one seeks God's will in everything.* Freedom by itself "is insufficient: it needs a guide, a North Star."[12] God's will for us is made known in many ways; among others, through the suggestions we receive in spiritual direction.

"Educating our will" means wanting to be guided with ever more refinement by what God wants of us. This is the compass

---

11. The determination to be a saint has to be so strong that not even the defects one sees in the person giving guidance should be able to hinder the soul on its path towards God. "What a pity that whoever is in charge doesn't give you good example! But, is it for his personal qualities that you obey him? Or do you conveniently interpret Saint Paul's 'obey your leaders' with a qualification of your own—'always provided they have virtues to my taste'?" (St. Josemaría Escrivá, *The Way*, no. 621).

12. St. Josemaría Escrivá, *Friends of God*, no. 26.

that marks out the path of our life, rather than being led by "what I like," the fear of "what others might say," or by laziness and seeking comfort. Striving to stay close to God brings with it the realization that in this way we are ever more free: "What do you want from me, Lord, so that I may freely do it?"[13]

St. Paul warned the first Christians not to use their freedom as an excuse for acting badly: "You were called to freedom, brethren; only do not use your freedom as an opportunity for the flesh" (Gal 5:13). And St. Peter insists, "Live as free men, yet without using your freedom as a pretext for evil; but live as servants of God" (1 Pet 2:16).

Along with personal initiative, we have to foster in souls the virtue of obedience, grounded precisely on the *responsible freedom* of a person who seeks to do God's will. By this virtue we imitate our Lord in a special way: "To carry out the will of the Father, Christ inaugurated the kingdom of heaven on earth and revealed to us the mystery of that kingdom. By his obedience he brought about redemption."[14] He did so not by his miracles, but by renouncing his own will. St. Paul stresses how much Christ loves this virtue: although being God, "he humbled himself and became obedient unto death, even death on a cross" (Phil 2:8), accepting the most shameful of deaths possible in that day and age, reserved for the worst criminals.

Moments of special struggle and temptation can be an excellent occasion to make one's own the teaching of Sacred Scripture: *Vir oboediens loquetur victoriam* (Prov 21:28, Vulgate), the one who obeys attains victory.

The function of a spiritual guide is formally distinct from the minister of the sacrament of confession. These are two essentially distinct actions, even though it may be the same priest who carries out both with the same person. In the sacramental

---

13. Ibid.
14. *Lumen Gentium*, no. 3.

internal forum, there is a very strict duty to guard the seal of everything said in confession—as all priests know and live very well. What is said in confession is a secret conversation that the penitent has directly and exclusively with God.

In the sphere of spiritual accompaniment, a sincere and complete openness is required on the part of the faithful so that the person guiding can help and counsel effectively. This opening of one's conscience requires, in turn, a total reserve in regard to what is confidentially made known.[15]

SHOWING PRUDENCE

Respect for each person's conscience requires keeping complete silence regarding the content of these conversations. It is important to avoid even the slightest reference to defects, attitudes, possibilities, etc., that are known in spiritual direction. This is a fundamental moral principle to which one has to be extremely faithful. "The shepherd," St. Gregory the Great insists, "has to know how to keep silent."[16]

Any lack of prudence here would lead to a loss of trust and could undermine everything achieved. This trust, which upholds all spiritual guidance, can be undone by something very small.[17] A person who lacks discretion is incapable of giving spiritual direction to others. "Discretion is refinement of spirit."[18] And

---

15. See *Diccionario de espiritualidad,* cited, heading "Dirección espiritual," p. 625, col. b, "*Apertura de corazón.*"

16. St. Gregory the Great, *Regulae pastorali,* 2, 4. This is the criterion of all spiritual authors: "The director must strive to keep the most absolute reserve . . . and never fear going too far in the rigor and severity of his silence" (Royo Marin, *Teologia de la perfección cristiana*), p. 764.

17. "How can the total openness of the directed one that is required be preserved, if he sees that his spiritual director is not discreet, even if it is a matter of material in which discretion is not indispensable? It is preferable to sin by being overly discreet than the contrary: Trust can be lost through a very small thing" (Gustave Thils, *Santidad cristiana,* p. 543).

18. St. Josemaría Escrivá, *The Way,* no. 642.

nothing requires greater refinement than a conscience that has opened itself to another person in a confidential chat. Nor is it fitting to speak about the virtues or good qualities of those being guided, even when holding them up to others as a good example. Not even the most trivial detail mentioned in this conversation should be revealed. This is a "natural secret" that obliges in conscience. In this regard, the following advice is especially relevant: "Remain silent, and you will never regret it: speak, and you often will."[19]

When faced with indiscreet questions or with curious, unjust, or malicious inquiries, spiritual guides have an obligation of justice and charity not to reveal anything known through spiritual direction. They can make use of various ways of hiding the truth (without lying), especially when the person asking has no right to know the truth and acts as an unjust aggressor, losing thereby even the right not to be deceived. But "let us remember, moreover, that often it is our own fault if we are asked indiscreet questions. If we were more recollected and silent, people would not ask them of us, or at least they would do so only rarely."[20]

When one is indiscreet here and fails to keep this natural secret, it is almost always possible to trace this failure back to vanity—to the desire to give oneself importance by showing that one knows certain things others don't. A caricature of this silence is also possible when one lets on that one knows certain things but is not free to talk about them.

A sign of prudence and common sense in this very delicate matter is not to carry any notes referring to those who come for spiritual direction. Refinement here also entails not speaking with the persons themselves about spiritual matters outside the

---

19. Ibid., no. 639.
20. Garrigou-Lagrange, *The Three Ages of the Interior Life*, vol. II, p. 160.

proper time and place—for example, on the phone, in a hallway, etc. This is also one of the reasons why giving spiritual guidance by letter or similar means is not recommended.

THE HUMAN AND THE DIVINE

Those guiding others on the path to holiness must keep in mind that both the human and the supernatural dimensions are important in people's formation, for the life of grace is not foreign to or superimposed on human nature. Rather, grace enriches and elevates nature. "That is why the Church requires its saints to be heroic in practicing not only the theological virtues but also the moral or human ones. And it is why people who are truly united to God through the theological virtues of faith, hope, and love also perfect themselves humanly. They are refined in their relationships with others, loyal, affable, well-mannered, generous, sincere, precisely because they have placed all their affections in God."[21] A saint should possess all the characteristics of a truly human personality.

A Christian Personality

Human personality and supernatural life are not two distinct principles, two separate "nuclei." Rather, the human dimension has to be elevated and transformed by the higher one. Holiness leads a Christian to be both deeply supernatural in confronting the world and daily events and also, at the same time, deeply human: "Supernatural life always brings with it the attractive practice of human virtues."[22]

Much of the advice given will thus be aimed at preparing good soil—the natural virtues—so that the divine seed can grow

---

21. Álvaro del Portillo, *On Priesthood* (Dublin: Four Courts Press, 1980), p. 14.
22. See St. Josemaría Escrivá, *Furrow*, no. 566.

and develop normally.[23] Moreover, grace improves the soil into which the good seed falls. Christian life perfects human qualities, by giving them a higher end and more consistency. A Christian is more human—more a man, more a woman—when he or she is more a Christian.

Care for the natural virtues is therefore of great importance. Although grace can transform a person's life by itself, normally human virtues are also required. How can the cardinal virtue of fortitude take root, for example, in a Christian who fails to overcome himself in small habits of comfort or laziness, who is excessively concerned about the heat or cold, who lets himself be governed habitually by his moods, who is constantly thinking about himself or his comfort? How can one be optimistic in the face of daily circumstances, a consequence of a life of faith, if one is pessimistic and bad humored in daily life or at work? These natural virtues are, as it were, the foundation, the ground that is well disposed for sanctity, and therefore needs to be cultivated and developed through opportune counsels and suggestions. "A calm and balanced character, an inflexible will, deep faith, and an ardent piety, these are the indispensable characteristics of a son of God."[24]

Spiritual accompaniment should seek to foster each one's own personality, and not produce a reflection of the person directing the soul. Those guiding others must try to strengthen each person's human qualities and help to direct these to God so they become part of the struggle for sanctity. Human personality requires the possession of sure criteria, solid principles that help give focus to every event. This Christian way of viewing

---

23. "Once a person is striving to improve in the human virtues, his heart is already very close to Christ. If he is a Christian, he will realize that the theological virtues (faith, hope, and charity) and all the other virtues which God's grace brings with it are an encouragement never to neglect the good qualities he shares with so many of his fellow men" (St. Josemaría Escrivá, *Friends of God*, no. 91).

24. St. Josemaría Escrivá, *Furrow*, no. 417.

the world manifests itself in every situation and gives rise to a "unity of life." Mature personality is also shown in a strong will to act in accord with one's beliefs. Therefore, inconsistency, acting out of caprice, and doing what one finds more pleasant at the moment reveal a lack of character.

By contrast, a Christian personality requires a struggle to *die to oneself*, to one's selfishness and disordered attachments, so as to *live in Christ* and say with St. Paul: "for me to live is Christ" (Phil 1:21). He is the Model each of us has to imitate: "Make the foundation of my personality my identification with you."[25]

To be like our Lord, to become "another Christ," we have to contemplate him frequently: seeing how he loves, how he acts, how he deals with those around him. We need to imitate him in his self-giving and in his spirit of service, letting him take possession of us through grace: "It is no longer I who live, but Christ who lives in me" (Gal 2:20). Jesus comes to dwell in the depths of our soul, where he shapes our personality; we can even say that he thinks and acts in us, without our thereby losing our personal identity.

In directing souls, therefore, we can never forget the importance of grace, which is what underlies everything, nor can we set aside the human element. The spiritual edifice can only be constructed by building on each one's personal qualities. The apparent "showy" virtues of sanctity would be of no value if not united to the ordinary virtues of daily life. "That would be like adorning yourself with magnificent jewels over your underwear."[26]

---

25. St. Josemaría Escrivá, *Christ Is Passing By*, no. 31. See also *The Forge*, no. 468. Through this identification with Christ, we can see why a Christian's presence in the world—one's way of being and acting in every circumstance—is always an apostolic presence, like that of Christ himself.

26. St. Josemaría Escrivá, *The Way*, no. 409.

Developing Human Virtues

Great care has to be taken not to impede the growth of the humanly noble qualities that God has placed in each person; instead, we need to foster and strengthen them. Our Lord wants each person to grow in the human virtues of optimism, industriousness, generosity, order, toughness, cheerfulness, cordiality, sincerity, capacity for friendship, and truthfulness. First of all, because we have to imitate Christ, perfect God and perfect Man. In him we see the fullness of all the human virtues; while being God, he was also deeply human. "He dressed as people did in those days; he ate the usual food, behaved according to the customs of the place, race, and time to which he belonged. He placed his hands on people, he gave instructions, he became angry, he smiled, wept, argued, felt tiredness, hunger and thirst, anguish and joy. And the union between the divine and the human was so complete, so perfect, that all his actions were, at the same time, both divine and human. He was God, but liked to call himself the Son of Man."[27]

Christ demanded of everyone the human perfection contained in the natural law (see Mt 5:21); he formed his disciples not only in the supernatural virtues, but also in the human ones, in sincerity and nobility, and he insisted that they be men of discerning judgment. He was hurt by the lack of gratitude of some lepers he had cured and the neglect of small points of courtesy and human refinement. So great was the importance Jesus gave to human realities that he said to his disciples: "If I have told you earthly things and you do not believe, how can you believe if I tell you heavenly things?" (Jn 3:12).

These natural virtues also have great importance in the apostolate, for a Christian in the middle of the world is like "a

---

27. Federico Suarez, *The Priest and His Ministry* (Dublin: Four Courts Press, 1979) p. 86.

city set on a hill," a "light on a stand" (Mt 5:15). And it is one's human qualities that first stand out: integrity, loyalty, nobility, courage. . . . Human virtues thus become instruments of grace to attract others to God. Professional prestige, friendship, simplicity, cordiality: all these human qualities help make other men and women more open to the message of Christ that we carry in the depths of our being. If others fail to see these virtues in us, it will be difficult for them to understand the supernatural virtues. If we are not truthful, how can our friends trust us? How can one make the true face of Christ known, if one isn't truly human?

Those who follow the Master closely demonstrate that their Lord is truly alive by habitual cheerfulness, through being serene in painful circumstances, in work that is well done, by sobriety and temperance, with a friendship that is always open to everyone.[28] "We have to act in such a way that others will be able to say, when they meet us: this man is a Christian, because he does not hate, because he is willing to understand, because he is not a fanatic, because he is willing to make sacrifices, because he shows that he is a man of peace, because he knows how to love."[29] Also because he is generous with his time, because he does not complain, because he knows how to do without what is superfluous.

The world needs the testimony of men and women who bear Christ in their hearts and are exemplary in human virtues. Pope Benedict XVI insisted: "To reach him we also need lights close by—people who shine with his light and so guide us along our way."[30]

"The Sacred Humanity of Christ. This is why I have always advised people to read books on the Lord's Passion. Such works, which are full of true piety, bring to our minds the Son of God,

---

28. "How I wish your bearing and conversation were such that, on seeing or hearing you, people would say: This man reads the life of Jesus Christ" (St. Josemaría Escrivá, *The Way*, no. 2).

29. St. Josemaría Escrivá, *Christ Is Passing By*, no. 122.

30. Pope Benedict XVI, *Spe Salvi*, no. 49.

a Man like ourselves and also true God, who in his flesh loves and suffers to redeem the world.

"To follow Christ—that is the secret. We must accompany him so closely that we come to live with him, like the first Twelve did; so closely, that we become identified with him. Soon we will be able to say, provided we haven't put obstacles in the way of grace, that we have put on, have clothed ourselves with our Lord Jesus Christ (see Rom 13:14). Our Lord is then reflected in our behavior, as in a mirror. If the mirror is as it ought to be it will capture our Savior's most lovable face without distorting it or making a caricature of it; and then other people will have an opportunity of admiring him and following him.

"I have distinguished as it were four stages in our effort to identify ourselves with Christ: seeking him, finding him, getting to know him, loving him."[31]

What Should Always Be Present

Those who guide others have to ask themselves frequently what the goal is. What we are seeking to attain is holiness, intimacy with the Three Persons of the Most Blessed Trinity, which means traveling the path clearly marked out by the saints, closely accompanied by our Lady. But we also need some basic "rules for building well,"[32] key norms that orient the interior struggle, although always in accord with each one's specific spiritual situation.

Among these fundamental "key ideas"[33] that we always need to keep in view, the following are especially important: the source

---

31. St. Josemaría Escrivá, *Friends of God*, nos. 299–300.
32. This figure of speech—norms or rules for building—is taken from the writings of St. Paul. For example, when addressing the Christians at Corinth he writes: "According to the grace of God given to me, like a skilled master builder I laid a foundation. . . . Let each man take care how he builds upon it" (I Cor 3:10). He makes clear, however, that these "rules" are in no way meant to provide a "closed system."
33. See St. Josemaría Escrivá, *Furrow*, no. 884, and *The Forge*, no. 859.

of all holiness is God (and therefore we cannot attain sanctity by "force of arms"); the reality of our divine filiation, which imbues a Christian's being and acting; the compatibility of great ideals with a struggle in the little things of each day; unity of life, the consequence of knowing we are God's children; sanctification of work, the "hinge" for holiness in the midst of the world.

These points will provide us with the topics for the rest of this chapter.

Struggling for Love: Confidence in God's Help

As St. Augustine said succinctly: "God, who created you without you, will not save you without you."[34] He thus stresses the need for our personal correspondence to grace. We are not inert beings that God draws towards himself like stones without a will. But it's also true that the only one who can save and sanctify us is God, who is more determined to attain this goal than we are. He is the one who gives opportune help and disposes events so that his children can reach the home of their Father. Certainly, without our personal correspondence, his grace would become as ineffective as water poured into a broken pitcher. God grants his grace abundantly, but he takes seriously our personal freedom and responsibility; without our own effort we will never grow spiritually. But those directing others should also never forget that the Holy Spirit is the Sanctifier, who with infinite love wants everyone to be holy and who wants this with an efficacious will.

This essential truth—God's own "interest" in our attaining holiness—brings with it the need to interiorize an attitude of trust at the hour of struggle. We need to fight, not "by force of arms" in a voluntaristic way as though the victory depended only on our own effort, but with complete abandonment to God's action. Each

---

34. See St. Augustine, *Sermon* 169, 11, 13. In another place, the saint says: "The mercy of the one who calls (God) is not sufficient: the obedience of the one called is also required" (*On 83 Diverse Questions*, 1, 2, 13).

one should be able to say: "I love the Will of my God and that is why, abandoning myself completely into his hands, I pray that he may lead me however and wherever he likes."[35]

The voluntaristic person tends to trust above all in his own strength and experience, forgetting that without God's grace nothing can be achieved: "Without me you can do nothing" (Jn 15:5). One who trusts in himself ordinarily wants clear and simple rules that he can apply in a rigid and mechanical way, and since a struggle based on human strength fails to yield great results, he becomes discouraged and loses hope.

"So we know and believe the love God has for us" (1 Jn 4:6), writes St. John, recalling his own experience close to the Master. God loves each of us with infinite tenderness. This is the consoling truth that should preside over the soul's struggle to improve. It is important to insist on this point again and again until it imbues every corner of one's soul: the Son of God "loved me and gave himself for me" (Gal 2:20). Every act of Christ's heart and will was directed to our redemption—to *my* redemption. He wanted to gain for us all the help we needed to be faithful in following him and to make it easier for us to return if we have gone astray. He joyfully accepted every possible suffering and disgrace for us. The certainty of our Lord's love brings us consolation even in the hardest moments of our lives.[36]

---

35. St. Josemaría Escrivá, *The Forge*, no. 40.

36. Christ calls men by the titles of brother and friend, and unites his fortunes so intimately with them that anything one does for another, is done for him (see Mt 25:40). The Gospel writers constantly tell us that he felt compassion for the people (see *Mk* 8:2). "He had compassion on them, because they were like sheep without a shepherd" (Mk 6:34). He was always moved by others' misfortune and sorrow. He could not say no when he saw the suffering of the Syrophenician woman—even though a Gentile (see Mk 7:26). He assisted all those who came to him, even when they criticized him for breaking the Sabbath (see Mk 1:21). And he associated with publicans and sinners, even when that scandalized those who thought themselves faithful observers of the Law. Even in the midst of his own agony, he told the good thief: "Today you will be with me in paradise" (Lk 23:43). He welcomed rich men like Nicodemus, Zacchaeus, and Joseph of Arimathea, and the poor like Bartimaeus, a beggar who, after being cured, "followed him on his way" (Mk 10:52).

On seeing a person's mistakes and weaknesses, we need to insist on this truth: we can always count on the loving help of our Lord to return to the right path, since it is he who helps us to keep fighting. As St. John Chrysostom wrote: "A leader on the field of battle has a greater estimation for the soldier who, after having fled, returns and attacks the enemy with zeal, than for him who never turned his back, but neither did he perform an act of bravery."[37]

It is good to remind people that sanctity doesn't mean never making mistakes. Sanctity can also be attained by one who seriously strives not to fall and who, despite this effort, does make a mistake, but who always repents with humility and continues fighting with optimism, doing so above all to "give joy" to God.[38] A person who truly loves seeks to make the beloved happy, even when it requires sacrifice. Blessed John Paul II once asked: "What is holiness?" And he answered: "It is precisely the joy of doing God's will."[39]

Holiness is not a question of a superhuman ascetical effort to attain specific goals, as though striving for perfection by oneself for some sort of "self-perfection." Rather, it means growing in love for God, the source and goal of every virtue. In spiritual guidance, stress should be placed not so much on the material fulfillment of a particular virtue, as on the love for God that is put into the struggle to fulfill it. It is not a matter of

---

37. St. John Chrysostom, *Commentary on the Letter to the Corinthians*, 3.

38. St. Teresa often spoke about trying to please or "give joy" to God, "making him happy": "To love is to want to please God in everything" (*Mansions*, IV, 1, 7); "The desire to please God and faith make possible what is not possible naturally" (*Foundations*, 2, 4); "Self-love . . . is to want to please ourselves more than God" (Ibid. 5, 4); "God is more pleased with obedience than with sacrifice" (Ibid., 6, 2); "This house is a heaven . . . for anyone who is only happy in making God happy and is not concerned with her own happiness" (*The Way of Perfection*, 13, 7); "What do kings and lords matter to me . . . or making them happy, if, although it be in something very small, I have to make God unhappy for them?" (Ibid., 2, 5).

39. John Paul II, *Homily*, January 18, 1981.

compiling a spotless record but of struggling to fulfill lovingly God's will.

Christ knows the depths of the human heart, and despite all the wretchedness it can harbor, he always sees its capacity for good. "Jesus' look penetrates the veil of human passions and reaches the depths of the human heart, where one is alone, poor, and naked."[40] He understands us and encourages us to continue struggling. His loving look sees our immense possibilities for good and also the weaknesses that are so often a reality in our lives. Christ knows what is within man. "He alone knows it!"[41] And nevertheless he asks us to follow him: "Come, follow me" (Mt 4:19).

Our Lord's love for us is the all-encompassing reality that shapes the struggle for sanctity. It is the reality that enables us to renew our spirits and regain our joy, despite any sorrows and setbacks. And it is this reality that has to guide all the advice given in spiritual direction.

The spiritual life of any saint is the story of Christ's love. This love impels forward every effort towards sanctity and lies at the very heart of all spiritual accompaniment. At times some people, if they have not been fully faithful to our Lord, may think he is upset and angry with them, and the devil makes use of this falsehood to distance them from God when their need is greatest to draw close to him. It is then that they need to recall with special force the parables of divine mercy: the prodigal son, the lost sheep, and the lost coin that brings joy when found.

We often need to remind souls that every moment is appropriate for beginning again with trust. Our Lord does not want anyone to be cast down by the negative experience of past weaknesses and sins. We need to assure such people that they are never alone in the struggle, that struggling against defects to

---

40. Karl Adam, *Jesucristo* (Barcelona: Herder, 1967), p. 112.
41. John Paul I, *Homily*, October 22, 1978.

"give joy" to our Lord, to behave as he wants, will propel them far along the path of virtue.

As God's Children

St. Paul confided to Timothy how the Lord had had mercy on him and made him an apostle despite his having been a "blasphemer and persecutor" of the Christians. "The grace of our Lord," he wrote, "overflowed for me with the faith and love that are in Christ Jesus" (1 Tim 1:12–14). All Christians can attest that God has poured out his grace on us abundantly. He created us, and bestowed on us gratuitously the greatest dignity possible: that of being his children through grace, becoming *domestici Dei*, members of his own family (see Eph 2:19). This truth should fill to overflowing a Christian's supernatural life, and come up again and again in spiritual direction. It is like the string of a necklace tying the pearls together, giving unity to all of life's events: the happy moments, the times of sickness, the death of a loved one. . . .

When giving guidance to others, it's important to stress how deeply divine filiation should affect our whole life. Our very being and all our actions should be transformed by the reality that we are children of God.

Therefore the path for growing in holiness, for sharing intimately in God's own life, is an ever-greater appreciation for our divine filiation. "We are not only called children of God; we really are such. God, in a superabundance of goodness, not only wants us to treat him like a father, but, in an incomparably greater outpouring of his love, he has adopted us as his children in a true, though limited and partial, sense. He makes us sharers in the only divine filiation that is so in the strict sense: that of the Second Person of the Most Holy Trinity, the Only Begotten Son of the Father. "See what love the Father has given us, that we should be called children of God; and so we are" (1 Jn

3:1). "Sons of God, brothers of the Word made flesh, of him of whom it was said: 'In him was life, and the life was the light of men' (Jn 1:4). Children of the light, brothers of the light: that is what we are." [42, 43]

When giving advice to souls, it is good to point out often the many practical consequences of this reality. Our prayer will be that of a child speaking with its father, for we come to realize that, although he is the Supreme Being and Omnipotent Creator, he is also truly our Loving Father. Interior life is grounded not on a solitary struggle against our defects in search of some form of "self-perfection," but rather on abandoning ourselves into the strong arms of the Father, and on an ardent desire shown in deeds to "give joy" to our Father God, who loves each of us infinitely. Therefore, divine filiation is not one aspect among many of our Christian identity; in some way it includes all the others. It is a particular way of being, a specific relationship that is ontologically distinguished from the other supernatural gifts: sanctifying grace, the virtues, the gifts of the Holy Spirit. But if we consider God's saving plan, we can say that all these other gifts are given with a view to receiving this "adoption."

42. See St. Josemaría Escrivá, *Christ Is Passing By*, no. 66.

43. Fernando Ocáriz, *El Sentido de la Filiación Divina* (Pamplona: Eunsa, 1982), pp. 179–181.

"To participate in the divine filiation of the one who is the Only Begotten—the Only Son of the Father—speaks to us of possessing partially, in a limited way, what in him subsists in infinite fullness . . . being children of God in a true but partial sense—that is to say, participating in the filiation of the Word—reveals to us that we are *sons of God in the Son*, because without ceasing to be the Only Begotten, he is the First Born among many brethren (cf. Rom 8:29)" (Ibid., p. 181).

"Divine filiation is not a particular virtue with acts proper to it. Rather it is a permanent condition of the person, the subject of virtues. One doesn't behave as God's child part of the time. All our activity, the exercise of each virtue, can and ought to express our divine filiation. 'We are children of God all day long, even though we set aside special moments for considering it, so that we can fill ourselves with the awareness of our divine filiation, the essence of true piety' (*Conversations*, no. 102)" (Ibid., pp. 193–194).

Divine filiation provides a firm grounding for our life and a special way of confronting all of life's events. God is always the support and strength of our soul, the refuge where again and again we can seek assistance.

By identifying us with the Son, our divine sonship also leads to seeing events and judging them with his eyes; to obeying like Christ, who became obedient even unto death (see Phil 2:8); to loving and forgiving as he did. We come to act always as children who know they are in the presence of their Father God, trusting and serene, feeling understood, forgiven, and encouraged to continue forward. Our faith is the faith of a son or daughter of God. We work as a child of God. Our fortitude, our joy, and our freedom are all deeply marked by the reality that we are God's children. Thus one is always cheerful and optimistic, never falling prey to anxiety.[44]

God may also permit someone who is seriously struggling for holiness to feel lost, useless, confused, failing to understand, *despite wanting to be completely God's*, what is happening in one's life or surroundings.[45] This is the moment to help that person to be faithful to God's will, with complete docility, even though he or she may not understand why our Lord is acting in this way. If God, who is our Father, permits this state of interior

---

44. "Optimism? Yes, always! Even when things seem to turn out badly: perhaps that is the time to break into a song, with a *Gloria*, because you have sought refuge in him, and nothing but good can come to you from him" (St. Josemaría Escrivá, *Furrow*, no. 90).

45. The saints describe this situation of complete obscurity in many different ways. But they always advise complete trust in God, who never abandons us. As St. Josemaría Escrivá wrote: "In those moments when one does not even know what the will of God is, and one protests: 'Lord, how can you want this, which is bad, which is intrinsically abominable'—as the humanity of Christ complained in the Garden of Olives—when it seems as though one's mind is going mad and one's heart is breaking. . . . If at some time you feel this falling into a vacuum, I advise that prayer that I repeated many times next to the grave of a beloved person: *Fiat, adimpleatur, laudetur atque in aeternum superexaltetur iustissima atque amabilissima* . . ." (cited in Francisco Fernandez-Carvajal, *Hablar con Dios*, vol. IV pp. 788–789). "May the most just and most lovable will of God be done, be fulfilled, be praised, and eternally exalted above all things. Amen, Amen." (St. Josemaría Escrivá, *The Way*, no. 691).

darkness, he will also grant the soul that momentarily seems to be blind the grace and assistance required to accept this trial. "Father, if thou art willing, remove this cup from me; nevertheless not my will, but thine, be done" (Lk 22:42).

Abandonment into God's hands without setting any conditions brings an unbreakable peace. Amid the deepest darkness, one will feel the powerful and gentle arm of our Father God who upholds us. Let us help anyone in this situation to repeat slowly a simple and trusting prayer that will foster abandonment in God's hands: "May the most just and most lovable will of God be done, be fulfilled, be praised, and eternally exalted above all things. Amen, Amen."

"You will show me the path to life, fullness of joy in your presence, the delights at your right hand forever" (Ps 16:11), proclaims the Psalmist. And there is no deeper joy—also amid destitution and darkness, when God permits it—than that of a child of God who abandons itself into the hands of its Father. This supernatural joy, so closely tied to the Cross, is one of the Christian's most intimate secrets. The realization that we are truly God's children frees us from internal tension and brings peace, even in the hardest moments. And when, through weakness, we do go astray, we will return repentant and trustingly to our Father's house.

Filiation and Fraternity

It is important to teach people the special strength that Christian and human fraternity acquire in light of our divine filiation.[46] We are brothers and sisters, above all, because we are children of the one Father, who unites us to himself with the supernatural bond of charity. The realization that we are God's children

---

46. "Our being children of God *in Christ* confers on Christian fraternity some very specific supernatural characteristics. This fraternity is truly unity: *we are all one in Christ* (Ocáriz, *El Sentido de la Filiación Divina*, pp. 190–191).

is shown in our mutual respect and refinement, in a spirit of service, in helping one another on the path to God. . . . In the Gospel our Lord asks his followers to purify their vision in order to see others clearly. "Why do you see the speck that is in your brother's eye, but do not notice the log that is in your own eye? First take the log out of your own eye, and then you will see clearly to take out the speck that is in your brother's eye" (Lk 6: 41–42). The Master asks us to set aside the prejudices forged by our own faults, especially the pride that leads us to focus on others' weaknesses and minimize our own. Our Lord exhorts us to see others as brothers and sisters, specially loved by God. He asks us to see them—first of all, those at our side—as what they are: children of God, with all the dignity of that marvelous title.

"We have to behave as God's children toward all God's sons and daughters. Our love has to be a dedicated love, practiced every day and made up of a thousand little details of understanding, hidden sacrifice and unnoticed self-giving. This is the 'good aroma of Christ' that made those who lived among our first brothers in the faith exclaim: See how they love one another!"[47]

Behaving as God's Children Toward All God's Sons and Daughters

We have to see people as Christ sees them, with love and understanding—both those who are nearby and those who seem further away. All are God's children—his creatures—and all are called to the warmth of the Father's house. This fraternity is also what spurs us on in the apostolate, to strive to make use of all the means to bring souls to God.

Thus we will help others to travel through life with serenity and peace, "doing good" (see Lk 18:17), like Jesus Christ,

---

47. St. Josemaría Escrivá, *Christ Is Passing By*, no. 36.

our Model, in whom we learn to be children of God the Father and to behave as such. Every Christian struggling for holiness is *Christ who is passing by* among men and women in the world.

Spiritual Childhood

Divine filiation also leads us to *spiritual childhood*, for God wants us to behave in accord with our true condition—as needy children who turn to him for help. Our Lord insisted: "Truly, I say to you, whoever does not receive the kingdom of God like a child shall not enter it" (Lk 18:17). For many people, discovering the path of childhood has meant the definitive beginning of a true interior life. The spiritual counselor will need to discern the right moment to suggest that a soul, with full freedom, begin traveling this path of great simplicity and trust.

The life of spiritual childhood leads to simplicity and humble abandonment, but not to immaturity and childishness. Being "infantile" is a caricature of what it means to be a small child before our Father God. This immaturity of the mind, heart, and emotions is closely linked to a lack of self-discipline and struggle. It is an attitude that may accompany some people during their entire life, right up to old age, without their ever truly becoming children before God. True spiritual childhood brings with it maturity of mind shown in supernatural vision, weighing events in the light of faith and with the assistance of the gifts of the Holy Spirit. Along with maturity it brings simplicity, a lack of complication. It is impossible to make progress on the path of spiritual childhood if one's life is a complicated tangle of ever fluctuating desires and emotions, with a capricious conduct guided solely by concern for one's ego.

By contrast, the one who is truly a child before God, who recognizes with simplicity his own neediness, is concerned only about the glory of his Father, as our Lord Jesus Christ was during his earthly life. A true child, a true son, lives and speaks continually with his Father and asks him for whatever he needs.[48]

GREAT IDEALS AND THE LITTLE THINGS OF EACH DAY

We have to help souls to embrace great ideals, since God is calling all men and women to the greatest ideal, to sanctity. At the same time, these ideals have to be grounded on a specific daily struggle in little things.

To chip away at deeply rooted defects (laziness, selfishness, envy, etc.), we will often suggest particular points of struggle. This will involve setting goals that might seem quite limited: getting up on time; being orderly in following a schedule and caring for items of personal use; serving others so that they hardly notice it; suggesting to a companion at school or work that he or she accompany us on a visit to our Lord in a nearby church; thinking less of one's own health and personal concerns; being careful in choosing a television program or turning it off if it seems inappropriate.

In the ascetical struggle, we must have our feet firmly planted on the ground, even if our heart is in heaven. God wants souls to have specific desires shown in deeds to love him a little more each day. And he wants us to give expression to our great ideals by struggling in what might seem of little importance.[49]

---

48. The reality of our divine filiation has always consoled the saints. "I am only a small child," St. Augustine said, "but my Father lives forever and is my greatest protector" (*Confessions*, 10, 4, 4).

49. "Have you seen how that imposing building was built? One brick upon another. Thousands. But, one by one. And bags of cement, one by one. And blocks of stone, each of them insignificant compared with the massive whole. And beams of steel. And men working, the same hours, day after day. . . . Have you seen how that imposing building was built? . . . By dint of little things!" (St. Josemaría Escrivá, *The Way*, no. 823).

We may often encounter individuals who think that sanctity involves extraordinary events and is attained only by great trials and martyrdom. They mistakenly think that a Christian life lived with all its consequences is something for only a few exceptional people, and that our Lord is satisfied if most people lead a second-rate Christian life. But we have to insist that our Lord calls everyone to holiness. The busy mother who hardly has time to carry out her housework, but who works out of love and is faithful to a plan of spiritual life and is apostolic, can truly be a saint.[50] Likewise, the businessman, the student, the employee in a large store, or the owner of a vegetable stand. . . . The Holy Spirit's words are addressed to everyone: "This is the will of God, your sanctification" (1 Thess 4:3). He makes use of all the circumstances in our lives and grants us all the necessary graces to attain this goal.

Sanctity in Ordinary Work

For centuries, many thought that to be a good Christian all that was needed was a life of piety, with no connection to one's daily work. Moreover, this often went hand in hand with the conviction that the secular concerns of daily life were an obstacle to encountering God and living a fully Christian life.[51] We need to understand very well and teach others that it is precisely in the midst of these daily happenings that one must find our Lord and attain holiness. Jesus' hidden life teaches us the value of work, of unity of life, for by his daily effort he was redeeming

---

50. Whatever one's daily work, this point from *Furrow* can be of great assistance: "You are writing to me in the kitchen, by the stove. It is early afternoon. It is cold. By your side, your younger sister—the last one to discover the divine folly of living her Christian vocation to the full—is peeling potatoes. To all appearances—you think—her work is the same as before. And yet, what a difference there is! It is true: before she *only* peeled potatoes, now, she is sanctifying herself peeling potatoes" (St. Josemaría Escrivá, *Furrow*, no. 498).

51. See Jose Luis Illanes, *La Sanctification del Trabajo* (Madrid: Palabra, 2001), p. 44ff.

the world. Ordinary Christians who live in the heart of the world have to imitate especially those years of the Master's life spent without human glamour. This was St. Josemaría Escrivá's teaching throughout his whole life.

Work not only should not distance us from our final goal; it is the specific path for growing in Christian life. Therefore Catholics should never forget that, besides being citizens of the world, they are also citizens of heaven, and therefore should always conduct themselves in a manner worthy of their Christian vocation (see Phil 1:27; 3:6)—always cheerful, irreproachable in their conduct, showing understanding towards all (see Phil 4:8). They should be both good workers and good friends, open to every authentic human value. "For the rest, brethren," St. Paul exhorted the Christians at Philippi, "whatever is true, whatever is honorable, whatever is just, whatever is pure, whatever is lovely, whatever is gracious, if there is any excellence, if there is anything worthy of praise, think about these things" (Phil 4:8).

Therefore, one who provides spiritual guidance to others should teach them to turn their work into prayer, to seek God's glory and the good of all mankind in their daily tasks. They should seek our Lord's help when beginning each task and in confronting the difficulties their work entails, giving thanks when a task, or the day's work, has been finished. Work then becomes a daily path to God. "This is why man ought not to limit himself to material production. Work is born of love; it is a manifestation of love and is directed toward love. We see the hand of God, not only in the wonders of nature, but also in our experience of work and effort. Work thus becomes prayer and thanksgiving, because we know we are placed on earth by God, that we are loved by him and made heirs to his promises."[52] Work should *be born of love, manifest love, be*

---

52. St. Josemaría Escrivá, *Christ Is Passing By*, no. 48.

ordained to love. We thereby give glory to God and draw closer to him each day. And through our work we assist all mankind, our brothers and sisters.

Work, a means of sanctity for a Christian when carried out in union with Christ, is a source of grace for the whole Church, for we are "the Body of Christ and members united with the other members" (1 Cor 12:27). Work is also a means for furthering the human progress of society.[53] Moreover, in the exercise of one's profession, a Christian encounters, in a natural way, without setting out to teach others, many opportunities to make the Church's teaching known and to bring people closer to our Lord: one's colleagues at work, friends, clients, acquaintances. We do so by our friendly conversation, by commenting on a current news item, or by listening to someone's personal or family problems. If we ask for assistance, the Holy Spirit will give us the words we need to encourage and help others and, although it may take time, to draw them closer to Christ.

With the help of grace, through our earthly activities we are striving to attain heaven.[54] Far from neglecting temporal tasks, we want to imitate Christ, who worked as a carpenter for the greater part of his life. Catholics by their faith "are

---

53. "Sweat and toil, which work necessarily involves in the present condition of the human race, present the Christian and everyone who is called to follow Christ with the possibility of sharing lovingly in the work that Christ came to do (see Jn 17:4). This work of salvation came about through suffering and death on a cross. By enduring the toil of work in union with Christ crucified for us, man in a way collaborates with the Son of God for the redemption of humanity. He shows himself a true disciple of Christ by carrying the cross in his turn every day (see Lk 9:23) in the activity that he is called upon to perform" (Bl. John Paul II, *Laborem Exercens*, no. 27).

54. The Magisterium of the Church recalls the value of work and exhorts Christians, "as citizens of two cities, to strive to discharge their earthly duties conscientiously and in response to the Gospel spirit" (Vatican II, *Gaudium et Spes*, no. 43; cf. Bl. John Paul II, *Laborem Exercens* and *Centesimus Annus).*

more obliged than ever to measure up to these duties, each according to his proper vocation."[55]

We have to raise our eyes frequently to heaven, our definitive homeland, while keeping our feet firmly planted on the ground. Each of us has to work with intensity in order to give glory to God, sustain our own family, and serve society. Without serious work done conscientiously, it is very difficult, perhaps impossible, to attain sanctity in the midst of the world. And those who are sick or disabled should strive to gain heaven by offering up their infirmity or sufferings. The person giving spiritual guidance should never lose sight of the fact that work is the natural medium for developing all the virtues.[56]

Work is the means to support oneself, and it is a privileged place for the development of the human virtues: constancy, tenacity, a spirit of solidarity, order, and optimism in the face of difficulties. Work is also an opportunity to exercise and grow in the theological virtues of faith, hope, and charity. Supernatural life fosters a "spirit of charity, of harmony, of understanding."[57] It spurs us to uproot from our life "attachment to our own comfort, the temptation to selfishness, the tendency to be the center of everything,"[58] and "to show the

---

55. Vatican II, *Gaudium et Spes*, no. 43.

As is only natural, work done for God should conform to the moral norms that make it upright and good. Therefore the spiritual guide should be alert to ensure that those being guided know very well the moral norms referring to work in the fields of commerce, medicine, nursing, law . . . They also should be aware of the duty to make a return for the salary one receives, to provide a just payment to those who work in the company, etc.

56. "Make no mistake about it. Man's duty to work is not a consequence of original sin, nor is it just a discovery of modern times. It is an indispensable means that God has entrusted to us here on this earth. It is meant to fill out our days and make us sharers in God's creative power. It enables us to earn our living and, at the same time, to reap 'the fruits of eternal life' (Jn 4:36)" (St. Josemaría Escrivá, *Friends of God*, no. 57).

57. St. Josemaría Escrivá, *Conversations*, no. 35.

58. St. Josemaría Escrivá, *Christ Is Passing By*, no. 158.

charity of Christ and its concrete expression in friendship, understanding, human affection, and peace."[59]

The one giving direction must stress the value of work—from a strictly spiritual point of view—as the ordinary means for obtaining holiness while living in the world. Laziness, idleness, and sloppy or badly finished work are in themselves important defects that distance us from God and hinder the development of a true supernatural life because they prevent one's talents from bearing fruit, as our Lord required of us (see Mt 25:24). In addition, they bring in their wake many grave consequences. "Idleness teaches much evil," says Sirach 33:27, for it impedes human maturity, weakens character, and opens the door to concupiscence and temptation. Part of teaching people how to work well involves teaching them how to relax, which is not the same as "dissipation" or "shirking one's duties."

Apostolate: The Overflow of Supernatural Life

Those who guide others in their Christian life also need to foster the unmistakable sign of ascetical struggle, founded on divine filiation: apostolate.[60] Anyone who wants to follow our Lord closely must be interested in the salvation of all souls, as was the Master. People who truly live their faith become a source of light for those around them, in their place of work and among their friends and acquaintances.[61] In accord with each one's circumstances and temperament, Christians

---

59. Ibid., no. 166.
60. Apostolate, as a topic of spiritual guidance, is dealt with in the Appendix of this book.
61. "The apostolic concern which burns in the heart of ordinary Christians is not something separate from their everyday work. It is part and parcel of one's work, which becomes a source of opportunities for meeting Christ. As we work at our job, side by side with our colleagues, friends and relatives and sharing their interests, we can help them come closer to Christ" (St. Josemaría Escrivá, *Friends of God*, no. 264).

should carry out an intense apostolate, for they know that their Father God has given them the world as their inheritance (see Ps 2), telling them: "Go and work in the vineyard today" (Mt 21:28).[62]

But this requires that Christians truly fulfill St. Paul's exhortation to the Philippians: "Have this mind among you that was in Christ Jesus" (Phil 2:5). It "requires that all Christians should possess, as far as humanly possible, the same dispositions as those which the divine Redeemer had when he offered himself in sacrifice: that is to say, they should, in a humble attitude of mind, pay adoration, honor, praise, and thanksgiving to the supreme majesty of God."[63] This self-offering is realized principally in the Holy Mass, the bloodless actualization of the sacrifice of the Cross, where we offer our daily work and endeavors, our family life, our rest, and the very trials that life brings with it. Everything in our life is turned into a means of co-redemption, of apostolate.[64] When the Eucharistic sacrifice ends, we go forth to meet life with

---

62. *"God calls me and sends me forth* as a laborer in his vineyard. He calls me and sends me forth to work for the coming of his Kingdom in history. This personal vocation and mission defines the dignity and the responsibility of each member of the lay faithful and makes up the focal point of the whole work of formation. . . . In fact, from eternity God has thought of us and has loved us as unique individuals. Every one of us he called by name, as the Good Shepherd 'calls his sheep by name' (Jn 10:3). However, only in the unfolding of the history of our lives and its events is the eternal plan of God revealed to each of us. Therefore, it is a gradual process, in a certain sense, one that happens day by day" (*Christifideles Laici*, no. 58).

63. Pius XII, *Mediator Dei*, no. 81.

64. Bl. John Paul II, referring specifically to priests, but with words applicable to all of the faithful, teaches that charity and concern for others have their source in the Mass, the center and root of Christian life: "Indeed, the Eucharist re-presents, makes present once again, the sacrifice of the cross, the full gift of Christ to the Church, the gift of his Body given and his blood shed, as the supreme witness of the fact that he is head and shepherd, servant and spouse of the Church. Precisely because of this, the priest's pastoral charity not only flows from the Eucharist but finds in the celebration of the Eucharist its highest realization—just as it is from the Eucharist that he receives the grace and obligation to give his whole life a 'sacrificial' dimension" (*Pastores dabo vobis*, no. 23).

the same sentiments as Christ had in his earthly existence: forgetting about ourselves and ready to give our life for others to bring them to God.

The Christian life, as we've already stressed, means imitating Christ's life, sharing in the Son of God's way of being. In advising others spiritually, we should teach them to see, feel, act, and react as Christ did. Jesus looked at the crowds and had compassion on them because they were "like sheep without a shepherd" (Mt 9:36), with no clear direction in life. So great was Christ's love that he wasn't satisfied until he gave his own life for us on the cross. This same love has to fill the heart of anyone who follows Christ, leading him or her to have compassion on all those still separated from our Lord and strive to help them to come to know the Master.[65]

Apostolate is firmly rooted in the Mass, from which it draws all its effectiveness, since it is simply the realization of the redemption in time through Christians. Christ "came on earth to redeem everyone, because 'he wishes all men to be saved' (1 Tim 2:4). There is not a single soul in whom Christ is not interested. Each soul has cost him the price of his Blood" (see 1 Pet 1:18–19).[66] We too have to be concerned about every soul, since Christians are called to look at the world "with the eyes of Christ himself."[67] We will see others as our Lord sees them to the extent that we identify ourselves with him.

---

65. The Magisterium of the Church has repeatedly reminded us that "the Christian vocation by its very nature is also a vocation to the apostolate" (Vatican II, *Apostolicam Actuositatem*, no. 2). Bl. John Paul II insisted that the lay faithful, "precisely because they are members of the Church, have the vocation and mission of proclaiming the Gospel: they are prepared for this work by the sacraments of Christian initiation and by the gifts of the Holy Spirit" (*Christifideles Laici*, no. 33). Therefore, it is impossible to understand how a good Catholic could not be an apostle.

66. St. Josemaría Escrivá, *Friends of God*, no. 256.

67. John Paul II, *Redemptor Hominis*, no. 18.

The spiritual counselor should encourage the apostolic initiatives of those he is guiding and make clear that, for apostolic zeal to bear fruit, it has to be the "superabundance"[68] of our love for God. If apostolic zeal and a concern for the welfare of souls are lacking, it's a clear sign that one's identification with our Lord has to grow.[69] The desire to co-redeem with Christ is what gives meaning to everything else. Apostolate is not something "added on" to our spiritual life, but rather "the precise and necessary outward manifestation of interior life."[70]

Unity of Life

Another essential point when guiding souls is the need to foster a true unity of life, grounded on the awareness of being a child of God in every circumstance. Following Christ means making him the aim of all our actions in order to become identified with him. The interior life is, in essence, "an effort to build up a unity of life, seconding the work of grace. At first, this involves a wide variety of ascetical practices with no evident unity. But this apparent diversity and complexity—which, in reality, is always unitary as regards its end—is resolved in a higher unity. As a Christian grows in grace, his or her actions become more and more explicitly informed by

---

68. See St. Josemaría Escrivá, *Friends of God*, no. 239. And also this passage: "I find it very hard to believe in the supernatural effectiveness of an apostolate that is not based, is not solidly centered, on a life of constant conversation with Our Lord. Yes, right there in our work; in our own home, or in the street, with all the small or big problems that arise daily. Right there, not taken away from those things, but with our hearts fixed on God. Then our words, our actions—our defects!—will give forth the *bonus odor Christi* (2 Cor 2:15) the sweet fragrance of Christ, which other men will inevitably notice and say: 'Here is a Christian'" (*Friends of God*, no. 271).

69. "People have often drawn attention to the danger of deeds performed without any interior life to inspire them; but we should also stress the danger of an interior life—if such a thing is possible—without deeds to show for it" (St. Josemaría Escrivá, *The Forge*, no. 734).

70. St. Josemaría Escrivá, *Christ Is Passing By*, no. 122.

charity, until the moment arrives when they are no longer seen as diverse."[71,72]

We can never fall into the mindset that some of our time is for God and the rest is for study or work. All time is God's gift, and all of it should be directed to him.[73] We have only one life, which is ordered by God with all of its actions and activities.[74] Unity of life is attained when we seek God's glory in all our actions—in our work, with our family, playing sports. This requires frequently rectifying our intention, striving to uproot the self-love and vainglory to which every human heart is so readily prone.

The effort to live always as a child of God, the focal point of unity of life, is shown in our work, which we need to direct to God; in our life at home, which we strive to fill with peace

---

71. Ignacio de Celaya, *Unidad de Vida y Plenitud Cristiana*, (Pamplona: Eunsa, 1985), p. 326.

72. "We start with vocal prayers which many of us have been saying since we were children. . . . First one brief aspiration, then another, and another . . . till our fervor seems insufficient, because words are too poor . . . : then this gives way to intimacy with God, looking at God without needing rest or feeling tired. We begin to live as captives, as prisoners. And while we carry out as perfectly as we can (with all our mistakes and limitations) the tasks allotted to us by our situation and duties, our soul longs to escape. It is drawn towards God like iron drawn by a magnet. One begins to love Jesus, in a more effective way, with the sweet and gentle surprise of his encounter" (St. Josemaría Escrivá, *Friends of God*, no. 296).

73. The spiritual guide has to help people to ward off "the temptation . . . of living a kind of double life. On one side, an interior life, a life of relation with God; and on the other, a separate and distinct professional, social, and family life, full of small earthly realities" (St. Josemaría Escrivá, *Conversations*, no. 114). The Second Vatican Council warned that "this split between the faith which many profess and their daily lives deserves to be counted among the more serious errors of our age" (*Gaudium et Spes*, no. 43).

74. The life of prayer has to penetrate and transform all of our daily activities. "Spirituality can never be understood as a collection of pious and ascetical practices set alongside a collection of rights and duties determined by one's circumstances. On the contrary, to the extent that they respond to God's will, these circumstances have to be taken up and given supernatural life by a particular way of developing a spiritual life, a development that has to be attained precisely in and through those circumstances" (Álvaro del Portillo, *On Priesthood*, p. 68).

and a spirit of service; and in our friendships, by which we can help others to draw closer to God. At every moment of the day or night, we struggle to be, with the help of grace, men and women of integrity, who don't bend with the wind and easily set aside their Christian principles, or who restrict their conversation with God to moments when in Church or on their knees. Therefore, in giving spiritual advice we need frequently to remind people that, in the street, at work, during sports, or in a social gathering, they have to be always the same person: sons or daughters of God who reflect in an attractive way their determination to follow Christ in every situation. "Whether you eat or drink, or whatever you do, do all to the glory of God" (1 Cor 10:31), St. Paul told the early Christians.[75]

All noble human realities are ordered by Christ—who is in the center of our soul—and should lead to him. Just as human love means loving someone at every moment and not just at specific times, so too we need to teach souls that love for Christ should imbue all our actions. "In the world some days are always bad, but in God there are only good days."[76] All days are good when we are close to him, even though sorrows and setbacks will also be present.

Through the unity of life, we show others how Christ sheds light on every aspect of human life: at work, in business dealings, when striving to implement the Church's social doctrine. . . . We would have to doubt the sincerity of a person's

---

75. St. Basil, commenting on these words of St. Paul, said: "When you sit at the table, pray. When you eat bread, do so giving thanks to the One who is generous. If you drink wine, recall the One who has given it to us for our joy and the relief of sickness. When you get dressed, give thanks to him for what he has deigned to give you. When you contemplate the heavens and the beauty of the stars, cast yourself at God's feet and adore the One who, in his Wisdom, has ordered all these things. In the same way, when the sun rises and the sun sets, while you sleep and when you are awake, give thanks to God who created and orders all these things for your advantage, so that you may know, love, and praise the Creator" (*Homilia in Julittam Martirem*).

76. St. Augustine, *Expositions on the Psalms*, 33, 2, 17.

life of prayer if the effort to stay close to God didn't lead, as its natural consequence, to being cordial and optimistic, to being punctual and just at work, to making good use of time, to putting care into each task.[77]

Each day's difficulties and worries should nourish our daily conversation with God. At the same time, prayer should enrich all the circumstances of each day. Close to our Lord, a Christian learns to be a better friend of one's friends, to be just and loyal in one's work, to be more human, to be open to the needs of others. In spiritual guidance we have to give people the specific advice they need to attain a true unity of life. This advice should include asking for God's help in beginning each task, struggling to keep present to God, and frequently examining one's rectitude of intention—thus attaining the human and supernatural maturity that unity of life brings.

Referring to the daily life of Christians, Bl. John Paul II insisted, "There cannot be two parallel lives in their existence: on the one hand, the so-called 'spiritual' life, with its values and demands; and on the other, the so-called 'secular' life, that is, life in a family, at work, in social relationships, in the responsibilities of public life and in culture. The branch, engrafted to the vine, which is Christ, bears its fruit in every sphere of existence and activity. In fact, every area of the lay faithful's lives, as different as they are, enters into the plan of God, who desires that these very areas be the 'places in time' where the love of Christ is revealed and realized for both the glory of the Father and service of others. Every activity, every situation, every precise responsibility—as, for example, skill and solidarity in work, love and dedication in the family and the education of children,

---

77. "The unity of life of the lay faithful is of the greatest importance: indeed they must be sanctified in everyday professional and social life. Therefore, to respond to their vocation, the lay faithful must see their daily activities as an occasion to join themselves to God, fulfill his will, serve other people and lead them to communion with God in Christ" (Bl. John Paul II, *Christifideles Laici*, no. 17).

service to society and public life, and the promotion of truth in the area of culture—are the occasions ordained by Providence for a 'continuous exercise of faith, hope and charity.'"[78, 79]

Attaining a solid unity of life enables us to overcome the divisions caused by original sin and by our personal sins. "Our wounded human nature finds it difficult to reconcile the apparent opposition between the natural and supernatural, contemplation and action, doctrine and life, obedience and freedom. . . . In the teaching of St. Josemaría Escrivá, the overcoming of these apparent dilemmas is a natural and necessary consequence of the fullness of Christian life. And for the first time in the history of the Church, this effort is asked of the ordinary Christian, of the 'man in the street,' and not 'despite' being in the world, but precisely through being present in temporal realities."[80]

Another consequence of unity of life is overcoming human respects, the fear of "what others will say." If a Christian acts for God alone, the misunderstandings or criticisms of others will have little importance, for we are seeking to serve God above all things. And by striving to do so, we will come to realize that love for God shown in deeds is the greatest service we can render our brothers and sisters.

We do a great good to our family and to society when we endeavor to stay close to our Lord throughout the day: seeking the presence of God, putting effort into our daily prayer, frequent confession with real contrition. . . . And when we fail to struggle—whether through disorder, lukewarmness, or even the desire to take care of other activities that seem more urgent or more important—we can do great harm.

---

78. Vatican II, *Apostolicam Actuositatem*, no. 4.
79. Bl. John Paul II, *Christifideles Laici*, no. 59.
80. Celaya, *Unidad de Vida y Plenitud Cristiana*, p. 329.

Chapter 4

THE CONVERSATION

PLACE, FREQUENCY, DURATION

Jesus liked to spend many hours talking with his disciples. He listened to their experiences, answered their questions, gave them arguments to respond to the Pharisees' attacks. . . . We never see him showing impatience; rather, he seeks to start a dialogue with those who come to him: with Nicodemus, the beggar Bartimaeus, the rich young man. . . . He does so when exhausted from his travels, as we see with the Samaritan woman, and even on Calvary, when his suffering was most intense. On the cross he addresses words filled with hope to the good thief who begs for his help. Everyone who has recourse to him finds consolation and feels in harmony with his Person.[1]

If those giving spiritual guidance imitate Jesus, they will soon become true guides of the souls our Lord entrusts to them, with their quite different personalities and interests.

Christ, being God, was very simple and natural when conversing with people, and we are meant to learn from him.

---

1. "Wherever you may happen to be, remember that the Son of Man did not come to be served, but to serve. Be sure that anyone who wants to follow him cannot attempt to act in any other way" (St. Josemaría Escrivá, *The Forge*, no. 612).

Spiritual direction can occur in many different places. Jesus sometimes spoke with his disciples when staying in a house; other times, he did so in the countryside or on a boat, or while walking along a road. The circumstances too can vary, as befits people living in the world. The important thing is to choose surroundings that facilitate an atmosphere of trust, avoiding an overly formal environment. It's better, for example, not to chat where interruptions are frequent, or in a room where the telephone rings frequently. The conversations should have a family tone, even though the subject matter is quite important. And they should always take place with the prudent attention that each person requires.

Spiritual guidance is the conversation of a brother with his brother or a sister with her sister, of two friends, of a father with his son or a mother with her daughter.

According to a centuries-old custom in the Church, confirmed by wise experience, the confessional is the proper place for a priest to give spiritual direction to women. The Holy Curé of Ars was happy to hear men's confessions in the sacristy, but he would hear those of women only in the confessional. And St. Teresa, in her spiritual conversations with St. John of the Cross, applied to the letter the refrain: "Twixt holy man and holy maid, a wall of solid stone be laid!" The Curé of Ars did not have a pejorative view of women, nor did St. Teresa of men. The ones they distrusted were themselves. These were measures filled with common and supernatural sense, which anyone with a right intention easily understands.

These conversations should take place at a good moment, when circumstances, time pressures (although ordinarily these chats don't require a large amount of time), or tiredness after a hard day's work won't present an obstacle to speaking with the necessary calm and depth. Nor would it make sense to schedule spiritual direction for a time slot that interferes with someone's professional duties.

Order and Duration

Order—a set day and place—helps to ensure that spiritual direction is held with the required regularity, so that this marvelous means of spiritual progress doesn't get lost amid the many tasks that family and professional life entail. It can also sometimes be a good idea to advance the chat to an earlier time slot— for example, when there is an upcoming trip or circumstances require it.

The *duration* should be the time required to do it well. So as not to waste time, which is so valuable, the session should normally be fairly brief. But it is important never to shorten it brusquely, or give an impression of impatience or restlessness (for example, by placing it right before a meeting, looking at one's watch frequently, etc.). Brevity can be facilitated by letting people speak without interrupting them unnecessarily and trying to avoid topics with little or no connection to spiritual questions (for example, sharing a mutual interest). It is also good to seek out a quiet place for the conversation so that interruptions are kept to a minimum.

One should keep in mind that some people are very talkative by nature, while others are quite frugal in their use of words. It is good to help the talkative person get to the point without getting lost in marginal questions, which can sometimes be a cover to avoid bringing up something that may be more difficult to say. When people are quite sparing in their words, we will need to have patience and, without trying to overcome their reticence in a single day, try to win their trust so that, little by little, they speak more freely. Nor should we jump to the conclusion that someone lacks interior depth just because he or she finds it difficult—which is quite natural at first—to express what is going on in his or her soul and struggles to find the right words.

At times one will need to dedicate more time to souls in specific situations: for example, those in whom the Holy Spirit is stirring up desires of dedication to God or who have already begun along that path of greater generosity. A person who has recently discovered his or her vocation and has begun following Christ more closely must be cared for like a plant that has just taken root and is danger of being stepped on and crushed. Special attention should also be given to those in a period of more intense formation (for example, a spiritual retreat), and those going through serious family, professional, or moral problems.[2]

THE FIRST CONVERSATIONS

All those who came close to Christ were quickly won over by him. "So you are Simon the son of John? You shall be called Cephas" (Jn 1:42). And from that day on, the person destined to be the Prince of the Apostles stayed by his side. John and Andrew never forgot their moving conversation with the Master on the afternoon John the Baptist pointed to Jesus and said: "Behold the Lamb of God" (Jn 1:29). The Samaritan woman's life was changed by her meeting with our Lord next to the well of Sichar (see Jn 4:5ff), where, despite his great weariness, Jesus focused all his interest on winning over a soul.

Likewise in spiritual accompaniment, the first conversations are very important, sometimes definitively so. In those first chats we have to win that person for Christ, by the interest and attention we show and by our prayer. "The more deeply we come to understand their ways of thinking through kindness and love, the more easily will we be able to enter into dialogue with them."[3] Our model here should be the conversations our

---

2. "Your charity must be adapted and tailored to the needs of others, not to your own needs" (St. Josemaría Escrivá, *Furrow*, no. 749). Those who are sick also need spiritual attention, offered by listening to them and encouraging them to sanctify their suffering.

3. Vatican II, *Gaudium et Spes*, no. 28.

Lord held with those who came to him, with his quick grasp of their needs and concerns.

If the person has "come from afar" and has been lax in practicing the faith, it is enough to suggest some small and simple practices of piety that can help him or her to converse with our Lord (a visit to the Blessed Sacrament or a brief period of prayer, perhaps ten or fifteen minutes, or some meditative reading). Given the widespread doctrinal confusion today and ignorance about the fundamental truths of the faith, spiritual reading[4] should be one of the pillars of formation, since it provides the nourishment needed to make progress in the interior life.[5] It is important to find the right book that matches the special circumstances of each person.

The goal of these practices of piety is to strengthen, right from the start, each one's desire to follow Christ in the middle of the world, in their own particular family and professional circumstances. We have to help them confront life with joy and optimism, without sterile complaints, even though they may be going through a difficult or painful situation. For it is precisely there, *in that situation*, where they have to strive for sanctity.

Rather than focusing on eliminating defects, our objective is to instill in souls an eagerness to acquire virtues, as our Lord did, because many defects disappear when someone gets to know and begins to follow Jesus closely. Especially at the beginning, we need to set very specific and attainable goals and be alert for any discouragement when the fruit is slow in coming. It is also good to emphasize the importance of keeping the presence of God throughout the day, developing the unity of life that prevents dividing the day into watertight compartments. This may be

---

4. On this topic, see Chapter 2, section "A Teacher," subsection *Spiritual Reading.*
5. "If there is one thing for which modern conditions have produced a special necessity, it is the regular practice of spiritual reading" (Eugene Boylan, *This Tremendous Lover* (Westminster, MD: The Newman Press, 1948), p. 99.

quite challenging at first, but it becomes easier when souls come to understand that our whole life is for God, although we dedicate some moments especially to him. Prayer is integral for that unity of life; our conversation with God gives new meaning and vigor to our work, our rest, our friendships . . . and these realities, in turn, become material for our prayer, for an encounter with our Lord. We should assure souls, as St. Teresa of Avila said, that when one begins to live a true life of prayer, "If we don't let ourselves be conquered, we will obtain our goal, without a doubt."[6]

It is also good to remind those who are just beginning that they will encounter obstacles on the path leading to God: whether from the environment around them, or from their own lack of effort and their weaknesses and falls, whether of greater or lesser importance. But they should be confident that, with the help of grace, they will win out in the end if they are always ready to begin again with humility, with simplicity and openness. We can remind them that following Christ means encountering the Cross, which enriches and deepens love;[7] and that they will sometimes be tempted to reject it and to be happy with "simply being good" when God is calling them to be holy.

KNOWING HOW TO LISTEN

Hearing is not the same as *listening*. Those giving spiritual advice have to show a real interest in what the other person is saying: about their struggles and defeats, their joys and sorrows. It is impossible to imagine Jesus being distracted, with his mind on other concerns, when someone is asking him a question or

---

6. St. Teresa, *The Way of Perfection*, 23, 5 (Carmelite Studies translation, vol. II, p. 127).
7. "The way of perfection passes by way of the Cross. There is no holiness without renunciation and spiritual battle (see 2 Tim 4). Spiritual progress entails the asceticism and mortification that gradually lead to living in the peace and joy of the Beatitudes" (CCC, 2015).

opening their heart to him. We need only recall his dialogue with the rich young man or Nicodemus or Bartimaeus, where we see him focusing all his attention on the person speaking. "What do you want me to do for you?" (Mk 10:51), he asks the blind man in Jericho. When speaking with the Samaritan woman beside Jacob's Well, he forgets his own fatigue and puts all his attention into that dialogue, winning over a woman with a great soul, in spite of her sins.

Our Lord treated each person individually; each, with his or her limitations and virtues, sensed that he or she was appreciated and loved. This is a good model for the spiritual guidance we should give. Each person who comes to us to ask for advice or receive words of encouragement is an unrepeatable image of God, his son or daughter. We have to dedicate the attention and time needed to each one, as though there was no one else in the world, even when we find ourselves tired or with reduced strength. We have to take others' problems upon ourselves, out of charity and, at times, out of justice, because God is asking us to share that noble burden.[8] When we concern ourselves with others' problems, God takes care of our own.[9]

"Iuvenes Videntur . . ."

"When you are with someone, you have to see a soul: a soul who has to be helped, who has to be understood, with whom you have to live in harmony, and who has to be saved."[10] This

---

8. This is possible when we really love others, "but in order to love, great refinement is required, and much thoughtfulness, and respect, and kindliness in rich measure. In other words, it involves following the Apostle's advice: 'carry one another's burdens, and thus you will fulfill the law of Christ' (Gal 6:2). Then indeed we shall be living charity fully and carrying out the commandment of Jesus" (St. Josemaría Escrivá, *Friends of God*, no. 173).

9. "In the measure that we take care of God's concerns," St. Augustine teaches, "in that same measure, God will care for our own" (St. Augustine, *The City of God*, 11, 4).

10. St. Josemaría Escrivá, *The Forge*, no. 573.

attentive concern should be all the greater when it is a question of someone who has spent years striving to live close to God, but who, for whatever reason, is going through a bad time. We then need to keep clearly in mind the fruitful years of fidelity of the person speaking and foresee them continuing on that path once the crisis is overcome. We should always keep in mind that old proverb filled with wisdom: *Iuvenes videntur sancti sed non sunt: senes non videntur sed sunt*—"young people look like saints, but they aren't, while old people (those who have spent years struggling on the path towards God) don't seem to be, but in fact are saints." A person in this situation needs to find in spiritual direction a firm support,[11] sensing that he or she is closely accompanied.

It is important to show a hopeful attitude when speaking with someone going through a difficult time, stressing how much God still expects from them. "You asked me what you could do to prevent the loneliness of that friend of yours. I will tell you what I always say, because we have at our disposal a marvelous weapon which is the answer to everything: prayer. In the first place, you must pray. And then you must do for him what you would like others to do for you if you were in similar circumstances. Without humiliating him, you must help him in such a way that the things he finds difficult can be made easy for him."[12]

"Do for him what you would like others to do for you." We need to put ourselves in the other person's circumstances, without trying to apply a set prescription, and "help him in such a way that the things he finds difficult can be made easy for

---

11. This fraternal help can often be decisive for keeping others safely on their path. "In the midst of so much selfishness, so much coldness—everyone out for what he can get—I call to mind those little wooden donkeys. They were trotting on a desktop, strong and sturdy. One had lost a leg, but it carried on forward, supported by the others" (Ibid., no. 563).

12. Ibid., no. 957.

him." This will often require helping that person to make progress along an "inclined plane" as it were, gradually rising up to where God is waiting for him; it means encouraging him, making him see that he is appreciated and that he can overcome, with God's grace, the bad situation he is going through, always showing him a respectful and positive attitude. This affection and respect is in no way opposed to the exercise of the virtue of fortitude or being clear in one's advice.

"Knowing how to listen" also means having a firm grasp on each person's interior situation, which leads to "knowing how to speak," to being on target with one's advice and suggestions. "It would be a mistake, for example, to try to foster enthusiasm for one's duties, when that person is suffering from fatigue or boredom, or has a heavy heart that needs an outlet in tears. Rather, different 'keys' need to be hit to bring forth sounds that are harmonious and pleasing to God."[13]

Often it isn't easy to determine the right "key," and especially then we will need to ask God for light. But it is important to have a good grasp of the soul "strings" in order to provide real assistance in any circumstance. As St. Francis de Sales wrote in one of his letters: "When we discover that our lute is out of tune, we must neither break the strings nor throw the instrument aside; but listen attentively to find out what is the cause of the discord, and then gently tighten or slacken the strings, according to what is required." [14] The cause of the disharmony may be fatigue, problems in professional work, or a lack of generosity in some point of the ascetical struggle. To locate it exactly, we will need to dedicate more attention to that person, and perhaps also to wait; we may need to apply more supernatural means, asking the Holy Spirit for light.

---

13. "*En la madurez*," the magazine *Palabra*, no. 104, April, 1974, p. 28.
14. Jean Pierre Camus, *The Spirit of St. Francis de Sales*.

And we will need to learn, with humility, to "become a carpet" so that the others can walk confidently,[15] with no fear of tripping over an unexpected obstacle.

BEING UNDERSTANDING

Our Lord didn't send away those who followed him or cease to have regard for them because of their defects. The disciples' failings are all too evident in the Gospels. At times we see them react with envy and anger; they are eager to hold the first place, and they often fail to grasp the meaning of Christ's words. Nevertheless, the Master is patient with them. He knew very well how far they were from the virtues they needed to be the pillars of his Church, but he continued to trust in them and love them. He did the same with the crowds of people who came to him. He said, "Those who are well have no need of a physician, but those who are sick" (Mt 9:12) and "The Son of Man will not break a bruised reed or quench a smoldering wick" (Mt 12:20). Christ's mission was to bring salvation to souls.

God doesn't want our defects, but he makes use of them as a painter makes use of dark tones to better highlight the picture's brightness. Often our defects will help us to grow in humility and go more trustingly to our Lord, sensing our divine filiation more deeply. In short, our failings can help ground our interior life on more solid foundations.

Christ's charity leads those who guide others to imitate the Master, to show understanding for the defects of those who ask for help, to have a great heart in the face of their weaknesses. And they are never scandalized by anything, suppressing even a flicker of surprise when something out of the ordinary is mentioned: falls, shirking responsibility, abandoning the interior

---

15. See St. Josemaría Escrivá, *The Forge*, no. 562.

life after years of struggle . . . [16] Our Lord is asking us to help people just as they are, with all their defects. There are no ideal people in this world. Each person should feel treated like a unique jewel. We can never allow others to feel they aren't loved, as though they were an "object" worthy of study and even interest, but not appreciation. When we truly understand someone, it is easier to love that person as he or she is, and come up with the proper remedy. "A person who loves someone is not content with a superficial knowledge of that person, but strives to go deeply into everything that pertains to that person's interior state." [17] In a heart that opens itself with full sincerity, the spiritual guide will uncover the source of many of that person's faults, the proper remedy, and the means for encouragement to begin again on the path to holiness.

Showing Sympathy

Being understanding in spiritual guidance requires us to be kind and open to those who come in search of help, viewing them with sympathy. This virtue, so closely tied to charity, enables us to grasp the good that exists in each soul. Its foundation is our own personal humility, since we know very well, as St. Augustine said, that "there is no sin or crime committed by another person that I am not capable of committing by reason of my weakness, and, if I have not yet committed it, it is because God, in his mercy, has not permitted it and has preserved me in the good." [18] Being understanding also means not seeing as a fault or defect what, in reality, is simply a different taste or opinion.

---

16. "How mistaken parents, teachers, directors can be, when they demand absolute sincerity and then, when they are told the whole truth, are frightened" (St. Josemaría Escrivá, *Furrow*, no. 336).
17. St. Thomas Aquinas, *Summa Theologica*, I–II, q. 28, a. 2, c.
18. St. Augustine, *Confessions*, 2, 7.

It leads us always to assume that others are acting with a good intention or, in the case of doubt, to try to find a favorable interpretation. We have to be like a good critic who views a painting from the best possible angle so as better to appreciate all the colors and contrasts. The positive attitude that true understanding fosters leads to the firm conviction that everyone, each in his or her own place, is of use in God's service.

Being understanding means, at the same time, seeing a person's defects in the context of his or her good qualities and possibilities: each is like a field full of hidden riches that we have to bring to light.[19] We have to strive always to see the positive in others, especially when some fault of theirs might hide other qualities, and we must continue loving them.[20] This doesn't mean, of course, calling something bad good, or seeing their faults or defects as unimportant. Not showing surprise is quite distinct from ignoring falls or faults as though nothing had happened. A doctor isn't surprised to see symptoms of an illness, but he doesn't for that reason fail to try to cure it. True charity leads to a distinction between errors and sins, which should always be opposed, and the person who errs or sins, "who never loses the dignity of being a person even when he is flawed by false or inadequate religious notions."[21] The one who acts as a guide "will call error error, but the person in error he will correct with kindliness. Otherwise he will not be able to help him, to sanctify him."[22]

---

19. "Avoid the inclination common to those who tend to see rather—and sometimes only—what is not going well, the mistakes. Be filled with joy and be assured that the Lord has granted to all the capacity to become holy precisely by fighting against their own defects" (St. Josemaría Escrivá, *Furrow*, no. 399).

20. "You have to love your fellow men to the point where even their defects, as long as they do not constitute an offence against God, hardly seem to you to be defects at all. If you love only the good qualities you see in others—if you do not know how to be understanding, to make allowances for them and forgive them—you are an egoist" (St. Josemaría Escrivá, *The Forge*, no. 954).

21. Vatican II, *Gaudium et Spes*, no. 28.

22. St. Josemaría Escrivá, *Friends of God*, no. 9.

Being understanding brings with it an open and welcoming attitude that leads to a quick grasp of the situation others are in and to a true appreciation of them, all the more so when their need is greater. This requires "putting ourselves in the other's shoes": "You will then see the various issues or problems calmly. You will not get annoyed. You will be more understanding. You will be able to make allowances and will correct people when and as required. And you will fill the world with charity."[23] We will do so especially with those our Lord has entrusted to us as our "small flock."

This effort does not require any particular techniques of psychology, but only Christ's charity,[24] an effective charity made a reality in each specific situation.

Truth with Charity

St. Paul reminded the first Christians at Ephesus that they had to spread the truth with charity: *veritatem facientes in caritate* (see Eph 4:15). The same rule holds for our effort to be understanding in spiritual direction. The truth—the goals set, the advice given—has to be presented integrally, without compromises or false compassion. At the same time, it should be done in a friendly and positive manner, well suited to the person's real situation, and never in a bitter or annoyed way, or a heavy-handed one. We should always seek an excuse for any mistakes or weaknesses, while taking into account each one's capacity to respond freely. This clear and kind manner in presenting the

---

23. St. Josemaría Escrivá, *The Forge*, no. 958.

24. "Practice a cheerful charity which is at once kindly and firm; human and at the same time supernatural. It should be an affectionate charity, knowing how to welcome everyone with a sincere and habitual smile, and how to understand the ideas and the feelings of others. In this way, with gentleness and strength, and without concessions in matters of personal morals or in doctrine, the charity of Christ—when it is being well lived—will give you a spirit of conquest. Each day you will have a greater desire to work for souls" (St. Josemaría Escrivá, *The Forge*, no. 282).

truth will help people to receive the advice and suggestions more positively and to strive eagerly to improve.

"Almighty God allowed the one he had prepared to be the visible head of his whole Church, to be frightened by the words of a maid and to deny him. We know that this occurred by special providence so that the one who was to be the shepherd of the Church should learn by his fault to be merciful to others. That is, first he made him know himself, and then he put him at the head of the others, so that he would learn by his own weakness how much mercy he had to show for the weaknesses of others."[25]

St. Peter gives us a moving example of how to be understanding without disfiguring or watering down the truth when he addresses those responsible for Jesus' death: "You denied the Holy and Righteous One, and asked for a murderer to be granted to you, and killed the Author of life. . . . And now, brethren, I know that you acted in ignorance . . . Repent therefore, and turn again" (Acts 3:14–19). The apostle tells them that they acted "in ignorance," and that he seeks only their good, their redemption: "Repent therefore, and turn again."

The effort to be understanding will often be shown by remaining calm, while pointing out the required remedies at the right moment, demanding of others without becoming tiresome.

"Continue speaking out," St. John Chrysostom recommended, "without growing weary, acting always in a kindly and pleasant way. Don't you see what painters do, how much they rub out, how much they insert, when they are painting a beautiful face? Well then, don't prove inferior to these. For if they put such care into painting a bodily image, how much more diligence should we put into fashioning a soul, leaving no stone unturned in order to do so as perfectly as possible."[26]

---

25. St. Gregory the Great, *Homilies on the Gospels*, 21.
26. St. John Chrysostom, *Homilies on the Gospel of St. Matthew*, 30.

Let us not forget that God loves people just as they are, even with their defects and deficiencies, as long as they are fighting to overcome them. When someone feels understood and appreciated, it is easier to allow himself or herself to be helped and really to struggle. And we will always keep in mind that, when there is real struggle, souls "improve with time"[27]—and that we can shorten this time with our prayer and mortification, our interest and affection.

BEING PATIENT

The road leading to holiness is a long one. Our Lord usually doesn't grant graces (although he could) that immediately suppress defects and weaknesses. Neither did he do so with those he chose to continue his work in the world. The Gospels show us that Jesus was patient with his disciples' defects and their failures to understand his words. We see how he counted on time, because each soul has its own pace: sometimes slow; other times, impelled by the wind of grace, more rapid.

The Master gives us an example of unwavering patience. He says of the crowds that come to see him: "Seeing they do not see, and hearing they do not hear, nor do they understand" (Mt 13:13). But in spite of everything, we see him untiring in his preaching and dedication to the people, continuously traveling the roads of Palestine. Even the Twelve closest to him don't seem able to grasp his teaching: "I have yet many things to say to you," he told them on the eve of his departure, "but you cannot bear them now" (Jn 16:12). Yet later each would be a faithful witness to Christ and his gospel.

Neither is our Lord discouraged today by people's lack of responsiveness; he knows the capacity for good that each soul

---

27. *Friends of God*, no. 78.

harbors and does not give up on anyone, even though they haven't always responded as he hoped. He himself said that he would never "break a bruised reed or quench a smoldering wick" (Mt 12:20). The pages of the Gospel are a continuous testimony to this truth: the parable of the prodigal son, of the lost sheep, of the fig tree without fruit that is granted another opportunity. . . .

Channels of Grace

Our Lord has also foreseen each Christian's struggle for sanctity today and the need to respect each one's ability to respond. It is our job, in spiritual direction, to be patient channels of grace, always to facilitate the action of the Holy Spirit, helping souls aspire to the high goal of sanctity. If our Lord doesn't tire of giving his help, how can we, who are simply instruments, become discouraged? If the carpenter's hand holds firmly to the wood, how can the plane be reluctant to carry out its work?

Patience is part of the virtue of fortitude and closely tied to humility. It leads to accepting reality as it is, within the timetable each person requires, without forcing things. It enables us to accept our own limitations and those of others.

Patience is more than a character trait; it is a gift of God, which we need to ask for in prayer. "From him comes my patience," proclaims the Psalmist (Ps 61:5), while St. Paul lists it among the fruits of the Holy Spirit (see Gal 5:22). Patience is intimately linked to hope and charity.

If we posses this virtue, we won't become upset if the advice we give sometimes seems to fall on deaf ears, or we find ourselves repeating the same counsels over and over. We know that everyone preserves in the depths of his or her soul—like good wine in a wine cellar—a deep longing for God, for sanctity, which we have to bring to light. Nevertheless souls—our own as well—have their proper time and hour, which we need to respect, as the farmer does the seasons and the soil. Didn't the Master say that the kingdom of God is like a property owner who went out at different hours of the day to hire workers for his vineyard (see Mt 20:1–7)?

Charity is imbued with patience, St. Paul says (see 1 Cor 13:4). Patience is indispensable for spiritual guidance, which is a refined expression of charity. Our Lord asks us to have the measured calm of the sower, who scatters the seeds of grain over ground that has been previously prepared and then follows the rhythms of the seasons, waiting for the right moment without becoming discouraged, confident that the tiny sprouts will one day become a field of rich grain. He wants us to imitate the urgency of the farmer to harvest the crop once it is ripe, without losing a day, since a sudden storm could wreak havoc on it.

"Love bears all things, believes all things, hopes all things, endures all things" (1 Cor 13:7). "Charity," says St. Augustine, "is like a safe ship. It can carry a heavy weight without fear of being sunk by it."[28] Charity enables us to bear serenely and cheerfully the defects and mistakes of others, without becoming discouraged, waiting for the right time and moment.[29]

The patience we see in our Lord cannot be confused with indifference or neglect; rather, it is a strong and tenacious perseverance to attain the goal as quickly as possible.[30] It would be a great mistake to be happy with the slow pace of a soul who

---

28. St. Augustine, *Expositions on the Psalms*, 129, 41.

29. We have to have at least the same patience and charity that the Lord and others have shown to us. "Try to bear patiently with the defects and infirmities of others, whatever they may be, because you also have many a fault which others must endure" (Thomas à Kempis, *The Imitation of Christ*, 1, 16, 2).

30. "To be patient means to preserve cheerfulness and serenity of mind in spite of injuries that result from the realization of the good." (Josef Pieper, *The Four Cardinal Virtues* [Notre Dame, IN: NDP, 1966], p. 129).

could advance quickly on the path of sanctity.[31] But it would also be a lack of supernatural sense to try to force someone to hurry who isn't even able to walk. We have to fight against any impatience and ill temper when it seems that someone is failing to make progress, trying always to be positive and optimistic. And if we ever have to reprimand anyone, it should be done with words that are encouraging and filled with understanding and affection.

Beginning Again

Being patient in spiritual guidance means fostering the desire that "souls aim very high," while also doing everything possible to help them begin again if a fall occurs. We can encourage them to get up and start over, selecting other remedies, if need be, from the ample pharmacopeia Christian asceticism contains. This virtue leads us to keep a hopeful attitude even when we fail to see any fruit, doing the hard work of the farmer who ploughs the soil, opens furrows, sows the grain at the right moment, and uproots weeds, watching over the crop with vigilant care. We need the vigilance of a doctor who doesn't give up on a sick person but tries one medicine after another, always hoping for a cure.[32] If a particular remedy doesn't work, we try another one: changing the

---

31. "Grace, like nature, normally acts gradually. We cannot, properly speaking, move ahead of grace. But in all that does depend on us we have to prepare the way and cooperate when God grants grace to us. Souls have to be encouraged to aim very high; they must be impelled towards Christ's ideal. Lead them to the highest goals, which should not be reduced or made weaker in any way. But remember that sanctity is not primarily worked out with one's own hands. Grace normally takes its time, and is not inclined to act with violence. Encourage your holy impatience, but do not lose your patience" (St. Josemaría Escrivá, *Furrow*, no. 668).

32. St. John Chrysostom said: "Suppose one of you was suffering an affliction of the eyes and I was a doctor. If after applying the ointments and salves, without doing much good, I retired from the case, wouldn't the patient come to the door of my office crying out and accusing me of negligence, for I have left him with his ailment? If I respond to his reproaches by saying that I have already cured him once, would he be satisfied? Obviously not; he would reply: 'What did I get out of all this, if I am still sick?' Well, apply the same to your souls" (*Homilies on the Gospel of St. Matthew*, 88, 3).

particular examination, suggesting a new book for spiritual reading, advising them to bring specific topics to their prayer. When someone fails to assimilate what we say and the fruit is slow in coming, we should follow St. Augustine's advice: it is better "to speak more to God about him than to him about God."[33]

When a soul is slow to make spiritual progress, it should spur the one guiding that person to be more generous in prayer and mortification, with a greater struggle in that point where the soul needs to advance. And we should intercede for that soul before God: "Let it alone, sir, this year also, till I dig about it and put on manure. And if it bears fruit next year, well and good" (Lk 13:6–9). We should also consider in our prayer whether the goals we have set are specific enough, and whether we are really asking that person to give more, doing so with affection but also with fortitude.

Often spiritual direction means encouraging people, calmly and affectionately, to take a small step forward, giving each person what is needed at the right moment and in the right dosage. We should never forget that the goal is very high, and that our Lord ordinarily doesn't grant at once all the graces needed to attain sanctity. Some can go quickly right from the start, while others find even a tiny step hard to take. We have to accompany each person at his or her own pace, while doing what we can to help him or her progress more rapidly. At times it could happen that someone, after many years of dedication, becomes tired of struggling to be generous. We would encourage a person in that situation to begin again, and show them even more affection and support, like the stake that holds up a weak plant.[34] And we will try to suggest specific and attainable goals, using the "gift of tongues" that knows how to make the ascetical struggle attractive.

---

33. St. Augustine, *How to Catechize Beginners*, 11, 16.
34. The stakes to which weak or broken plants are tied by a gardener to help them continue growing.

A spiritual guide carried away by impatience could easily "destroy with a sudden impulse what has been built up over time with persevering and diligent work, since by impatience one loses the virtue of charity, the mother and guardian of all the virtues."[35] Such a reaction could result in a person's going away just when he or she most needed help. But if that individual is sincere, God will grant his grace also in this situation, helping the person to see that this is no reason to separate from him. Nevertheless, the guide's mission is to make the path easier and not to put up obstacles.

KNOWING PEOPLE WELL

Jesus was very aware of the specific needs of those around him. Andrew, Peter, John, the centurion at Capharnaum, the good thief, Nicodemus, and so many others—all received his attentive and affectionate concern. But our Lord didn't call them to follow him in the same way, or teach them in the same manner, or apply the same remedy. The dialogue he carried on with Nicodemus when the latter came to see him at night is very different from the parables he addresses to the crowds. In different ways, he made himself understood by everyone.

In spiritual accompaniment, we need to get to know people well, so that we don't apply generic remedies or rules. Each soul must be led in a unique way. This isn't a matter of "acting as a psychologist" or reducing grace to a human reality, but of really getting to know people, their interior world and environment, their real problems and concerns.

We have to accept each person as each one really is. Although souls are in many ways similar, we have to avoid generalities, whether positive or negative, in order to find the right

---

35. St. Gregory the Great, *Regulae Pastoralis*, III, 9, 43.

remedy. It does little good to tell someone: "You are disordered" or "You are selfish," if we don't help that person to get down to specifics in the struggle to overcome these defects. Therefore, we have to know each person very well in order to pinpoint the source of his or her failings.

This discernment requires, in the first place, the light of the Holy Spirit, who is the true interior Master and knows the intimate truth of each person. To find the right prescription in each case, we need to ask insistently for the gift of counsel. With the Holy Spirit's prompting, we will quickly find the right suggestion for each particular situation, almost by instinct, as it were, with no need for laborious reasoning.

We will get the grace needed to give the right advice by praying for the person we want to help. And when special situations arise, it may also be necessary to consult, with discretion and refinement, someone with the required experience. Then "the Holy Spirit, who dwells in the heart of the upright, will inspire them like a doctor as to what they ought to say."[36] St. Thomas expressly taught that "all good counsel about the salvation of mankind comes from the Holy Spirit."[37] It is he who gives us the right medicine for each situation, and in the proper dosage.

We need to have frequent recourse to the Holy Spirit, asking him to make us good instruments. He will give us holy inspirations, the right advice for each person, and the strength needed to communicate it effectively. The Holy Spirit will help us employ the means needed—prayer and mortification—to perceive his inspirations; he will grant us the humility required to serve souls without seeking to receive anything in exchange, and with the fortitude to confront any discouragement that may arise.

---

36. St. Cyril, *Catena Aurea*, vol. III, p. 77.
37. St. Thomas Aquinas, *About the Our Father*, 1, c, 153.

One of the greatest obstacles that those giving guidance could place in the way of the Paraclete's action is attachment to their own judgment and experience without making use of the supernatural means. This could even lead to giving advice that isn't suited to what a person really needs at that moment,[38] or to giving general "prescriptions" that have little or no effect. Although spiritual direction is a deeply human reality, it is only the Holy Spirit who can sanctify someone—hence the great importance of fostering personal humility in order to readily receive his gift of counsel.

Along with the supernatural means, we also need to show an affectionate interest in those who come seeking assistance. This interest includes whatever can help to advise them more effectively: interior dispositions, positive qualities as well as defects, important circumstances from their past, friends, family situations, health, difficulties at work, and any overriding feelings (pessimism, euphoria, anger at someone) so as to evaluate objectively what they say. And together with their words, specific deeds: the apostolate they are carrying out with friends and family members, grades in the case of students, generosity in giving alms, good use of time, etc.

FOSTERING SIMPLICITY

The advice given should seek to help souls become steadily less complicated and tangled inside. We need to help them to forget about themselves, to give themselves to others in their family, at work, and in every situation. This same naturalness will lead

---

38. St. Teresa also had experience of "learned" people guided only by their own insights, "who want to be so rational about things and so precise in their understanding that it doesn't seem anyone else but they with their learning can understand the grandeurs of God. If they would only learn something from the humility of the most Blessed Virgin!" (*Meditation on the Song of Songs*, 6, 7, Carmelite Studies translation, vol II, p. 253).

to correcting oneself when a mistake is made or when new data change the parameters or solution of a problem.

Teaching souls to be simple requires, first of all, that those giving direction live this virtue in their own way of speaking, avoiding technical terms that are hard to understand, fostering the atmosphere of a fraternal chat.[39] Then, we strive to help souls to be sincere.[40] Sincerity helps prevent circumlocutions or long explanations and makes it easy to get right to the point. Complications often arise from a more or less conscious lack of sincerity, not wanting to recognize what humiliates us. When someone fails to go directly to the truth—hard, at times, as it is to accept—it leads to evasive replies and "smoke screens" and makes spiritual assistance difficult. A simple person speaks clearly and without fear, shunning half-truths and mental reservations.[41]

To help people grow in this virtue, it is good to ensure, especially with those just beginning, that the tone of the chat be fraternal and informal. At times we may need to help someone express what they are finding it hard to say, giving them the right words to do so and showing them that it is simpler than they think. We can encourage them that what they are saying is not anything especially new in the end: although people are very different, they are also very similar. We need to encourage

---

39. "Get rid of that 'self-satisfied air' which isolates your soul from the souls that approach you. Listen to them. And speak with simplicity; only thus will your work as an apostle grow in extent and fruitfulness" (St. Josemaría Escrivá, *The Way*, no. 958).

40. "When you open your soul, say first of all what you wouldn't like to be known. In this way the devil will always end up defeated. Lay your soul wide open, clearly and simply, so that the rays of God's Love may reach and illuminate the last corner of it" (St. Josemaría Escrivá, *The Forge*, no. 126).

41. This is how a spiritual author expresses it: "In our words, it is best not to speak too freely or quickly, or with pedantic and polished expressions; rather one should speak with gravity, directness and simplicity. It is also important not to be obstinate and stubborn, insisting on getting one's own way, because thereby one often loses peace of conscience, and even charity and patience, and one's friends" (Fray Luis de Granada, *Guia de pecadores*, p. 448).

souls to be specific and clear and go right to the heart of the matter, especially those souls that tend to be superficial or easily get caught up in unnecessary complications.

Opposed to simplicity, at least externally, is affectation in one's words and actions, the desire to call attention to oneself, pedantry, bragging, or an air of self-sufficiency—habits that make conversation with God and with others difficult. A simple soul is marked by a right intention, born of the desire to do God's will in everything, not seeking oneself. By contrast, "all that is tangled and complicated, the twisting and turning about one's own problems, all this builds up a barrier which often prevents people from hearing our Lord's voice."[42]

For people prone to complications, besides frequently recalling the need to "forget about oneself,"[43] it can be helpful to encourage them to control their imaginations, not giving free rein to fantasies or worries about future events that may never take place,[44] or exaggerating little slights that self-love can augment disproportionately, producing animosities based on unfounded or rash suspicions. A person who needs to grow in simplicity can be helped by a well-specified particular examination, presenting the struggle in a positive way. Often "becoming less complicated" comes down to "thinking more about others," trying to make life more pleasant for them. Those habitually concerned about the people around them have few

---

42. St. Josemaría Escrivá, *Friends of God*, no. 90.

43. This advice of "forgetting about oneself," always relevant for everyone, is especially so for people who tend to give excessive importance to "what others might think or say," to real or imagined offenses, etc.

44. St. Frances de Sales also advises us to put ourselves into the reality of each day in order to live with holy simplicity and without needless anxiety: "Let us make the firm resolution to serve God wholeheartedly our whole life, and not worry about tomorrow, which we don't have to think about. Let us concern ourselves in working well today; tomorrow will also come and will be called 'today,' and then we can think about it" (*Epistolario*, fragment 13 1, l.c., p. 766).

personal problems: they live the virtue of simplicity without any special effort.

We should give those who tend to be complicated advice that is easy to put into practice, encouraging them to examine their conscience and, whenever possible, aim it in a single direction.

TEACHING SOULS TO STRUGGLE

Often we will also be instrumental in helping people to acquire the fundamentals of Christian doctrine. A good doctrinal formation is the foundation for all spiritual life. But doctrine alone is not enough; it is also necessary to educate the will. We need to teach people to live the faith in the environment in which they find themselves, in each one's family and professional situation. The advice given should be imbued with practical sense. We have to teach souls to struggle, reminding them of what the Holy Spirit says: "Learn to do good" (Is 1:17), teaching them to exercise the virtues, because the desire to be good is not enough. The desire to live poverty and detachment in the middle of the world is not enough to be poor and detached. One needs to learn how to be poor while making use of earthly goods. Similarly, we need to teach people how to sanctify their work and practice all the other virtues.

The first step ordinarily will be clearing away obstacles that block the growth of the virtues: removing the stones and harmful weeds from the land where the good seed is to be sown and bear fruit—in other words, awakening the will to combat the sins that separate us from Christ and struggling to acquire the virtues that make us resemble him. The need to struggle, to fight, is intrinsic to the Christian life. In the order of grace (and also of nature), good does not come about on its own without our effort. Uprooting the defects and sins that disfigure the soul and acquiring the virtues that embellish it requires God's grace and our personal effort.

One of the weeds that is especially harmful and needs to be uprooted is "subjectivism"—making one's own tastes and interests the criterion for what is of value. "What sort of Christian perfection do you expect to achieve, if you are only following your whims and doing 'what you like'? All your defects, unless you fight against them, will produce bad works as a natural consequence. And your will, untempered by a persevering fight, will be of no use to you when a difficult occasion arises."[45] But if a soul is docile, the Holy Spirit will transform this tendency, even if deeply rooted, into the desire to do God's will in everything. "What does God want of me in these circumstances and at this moment?" This is the true North Star for a Christian, the guide that directs the footsteps of the saints.

We need to instill in souls the desire to do God's will, leading each one up an "inclined plane" as it were, always asking for a little more. It would be a great mistake for a spiritual director "to be content with a soul rendering four when it could be rendering twelve."[46] This inclined plane requires suggestions and counsels that lead a person to become accustomed to wanting what God wants, fighting in small things (accepting a setback with peace, considering important decisions in God's presence to see whether they are in accord with his will, etc.). Thus one will come to love the Cross, however heavy, if our Lord so disposes it for the soul's own good: a painful sickness, dishonor, interior darkness, or events that change the direction of one's life. Only a person determined to put God's will above any personal likes and interests will receive the light needed to discover it.

---

45. St. Josemaría Escrivá, *Furrow*, no. 776.
46. St. Josemaría Escrivá, *The Forge*, no. 628.

Self-Denial

"Get used to saying no,"[47] St. Josemaría Escrivá advised. We need to help souls learn to say *no* to selfishness in its many manifestations, and also to licit things out of love for God. "Unless a grain of wheat falls into the earth and dies, it remains alone" (Jn 12:24).

We need to say no, first of all, to laziness and comfort-seeking. The "law of sin" St. Paul speaks about (see Rom 7:23) becomes in many souls a "law of one's own tastes and whims." And this leads "to that disease of character whose symptoms are inconstancy in everything, thoughtlessness in action and speech, scatterbrained ideas: superficiality, in short."[48] The superficial person is moved by the law of caprice and is incapable of acting with firm and consistent criteria.[49] Saying *no* to many things means saying *yes* to our Lord, whom we find in each small task that we carry out.

To enable the Holy Spirit to act effectively in souls, we also need to warn people against the danger of reducing religion simply to sentiments, making interior feelings—"I feel a need for it," "I enjoy it"—the norm for one's relationship with God. Doing so does away with a supernatural outlook and therefore impedes any real advance in holiness. It can also easily lead to instability of character, to being carried away by passing enthusiasms, and losing heart at the first serious obstacle. The interior life then becomes simply a short-lived burst of light rather than a steadily

---

47. St. Josemaría Escrivá, *The Way*, no. 5.

48. St. Josemaría Escrivá, *The Way*, no. 17.

49. "Often, quite a little shock is enough to cast me down, a slight bitterness quickly fills me with distaste; and if some trial of crucifying sharpness falls upon me, I am crushed. I am a frail flower which dreads every touch of wind and rain, of sun and frost. The habit of pleasure has given my soul an effeminate temperament, which is incapable of enduring anything. And thus God's purifying operations, instead of bringing forth in me the fruits of progress, through my fault only contribute to increase my evil." (Joseph Tissot, *The Interior Life* [Westminster, MD: Newman Press, 1949], p. 151). Such is the reality of many souls, whom we have to strengthen little by little.

burning fire. The determined effort to fulfill God's will gives us the firmness needed to resist the ups and downs of daily life.

The advice given should aim at tempering these states of soul, taking advantage of the positive aspects while helping people realize that feelings—so important in one's union with God and in everything truly human—should not be the main driver of our actions. Feelings can be a great help, but they are only a help. "Love is not merely a sentiment. Sentiments come and go. A sentiment can be a marvelous first spark, but it is not the fullness of love."[50]

It is also important to stress the need to control one's imagination, which has such a great influence on the will. It is difficult, perhaps impossible, for someone to mature spiritually who goes about daydreaming in an unreal world, a product of one's fantasy, confusing—both in the human and in the divine—what truly is with what one would like it to be. The world of God's love, of holiness, is the real world. An uncontrolled imagination magnifies difficulties, leads to "mystical wishful thinking,"[51] and makes people timid and indecisive. As the Spanish refrain says, a person who daydreams has little stomach for the fight. We need to convince people of the need for interior mortification in this area, which helps them to remain in the presence of God and be attentive to others' needs. The imagination, when properly controlled, can also be of great assistance at the time of prayer, helping us to put ourselves into a Gospel passage as "another character in the scene."[52]

---

50. Pope Benedict XVI, *Deus Caritas Est*, no. 17.

51. "It is what I have repeatedly called 'mystical wishful thinking,' made up of useless day dreams and empty ideals: If only I hadn't married, if only I did not have this job, if only I had better health, or was younger, or had more time!" (St. Josemaría Escrivá, *Conversations*, no. 88).

52. "Make it a habit to mingle with the characters who appear in the New Testament. Capture the flavor of those moving scenes where the Master performs works that are both divine and human, and tells us, with human and divine touches, the wonderful story of his pardon for us and his enduring love for his children. Those foretastes of Heaven are renewed today, for the Gospel is always true" (St. Josemaría Escrivá, *Friends of God*, no. 216; see Ibid. no. 222).

Getting Down to Specifics

Besides awakening in souls the desire to struggle, we should remember that teaching people to struggle means *helping them to get down to specifics*. To do so, we have to know people very well—their real concerns, their environment, the difficulties they face, their daily schedule, what they read, the television shows they watch, the time spent on the Internet. . . . We have to listen attentively and patiently to their concerns and worries, which perhaps don't stem from an objective difficulty, but which for them, in their particular circumstances, are weighing on them and worrying them. At other times, with questions steeped in charity and understanding, we may encourage them to open their souls more fully. Thus we can help a person to take a step forward, to improve a little, to sanctify the difficulties being confronted, seeing in these the will of God and a way of growing in love.

Stress should be placed on the importance of "little things," which is where love for God is shown and also where the seeds of lukewarmness and infidelity abide. Tiny wounds might seem unimportant, "but when multiplied over the whole body they can be just as deadly as a serious chest wound."[53]

To help people get down to specifics in their struggle, the advice given should have immediate application to the interior battle, with resolutions that often can be fulfilled quite soon. By dint of one small step after another, great progress can be made. It would be a great mistake for those giving guidance on ascetical questions to be afraid to make demands, content to give vague and nebulous counsels that fail to challenge the person and get lost in generalities.[54] With supernatural sense,

---

53. St. Gregory the Great, *Regulae Pastoralis*, III, 33.

54. "From time to time you have to deal with souls as you would with a fire in the hearth, giving it a good poke to get rid of the embers, which are what shine most but are causing the fire of the love of God to die down" (St. Josemaría Escrivá, *The Forge*, no. 937).

the one guiding souls easily finds a way to be demanding in specific points, doing so with kindness, without asking about matters of conscience. When souls sense they are being challenged on their path towards holiness, they are thankful and eager to return. They see that the person listening to them truly appreciates them and has a real interest in leading them to God.

This friendly way of making demands means putting into practice Christ's words: the one to whom God has given five talents will be asked for five more. It means accompanying souls closely, opening up horizons, encouraging them to begin again with a sporting and cheerful spirit. A good rule is to ask souls for a little more than they can give, suggesting attainable goals that are related to one another.

This requires a greater effort at the hour of attending to those who come for spiritual direction, but it is a sacrifice full of joy, like the gardener who spends hours bent over his garden, lavishing loving care on it. Or like our Lord himself, who dedicated so many hours to forming his apostles.

Above all, those seeking guidance should realize very clearly that, when they open up their souls and unburden their concerns, they defeat the enemy and make real progress in their love for God, which is what truly matters in the end. Helping people to live better the virtue of sincerity is a sure path to victory. The help given here has repercussions in every area of the interior life.

Finally, before ending this section, we should mention the possibility of someone with a less than right intention coming to seek, perhaps unconsciously, advice that will favor their own selfishness and will "suppress with its apparent authority the voice of one's inner convictions." Such a person could even "go from adviser to adviser until we find a 'benevolent' one."[55] This could happen especially in more delicate areas that

---

55. St. Josemaría Escrivá, *Conversations*, no. 93.

demand sacrifices which the person concerned is not in the end ready to make, thus trying to make God's will conform to one's own will: in not having the generosity needed to be open to more children; in not struggling to live chastity during the time of engagement; in not being magnanimous when a vocation of greater commitment is sensed. . . . We have to help those in this situation to be more honest with themselves and with God and truly seek his will and not their own. What we can never do is to be an accomplice to their selfish attitude, allowing them to water down God's will.

A Positive Outlook

Those giving spiritual guidance take the place of Christ, who spent the last three years of his life teaching, curing, and guiding all who followed him. Therefore spiritual directors must see others as our Lord sees them, with understanding and optimism, "with the eyes of Christ himself."[56] Our Lord has his hopes placed in each soul, and he looks on each with the eyes of a father contemplating his child, whom he is always ready to help.[57] Jesus saw in those around him the capacity for good and generosity hidden in their hearts that others with a myopic vision were unable to discern. He discovered in Zacchaeus qualities his fellow citizens didn't recognize; in Matthew, who moved in the company of sinners, he found the capacity to be a great apostle; in the Samaritan woman, he saw her greatness of soul; and in the sinful woman who approached him in the house of Simon the Pharisee, her great capacity to love. . . .

---

56. John Paul II, *Redemptor Hominis*, no. 18.

57. Looking at others with faith leads us to avoid "the inclination common to those who tend to see rather—and sometimes only—what is not going well, the mistakes" and to be "filled with joy and be assured that the Lord has granted to all the capacity to become holy precisely by fighting against their own defects" (see St. Josemaría Escrivá, *Furrow*, no. 399).

Looking with eyes of faith will lead us to see in others their best qualities and to make demands in a positive and optimistic way. The advice we give, full of supernatural sense, will encourage them to continue struggling with cheerfulness and joy, eager to begin again. People should leave this fraternal conversation strengthened and renewed, with new eagerness for the struggle.

This hope-filled vision of souls, even when they are going through a bad situation, has deep roots in God's grace. St. Thomas Aquinas said, "God prepares those he chooses to carry out a mission in such a way that they are suited to carrying it out."[58] His grace will never be lacking for each soul to make a deep conversion and reach the goal of sanctity to which he is calling them. And the greater the need, the more abundant will be God's help. St. Augustine gives us a strong reason for hope: "When we struggle, God is not a spectator, like the crowds watching a game. God is helping us."[59] God is never neutral: he is always seeking our good. This certainty will help those guiding others to always be positive and optimistic, despite the difficult circumstances a specific person might be going through.

We should ask God for the light needed to communicate this spirit of trusting hope—a sporting spirit that imbues the struggle for sanctity with joyful optimism. "The struggle of a child of God cannot go hand in hand with a spirit of sad-faced renunciation, somber resignation, or a lack of joy. It is, on the contrary, the struggle of the man in love who, whether working or resting, rejoicing or suffering, is always thinking of the one he loves, for whose sake he is happy to tackle any problems that may arise."[60]

---

58. St. Thomas Aquinas, *Summa Theologica*, III, q. 27, a. 4, c.
59. St. Augustine, *Sermon*, 128, 9.
60. St. Josemaría Escrivá, *Friends of God*, no. 219.

In This Vineyard

Even when things are not going well (in one's profession, family, or in society at large), we can instill in souls this positive outlook on life, reminding them that complaining about how things are going with a pessimistic outlook is never pleasing to God, since it shows a weak faith.[61] It is *in this vineyard* and *in this field* where our Lord wants us to struggle joyfully for sanctity—in this family, in this society, with all its good qualities and bad. Each day God asks us to carry out his plans of redemption; in every situation we receive his efficacious supernatural help to grow in love for him and carry out a fruitful apostolate. Every day our Lord says to us: "You go into the vineyard too" (Mt 20:4). All earthly realities are to be sanctified and raised to the plane of grace.[62]

Once when the multitudes were pressing upon Jesus, the disciples, concerned by the late hour, told the Master that the people were hungry, since they had not brought provisions with them (see Mt 14:13–21). "This is a lonely place, and the day is now over; send the crowds away to go into the villages and buy food for themselves." The immediate reality was not very promising. But Jesus knew of "another reality," a higher one. He replied to them: "They need not go away; you give them something to eat." The disciples didn't understand him, replying: "We have only five loaves here and two fish."

The disciples see the objective reality. They know that with the amount of food at hand they cannot possibly feed a multitude.

---

61. "Christians are ordinary people, but their hearts overflow with the joy that comes when we set out to fulfill, with the constant help of grace, the will of the Father. Christians don't see themselves as victims, underrated, or restricted in their behavior. They walk, head on high, because they are men and women who know they are children of God" (Ibid., no. 93).

62. "Indeed, as a person with a truly unique life story, each is called by name, to make a special contribution to the coming of the Kingdom of God. No talent, no matter how small, is to be hidden or left unused (cf. Mt 25:24–27)" (Bl. John Paul II, *Christifideles Laici*, no. 56).

The same can happen to us when we make a human calculation of the possibilities we possess. A purely human objectivity leads to discouragement, since it means losing sight of the radical optimism of our Christian vocation, which has different roots. In spiritual guidance, it may lead to the mistake of demanding little of souls, convinced that "they cannot give more of themselves."

The apostles calculated correctly, they counted the available loaves and fishes; but they forgot to include Jesus—his power and nearness. The truth, the full reality, was very different. Being supernaturally realistic always leads to hope, because we count on God's grace and power and his constant action in souls.[63] Otherwise our role would be restricted to being good counselors, giving advice from an exclusively human point of view, when God is calling us to much more: He is calling us to act in his place.

Therefore, optimism in leading others along the path of holiness is not based on the absence of obstacles and personal mistakes, which in one form or another are always present, but on God who assures us: "I am with you always" (Mt 28:28). We can always rely on God's grace in guiding souls. With him we can do all things; victory is assured, even amid apparent defeats. Even if all seems lost, God never tires of giving us once more the help needed. This is the optimism that the saints had—the optimism we need to have ourselves and instill in others.[64] A person

---

63. "Don't be a pessimist. Don't you realize that all that happens or can happen is for the best? Your optimism will be a necessary consequence of your faith" (St. Josemaría Escrivá, *The Way*, no. 378).

64. "Reject your pessimism and don't allow those around you to be pessimistic. God should be served with cheerfulness and abandonment" (St. Josemaría Escrivá, *The Forge*, no. 217).

"In your work with souls—and all your activity should be work with souls—be filled with faith, with hope, with love, because all the difficulties will be overcome. To confirm this truth for us, the Psalmist wrote: *Et tu, Domine, deridebis eos: ad nihilum deduces omnes gentes*—'You, O Lord, will laugh at them: You will bring them to nothing.' These words confirm those other words: *Non praevalebunt*; the enemies of God shall not prevail. They will not have any power against the Church, nor against those who serve the Church as instruments of God" (Ibid., no. 637).

who teaches others the faith, says St. Augustine, referring to catechists, needs to be "joyful, because the greater one's joy when teaching, the more readily will the person listening accept his words."[65] Pessimistic and sad people can never be good guides.

Those beginning the spiritual path require special attention, since owing to their inexperience they are more easily disconcerted and discouraged by a mistake or weakness.[66] No matter what happens, we have to teach them to begin again, upheld by their trust in the Master and their own sincerity, even when the fall has been quite painful.

Optimism

Optimism in guiding souls, then, is a matter of faith, not of human temperament or circumstances. The spiritual guide knows that God uses everything for a greater good and produces fruit even from apparent disasters. Moreover, by means of contrition, he wins even "lost" battles. At the same time, we need to employ all the available human means (affection, punctuality, constancy), for these human means are the five loaves and two fish that our Lord used to work the miracle.

Christ wants us to give him the few loaves and fish that we have, and then trust in him. Some good results will arrive quickly, while our Lord will reserve the rest for the right moment and occasion, which only he knows; but in the end, the good results will certainly come.[67] We have to be convinced that, although

---

65. St. Augustine, *How to Catechize Beginners*, 2, 4.
66. See Joseph Tissot, *How to Profit from One's Faults* (New York: Scepter, 1996), p. 12–13.
67. "To win the battles of the soul, the best strategy often is to bide one's time and apply the suitable remedy with patience and perseverance. Make more acts of hope. Let me remind you that in your interior life you will suffer defeats and you will have ups and downs—may God make them imperceptible—because no one is free of these misfortunes. But our all-powerful and merciful Lord has granted us the precise means with which to conquer" (St. Josemaría Escrivá, *Friends of God*, no. 219).

we are nothing and can do nothing by ourselves, Jesus is at our side, and "all created reality is subject to his power and knowledge, and he will protect us by his inspirations against all ignorance and hardness of heart."[68]

The Christian's optimism is closely tied to prayer: "Christian optimism is not a sugary optimism; nor is it a mere human confidence that everything will turn out all right. It is an optimism that sinks its roots in an awareness of our freedom, and in the sure knowledge of the power of grace. It is an optimism that leads us to make demands on ourselves, to struggle to respond at every moment to God's calls."[69] It is an optimism far removed from that of selfish people who seek only a comfortable existence, and who close their eyes to the problems of those around them so as not to have to try to remedy them.

The optimism needed by those guiding souls is firmly in touch with reality. With eyes wide open, they confront the reality of evil without being overwhelmed by sadness. Nor do they give in to discouragement, since they know that their Father God will always bring forth disproportionate fruit from the field—these specific souls in these specific circumstances—that might seem fit for yielding only thistles and nettles.

Nor does an optimism founded on faith lead to an ingenuous and irresponsible neglect of the human means. We should never ask God to solve something that we can fix by our own effort.[70]

Another strong reason for optimism is the communion of saints. Those who follow Christ are united by a strong bond and share in the same life. Through the communion of saints

---

68. St. Thomas Aquinas, *Summa Theologica*, I–II, q. 68, a. 2, ad 3.
69. St. Josemaría Escrivá, *The Forge*, no. 659.
70. "I was amused by your vehemence . . . You said: 'I have only two arms, but I sometimes feel impatient enough to become a monster with fifty arms to sow and reap the harvest.' Ask the Holy Spirit for that effectiveness, for he will grant it to you!" (St. Josemaría Escrivá, *Furrow*, no. 616).

we form a single Body in Christ, and we can help one another effectively. At this very moment, someone is praying for us; someone is beseeching God for us by their work, their prayer, their suffering. The communion of saints makes available to us a mysterious but real help. In spiritual guidance, our prayer and mortification for souls will often be what spurs them to go forward.

Let us never forget that our Lord still works miracles when we put at his disposal the little that we possess.

Chapter 5

CORRESPONDENCE
TO GRACE

Correspondence to the motions and inspirations of the Holy Spirit is the soul's entire life. Grace in the soul is destined to grow continually (see Mk 4:26–32). If no obstacle is put in the way, it yields fruit without fail, due not to the one who sows or the one who waters, "but only God who gives the growth" (see 1 Cor 3:5–9).

The Holy Spirit constantly grants us the grace we need to be faithful. It is truly the Paraclete who guides souls. "Our divine Teacher holds his school within the souls of those who ask him and who really want to have him as their Teacher. . . . Words are not the medium he uses. He rarely speaks, and never at the beginning. If we really put into practice the lessons he teaches us, then he may speak, although little, just to show us that he is pleased. But the lesson has to be practiced properly, because in this school it is all a question of practicing what we are taught: if we do not practice it, the whole thing is finished: the school closes down, its doors are closed to us."[1]

If we fail to correspond to the Holy Spirit's inspirations, "the school closes down." Spiritual progress becomes impossible until once again the Consoler, if he wishes, inspires the soul with new

---

1. Francisca Javiera del Valle, *About the Holy Spirit* (New York: Scepter, 2007), pp. 43–44.

graces. "Although the school takes place in the center of our soul, nevertheless we cannot enter there unless the Teacher allows us. However much we may want to go in ourselves, we neither know the way nor have the ability. The only thing we can do in that case is to remain within ourselves and stand at the door, sincerely lamenting and regretting our loss unselfishly."[2] We would need to seek interior recollection, to strive to guard our internal and external senses, and to "sincerely lament"—purifying our previous faults by means of prayer and penance.[3]

THE PLACE OF THE HEART IN THE INTERIOR LIFE

Holiness consists in identifying our will with God's will. But this desire of ours is accompanied and perfected at every moment by feelings in our sensory appetite, in a way similar to how our intellectual knowledge is linked to the senses.[4] Traditionally, moral philosophy has used the word "passions" to designate these feelings or emotions.[5] Present in every human being, they "ensure the connection between the life of the senses and the life of the mind. Our Lord called man's heart the source from which the passions spring."[6]

---

2. Ibid., p. 44.

3. Mortification done with a spirit of reparation disposes the soul to hear the gentle but strong voice of the Paraclete. "Atonement: this is the path that leads to Life" (St. Josemaría Escrivá, *The Way*, 210). "When a child-like soul tells our Lord of its desires to be forgiven, it can be sure that it will soon see those desires fulfilled: Jesus will free the soul from the filthy tail that it drags in punishment for its past miseries. He will remove the dead weight that still remains from all its impurities and drags it down to the ground. He will free the child from all the earthly ballast in its heart so that it can rise up towards God's Majesty, and be enveloped in the living flame of his Love" (Ibid., no. 886).

4. R. Garcia de Haro, *La Vida Cristiana* (Pamplona: Eunsa, 1992), p. 296.

5. "The term 'passions' belongs to the Christian patrimony. Feelings or passions are emotions or movements of the sensitive appetite that incline us to act or not to act in regard to something felt or imagined to be good or evil" (CCC, 1763).

6. CCC, 1764.

The Passions and Their Influence on the Interior Life

There are many passions that influence human action. The most fundamental one is *love*, which inclines us towards the good and union with the person loved. *Desire* moves us to set out to attain a good that is absent. *Joy* is the result of attaining this good. *Hate* is opposed to love and arises when something is seen as evil; *aversion* is opposed to desire, and *sorrow* to joy. *Daring* spurs us to seek what is good despite the difficulties involved; *fear* leads us to distance ourselves from an evil that it is difficult to avoid, while *anger* spurs us to resist forcefully an evil we confront.

The passions in themselves are neither good nor bad; their moral value depends on the direction we give them.[7] The saints were never apathetic when faced with true human values. On the contrary, the saints are marked by a passionate love for God and for everything humanly noble.

Our passions facilitate the voluntary act and reinforce and perfect it. Joy helps us to work with greater intensity and care; daring is indispensable in the apostolate; fear, the holy "fear" of God, spurs us to separate ourselves from occasions of sin. "To love is to will the good of another," St. Thomas Aquinas taught.[8] "All other affections have their source in this first movement of the human heart toward the good. Only the good can be loved.[9] Passions 'are evil if love is evil and good if it is good.'"[10]

In colloquial language, and in the teaching of many spiritual writers, the word "passion" is often used with a negative connotation, as though it meant only the "bad passions" that we have to fight against and conquer. Passion so understood is a

---

7. St. Thomas Aquinas, *Summa Theologica*, I–II, q. 24.
8. Ibid., I–II, q. 26, a. 4.
9. St. Hilary of Poitiers, *Treatise on the Trinity*, Pl 10, 25–472, 8, 3, 4.
10. See CCC, 1766; the enclosed quotation is from St. Augustine's *City of God*, 14, 7, 2.

result of the disharmony introduced by original sin and aggravated by our personal sins. In this context, disordered passions are a big obstacle to reaching God and have to be fought against and dominated.[11] They blind us to the good because, rather than making God our goal, we pursue what brings pleasure or sensual satisfaction. Disordered passions weaken the will in the struggle for virtue and often leave behind a trail of filth.[12] They tie the soul down and impede it from soaring upward towards the love of God.[13]

Hence the importance in spiritual direction of helping people to control, purify, and order their passions, and to love only what leads to God. The goal in guiding people in the use of their freedom is not suppressing the passions (something impossible to achieve), but rather to order them and put them at the service of God's love, one's family, and the apostolate. A Christian personality requires the harmonious integration of the passions. Although we will always need to fight against the disorder introduced by original sin, Christian life entails, above all, the giving of a positive direction to the emotions and feelings, directing them towards the true good.[14]

---

11. St. John of the Cross points out that these disordered passions "are like restless and discontented children, who are ever demanding this or that from their mother, and are never contented. And even as one that digs because he covets a treasure is wearied and fatigued, even so is the soul weary and fatigued in order to attain that which its desires demand of it; and although in the end it may attain it, it is still weary, because it is never satisfied. . . . The soul is wearied and fatigued by its desires, because it is wounded and moved and disturbed by them as is water by the winds" (St. John of the Cross, *The Ascent of Mt. Carmel*, 1, 1, 11).

12. See Tanquerey, *The Spiritual Life*, nos. 789–793.

13. "For it comes to the same thing whether a bird be held by a slender cord or by a stout one; since, even if it be slender, the bird will be well held as though it were stout, for so long as it breaks it not and flies not away" (*Ascent of Mt. Carmel*, 1, 1, 11).

14. The passions can and should be directed towards the good:

—*Love* should be channeled, in the natural order to the family, to good friendships, to great ideals; and in the supernatural order to Christ (the most faithful and generous Friend), who is the Way to reach the Father, to the Holy Spirit, the Sanctifier, to Mary, to the angels and saints, to the Church, to all souls. (CONTINUED)

The spiritual director should also be watchful for any possible attachments and deviations in the realm of the affections and help channel the heart, with all the good passions that reside there, along the right path. Even greater attention has to be paid to this point when the person being guided has dedicated himself or herself entirely to our Lord.

Guiding the Emotions

Special care has to be taken, then, to teach people how to channel their feelings and emotions to our Lord and to other men and women, doing so in a way that is in accordance with the order desired by God's will. The first struggle has to be to purify the heart of selfishness, of the search for compensations. At the same time, one also needs to watch out for a heart that is "constricted," afraid of loving others because the human affections are seen as bad. The love that we contemplate in the Most Holy Humanity of Christ is both human and supernatural. We see his human warmth and tenderness both

---

—*Hatred* has to be directed towards sin, and the enemies of our soul (the world, the flesh, and the devil), and to all that could degrade us in the natural and supernatural order.

—*Desire* should be directed, above all, towards the eagerness to be holy, to do great things for God in this world, and to assist one's family and society.

—*Aversion* finds its noble object in fleeing from the occasions of sin, in diligently avoiding whatever could separate us from God.

—*Joy* is based on the fulfillment of God's will, the source of every true joy, in the realization that one is a child of God, and in contemplating all the good that exists in the world.

—*Sorrow* should be directed towards contemplating Christ's Passion, the sorrows of Mary, and our own failure, and that of so many others, to respond to grace.

—*Daring* needs to be directed towards overcoming the difficulties striving for sanctity entails, and in carrying out a fruitful apostolate within one's family, and among one's companions at work.

—*Fear* should be directed to the possibility of sin—the only true evil—and lead to fleeing from the occasions of sin.

—*Anger*, finally, has to become holy indignation for whatever offends God, leading us to make many acts of reparation.

when he addresses his heavenly Father and when he interacts with people. He is moved by a widowed mother who has lost her only son; he weeps for a friend who has died; he misses the gratitude of some lepers he has just cured of their infirmity. We see him always cordial, open to everyone, even in the anguished and sublime moments of his Passion. A person who seeks to make progress in the interior life strives to imitate our Lord: "Let this mind be in you, which was also in Christ Jesus" (Phil 2:5, Douay). We want to foster the same sentiments we see in the life of our Lord.[15]

In our emotions and feelings, we experience our own poverty, our need for protection, for affection, for happiness. And these sentiments, often very deep, can and should be channeled into our search for God, telling him that we love him and that we need his help to remain close to him. If our conduct were solely the result of a cold and rational choice, and if we tried to ignore the affective side of our being, we would not be living integrally as God wants, and in the long run we would find it impossible to love him at all. God created us with a body and soul, and we have to love him with our whole being—with all our heart, mind, and strength.[16] It is good to remember frequently that following Christ closely and growing in Christian life does not consist "in thinking much, but in loving much."[17]

---

15. Bl. John Paul II taught: "Man cannot live without love. . . . He remains a being that is incomprehensible for himself, his life is senseless, if love is not revealed to him, if he does not encounter love, if he does not experience it and make it his own, if he does not participate intimately in it. [Christ the Redeemer] 'fully reveals man to himself.' If we may use the expression, this is the human dimension of the mystery of the Redemption. In this dimension man finds again the greatness, dignity and value that belong to his humanity" (*Redemptor Hominis*, no. 10).

16. See CCC, 2083–2141.

A pure heart needed to contemplate God is in no sense an empty heart. "The heart has been created to love, do not doubt it. Let us therefore bring our Lord Jesus Christ into the love that we feel. Otherwise, the empty heart takes revenge and fills itself up with the most despicable vileness" (St. Josemaría Escrivá, *Furrow*, no. 800).

17. St. Teresa, *The Interior Castle*, I, 1, 7.

In loving God we return his own love for us, for he has loved us first (see 1 Jn 3:18). Every noble human love is a participation in God's love for creatures. He loves us with a unique and personal love, and he asks for all our love in return, in accord with each of our personal vocations. We have to love him through all the daily circumstances we encounter, whether pleasant or not.[18] Not only when we go to church to visit him or to receive Communion, but in the midst of our work, in our family, when sorrows or disappointments come, or when we receive some unexpected good news.

Feelings in Piety

St. Thomas Aquinas, when commenting on the precept to love God with our whole heart, points out that love can be fed by two sources: by our feelings and by our reason.[19] When our feelings are deeply involved, we don't know how to live without the one we love. But when we love with our reason, we follow the dictates of our intellect. The spiritual director should teach souls that God wants us to love him both ways: with our intellect, as intelligent beings, and also with our human heart, with the affection we have for those we love here on earth, with the only heart we have.

Nevertheless, the heart may sometimes find itself cold, as though the soul had fallen asleep, since our feelings come and go in a way we often have little control over. In spiritual direction, we can't allow someone in this situation to be content with following our Lord grudgingly, as though fulfilling a burdensome

---

18. "God has a right to ask us: Are you thinking of me? Are you aware of me? Do you look to me as your support? Do you seek me as the Light of your life, as your shield . . . as your all? Renew, then, this resolution: In times the world calls good I will cry out: 'Lord!' In times it calls bad, again I will cry: 'Lord!'" (St. Josemaría Escrivá, *The Forge*, no. 506).

19. St. Thomas, *Commentaries on St. Matthew*, 22, 4. St. Thomas is referring here to a remark by St. John Chrysostom.

obligation or taking a bitter medicine. We have to help them to do everything possible to get out of that situation: praying more aspirations, making more acts of love and reparation. . . . These are the "branches and twigs" that help keep the fire of God's love enkindled.[20]

But at times the Holy Spirit is the one who puts this dryness or disquiet in the soul. By doing so (often when other means and graces have not borne fruit), he seeks to spur the soul to make quicker progress and set higher goals in its struggle for sanctity.[21] And this can happen when someone is already giving a lot and being generous with our Lord. But God wants more from that soul because he wants to give more, and the soul must prepare itself to receive the new gifts and graces. The soul is perhaps being asked to cut "that fine thread—that chain, that chain of forged iron" which is preventing it from rising up to the higher peaks.[22]

The Holy Spirit stirs up in the soul these feelings of distaste and unease precisely because he sees that it can and should rise higher. "The spiritual man who has reached this stage is like a man who in climbing a mountain comes to a difficult spot where, to make progress, he must have a keener desire for the goal to be attained."[23] It is very important for the spiritual guide to know how to encourage a person in this situation to take this step forward and continue climbing.

---

20. "When you don't know how to go on, when it feels as if your fire were dying out and you can't throw fragrant logs on it, throw on the branches and twigs of short vocal prayers, of ejaculations, to keep feeding the blaze" (St. Josemaría Escrivá, *The Way*, no. 92).

21. "Consolations disappear, so that the soul may no longer be attached to them, for they are not God. If the soul is attached to them, it stops all the work of the divine life" (Joseph Tissot, *The Interior Life*, ch. 4, no. 16).

22. See St. Josemaría Escrivá, *The Way*, no. 170. Although it may be in matters that seem of little importance, "A heart which loves the things of the earth beyond measure is like one fastened by a chain—or by a 'tiny thread'—which stops it flying to God" (*The Forge*, no. 486).

23. Garrigou-Lagrange, *The Three Ages of the Interior Life*, Vol. II, p. 55.

This situation, as we already said, is very different from that of a person who is trying to make God's will compatible with attachments that lead one "to drink from the puddles of worldly consolations," [24] the "compensations" that hinder sincere friendship with our Lord. The spiritual guide has to be vigilant in discerning these two different kinds of aridity. For rather than being a passive purification that God permits or an unease that he himself sows in the soul, it could be the beginning of lukewarmness, of a lack of interior mortification, failing to prepare properly for prayer, or to purify one's intention so as to seek our Lord and him alone.[25]

We have to teach souls, with the help of grace, to love God with a firm will, and whenever possible with all the noble feelings of the human heart. With God's help, normally it is possible to

---

24. See *The Way*, no. 148.

25. One needs to distinguish clearly between the aridity that is a means of purification and of advancing in the spiritual life (if the person undergoing it is faithful) from the indifference that invades a soul due to lack of response to grace that gives free reign to one's feelings.

"In your life, there are two things that do not fit together: your head and your heart. Your intelligence—enlightened by faith—shows you the way clearly. It can also point out the difference between following that way heroically or stupidly. Above all, it places before you the divine greatness and beauty of the undertakings the Trinity leaves in our hands. Your feelings, on the other hand, become attached to everything you despise, even while you consider it despicable. It seems as if a thousand trifles were awaiting the least opportunity, and as soon as your poor will is weakened, through physical tiredness or lack of supernatural outlook, those little things flock together and pile up in your imagination, until they form a mountain that oppresses and discourages you. Things such as the rough edges of your work, your resistance to obedience; the lack of proper means; the false attractions of an easy life; greater or smaller but repugnant temptations; bouts of sensuality; tiredness; the bitter taste of spiritual mediocrity . . . and sometimes also fear; fear because you know God wants you to be a saint, and you are not a saint. Allow me to talk to you bluntly. You have more than enough 'reasons' to turn back, and you lack the resolution to respond to the grace that he grants you, since he has called you to be another Christ, *ipse Christus!*—Christ himself. You have forgotten the Lord's admonition to the Apostle: 'My grace is enough for you,' which is confirmation that, if you want to, you can" (St. Josemaría Escrivá, *Furrow*, no. 166).

reawaken dormant feelings and re-enkindle the heart, even when interior dryness is present.[26]

God sometimes treats those who follow him like an affectionate mother who, without her child expecting it, offers some candy as a reward or simply because she wants to show her small child special affection. And the boy, who has always loved his mother, is so happy that he volunteers to do anything needed, in his eagerness to show his appreciation. But that child would reject any thought that his mother didn't love him if she didn't offer him some sweets, and with common sense he would also see his mother's love when she corrects him or has to take him to the doctor. That is how souls are treated by our Father God, who loves us much more.

Lack of Feelings

When God grants abundant consolations to a soul and the struggle seems easy, the spiritual director must make sure that the person makes good use of these sensible consolations to draw closer to God—giving thanks,[27] showing greater generosity in the daily struggle and in the apostolate, striving to improve in some point.

---

26. "How can we fight against this tyranny of the feelings that can prevent us from loving truly? When we do everything to please God, when we try to make him happy in everything we do, without seeking excuses, when, in short, we try always to ensure that 'thy will be done,' we can be sure that our love for God is true. Although we will not always be victorious in the struggle, we are on the right path. We will win the final battle" (J. B. Cabaniña Majide, *Sentimiento y Amor de Dios*, p. 36).

27. Otherwise the soul may deserve to hear our Lord's words of complaint about the ungrateful lepers, who failed to return to give thanks for their cure. The only one who was grateful, the Samaritan, heard those consoling words: "Rise and go your way: your faith has saved you" (see Lk 17:11–19).

"When you give a present, you receive a simple and cordial 'Thank you,' and this 'thank you' is enough to show gratitude for your kindness, for it assures you that the person appreciates your generosity. And thus it is that I must act towards God, when he vouchsafes to give me his great present, which is suffering. 'My God, I thank thee!' How eloquent is this 'Thank thee!' . . . It tells God that I understand his action and his love. A word between friends says so much!" (Tissot, *The Interior Life*, ch. 8, no. 37.)

At the same time, one needs to make clear that the essence of love lies not in feelings but in our daily response, with or without feelings. Sensible consolations may disappear, and our Lord could even permit a sensation of being alone amid great temptations, although he is always nearby with his efficacious help. Biographies of St. Catherine of Siena recount how one night, after she had suffered great temptations and resisted them, Jesus appeared to her. She fell on her knees before him.

"Lord," she sobbed, "where were you when the temptations were assaulting me?"

"I was inside your heart, seeing how you were fighting," our Lord answered. He is always near to those who seek him and are faithful to him, even though we may not have any sensible experience of his presence.

This very lack of feelings and the experience of interior solitude, or suffering greater temptations when perhaps one is fighting to avoid the slightest thing that is displeasing to God, can be a special opportunity—as we said above—to take an important step forward in sanctity.[28]

To help those being guided to love God *with all one's heart*, it is good to advise them to go frequently to Christ's Most Holy

---

28. St. Catherine herself puts these words on our Lord's lips: "Among those who have become my trusted servants, there are those with faith without any servile fear. But this love is still imperfect, because what they seek in this service (at least to a great extent still) is their own benefit, it is their satisfaction and the delight that they take in me. The same imperfection is also found in the love that they feel for their neighbor. And do you know what shows the imperfection of this love? At the moment when they are deprived of the consolation that they find in me, this love is not enough and cannot sustain them. They languish and often become colder and colder towards me when, to exercise them in virtue and tear them away from their imperfection, I take away the spiritual consolations and send them difficulties and setbacks. Nevertheless I act in this way to attract them to perfection, to teach them to know themselves better, to realize that they are nothing and that by themselves they do not have any grace. Adversity should have as its effect to lead them to seek refuge in me, to recognize me as their benefactor, to unite themselves to me only by means of a true humility. . . . If they are not convinced of their imperfection, along with a desire to improve, it is impossible that they do not go backwards" (*The Dialogue*, ch. 60).

Humanity, recommending that they read the life of Christ or a narrative of the Passion. They should be encouraged to contemplate Christ as perfect God and perfect Man, to observe closely how he welcomes those who come to him for help with his merciful compassion, his love for all men and women. It will be especially helpful for them to meditate on the passion and death of our Lord on the cross, his unlimited generosity when suffering the most cruel torments.[29] Also of great help is considering the life of the Virgin Mary and the example of the saints, especially those most relevant to the soul's own situation. In addressing God, one can also make use of the words human love employs, and even convert songs of pure and noble human love into true prayer.

It can also be very helpful to teach people to practice some of the affectionate manifestations of piety (while not reducing love to these external signs), such as lovingly kissing a crucifix or looking at an image of our Lady. Thus they will be prevented from trying to reach God "by sheer will power" or by cold reasoning, which in the long run tires one out and impoverishes the soul's relationship with Christ. We should never forget that in striving to draw close to God, the heart is a precious help. "Your mind is sluggish and won't work. You struggle to collect your thoughts in God's presence, but it's useless: a complete blank! Don't try to force yourself, and don't worry. Listen closely: it is the hour for your heart."[30] It is the moment perhaps to make use of a few simple words, as when we were very young, repeating slowly some aspiration filled with piety and affection.

---

29. "For our consolation, the Holy Spirit has wanted to leave written testimony to Jesus' final battle. His human will resisted accepting the horrifying agony that awaited him, prelude to the shameful death by which—accepted with infinite Love—he would make satisfaction for our sins and open to us the gates of heaven. He even beseeches his eternal Father to free him from these sufferings that make his body tremble and cause him to sweat blood. . . . Who could understand better than he, who suffered them first, the difficulties that our feelings present in following him?" (J. B. Cabaniña Majide, *Sentimiento y amor de Dios*, p. 37).

30. St. Josemaría Escrivá, *The Way*, no. 102.

The Hour for the Heart

Once again I want to stress that, while never failing to value the feelings of the human heart, *love for God is not a question of sensible feelings*[31] (although God may grant them to us to help us be more generous). Love consists above all in the complete identification of our love with God's will, although our heart may be completely dry. Someone going through a period of interior dryness can find great peace in this teaching of St. Teresa of Avila. "Perhaps we don't know what love is," says the saint. "It doesn't consist in great delight but in desiring with strong determination to please God in everything, in striving, insofar as possible, not to offend him, and in asking him for the advancement of the honor and glory of his Son and the increase of the Catholic Church."[32]

Love is shown in the deeds our Lord wants from us: love is repaid with a love expressed in specific actions, fulfilling our duties towards God and neighbor even when this means "going against the grain." "The highest perfection," St. Teresa teaches, "does not consist in interior delights or in great raptures or in visions . . . but in having our will so much in conformity with God's will that there is nothing we know he wills that we do not want with all our desire, and in accepting the bitter as happily as we do the delightful when we know that his Majesty desires it."[33]

---

31. "This false view of love is very widespread today, which trivializes love and makes it equivalent to 'what I like' or 'what pleases me.' . . . It is urgent to restore to love its innate dignity . . . I don't love something because it pleases me. I love it because it is good (and this is true of both love for God and love for any person), and then it pleases me" (Carlos Cardona, *Metafísica del bien y del mal* [Pamplona: Eunsa, 1987], p. 128).

32. St. Teresa of Avila, *The Interior Castle*, IV, 1, 7 (Carmelite translation, p. 319).

33. Ibid., *Foundations*, 5,10 (Carmelite translation p. 120). The saint adds that when love is perfect "we forget about pleasing ourselves in order to please the one we love . . . even though the trials may be very great, they become sweet when we know we are pleasing God."

In our relationship with God, we must be led by faith and not by feelings.[34] Interior dryness is the opportunity to tell our Lord with greater sincerity that we are seeking only him. "As the flames of your first enthusiasm die down, it becomes difficult to advance in the dark. But that progress is the more reliable for being hard. And then, when you least expect it, the darkness vanishes, and the enthusiasm and light return. Persevere."[35]

Those who are just beginning to travel the path of prayer must be encouraged to persevere when these moments of dryness descend. They should know that "these trials are not spared anyone who takes prayer seriously,"[36] and therefore they are part of the normal path to holiness. These moments are a marvelous opportunity *to seek God for God himself,* to purify our intention, telling him repeatedly that we seek only him. The reward is a greater detachment from ourselves and a purer and more disinterested love.

Guarding the Heart

The book of Proverbs says, "Keep your heart with all vigilance; for from it flow the springs of life" (Prov 4:23). The heart is the symbol of the most intimate core of each person, "the seat of moral personality."[37] To guard one's heart means to guard one's intimacy, one's affections, the depths of one's soul. Hence an

---

34. To be guided by one's feelings "is to put the servant in charge of the house, and to get the master to abdicate. It is not sentiment that is bad, but the inordinate part assigned to it. In some souls, emotions are so much the whole of piety that they are convinced that they have lost all devotion when feeling disappears. If they only knew that this is just the moment to begin to have it" (Joseph Tissot, *The Interior Life,* ch. 3, no. 19–20, p. 54).

"To advance in interior life and apostolate, you do not need devotion that you can feel, but a definite and generous disposition of the will to respond to what God asks of you" (St. Josemaría Escrivá, *Furrow,* no. 769).

35. St. Josemaría Escrivá, *Furrow,* no. 789.

36. Congregation for the Doctrine of the Faith, *On Some Aspects of Meditation,* no. 30.

37. CCC, 2517.

important part of spiritual guidance is helping people to purify their hearts, keeping it for God and the pure loves he has destined for them, in accord with each person's specific vocation.[38]

Our Lord pointed out more than once that human actions stem from the heart, from what a person harbors inside; this inner core has to be kept pure and cleansed of all disordered affection, rancor, or envy. The heart is the source of all the good that later becomes a reality in a person's external conduct. It is where, with grace, a sincere piety in one's relationship with God takes hold along with a pure love for others, shown in understanding and cordiality towards one's neighbor.[39] This clean love increases the heart's capacity to see with the light of faith, while a heart that is stained produces spiritual blindness and selfishness. "For out of the heart come evil thoughts, murder, adultery, fornication, theft, false witness, slander" (Mt 15:19). Purity of heart is frequently seen in sacred Scripture as a prerequisite for drawing close to God, sharing in his life, seeing his face, and seeing other men and women as God's sons and daughters.[40]

---

38. "God, who works to lead me to Life, has two simultaneous operations to carry out, until his work in me is completed. He has to take away from me and to reclothe me. And He cannot do the one without the other. When the wheels of a machine are encrusted or rusty, cleaning must be done. There must be taking away, detaching, and purification. Then, when the metal is clean and bright, a suitable amount of oil or other lubricant is applied to make the wheels move with ease and rapidity" (Joseph Tissot, *The Interior Life*, ch. 3, no. 10).

39. "The 'pure in heart' are promised that they will see God face to face and be like him (see 1 Cor 13:12; 1 Jn 3:2). Purity of heart is the precondition of the vision of God. Even now it enables us to see according to God, to accept others as 'neighbors'; it lets us perceive the human body—ours and our neighbor's—as a temple of the Holy Spirit, a manifestation of divine beauty" (CCC, 2519).

40. "The sixth beatitude proclaims, 'Blessed are the pure in heart, for they shall see God' (Mt 5:5). 'Pure in heart' refers to those who have attuned their intellects and wills to the demands of God's holiness, chiefly in three areas: charity (see 1 Tim 4:3–9; 2 Tim 2:22), chastity or sexual rectitude (see 1 Thess 4:7; Col 3:5; Eph 4:19); love of truth and orthodoxy of faith (see Titus 1:15; 1 Tim 3:4; 2 Tim 23–26). There is a connection between purity of heart, of body, and of faith" (CCC, 2518).

An impure heart is not only a heart tied down by the disorder of sensuality, although lust always leaves a deep stain on the soul. It is also a heart marred by the immoderate desire for material goods; by the readiness to see others with distrust and envy and to hold grudges; by the selfishness that leads to thinking about oneself and overlooking others; by interior laziness that gives rise to daydreams and fantasies and hinders presence of God and intensity in work.

Affectivity

A clean heart requires keeping watch over our feelings and being prudent in not allowing the heart's tenderness to be given free rein where and when it shouldn't be, in accord with one's vocation and state. Those called to the path of marriage should guard their heart for their spouse, doing so not only at the beginning of the marriage but as the years go by. This requires constant care to channel affections properly, not allowing feelings to get entangled in real or imaginary compensations.

Spouses need to be reminded "that the secret of married happiness lies in everyday things, not in daydreams"—they should always strive "to love each other with the love of their youth. Anyone who thinks that love ends when the worries and difficulties that life brings with it begin has a poor idea of marriage, which is a sacrament and an ideal and a vocation."[41]

Our Lord has also asked some souls to give him their whole heart, without sharing it with another creature, and so they have an even more noble reason to keep it clean and free of all attachments. It would be very sad to allow the heart to become entangled in petty things that choke off God's love. God always gives the graces needed to keep our heart intact for him and for all souls out of love for him. And with his grace comes the

---

41. St. Josemaría Escrivá, *Conversations*, no. 91.

generosity and strength to cut off an attachment or rectify a disordered affection. At times the spiritual advisor will need to issue a reminder: "If the love of God is put into friendships, they are cleansed, reinforced and spiritualized, because all the dross, all the selfish points of view, and excessively worldly considerations are burned away. Never forget that the love of God puts our affections in order and purifies them without diminishing them."[42]

Guarding the heart requires drawing close to God and getting to know him. It requires imbuing our heart and all its feelings with his love, for a person whose heart is cold, whose prayer is tepid, and who lacks apostolic zeal would find it hard to ward off a desire for compensations, since the human heart is made for love and will never be satisfied with a cold and dry existence.[43]

Guarding our heart often begins with guarding our eyes.[44] Common sense and supernatural sense provide our eyes with a "filter," as it were, that prevents us from focusing on what shouldn't be looked at. And this happens with naturalness and simplicity, without doing anything strange, but also with the strength that comes from knowing the value of the treasure we are guarding: while in the street, at work, and in social situations. It is not a question of "not seeing" (since we need our sight in our daily activity in the world, at work, and in our human

---

42. St. Josemaría Escrivá, *Furrow*, no. 828.

43. "It is such a pity not to have a heart. How unfortunate are those people who have never learned to love with tenderness! We Christians are in love with Love: Our Lord does not want us to be dry and rigid, like inert matter. He wants us to be saturated with his love!" (St. Josemaría Escrivá, *Friends of God*, no. 183).

44. Christians, with the help of grace, combat concupiscence and the disorder introduced through original sin "by the virtue and gift of chastity, for chastity lets us love with upright and undivided heart; by purity of intention, which consists in seeking the true end of man . . . by purity of vision, external and internal; by discipline of feelings and imagination; by refusing all complicity in impure thoughts that incline us to turn aside from the path of God's commandments: 'Appearance arouses yearning in fools' (Wis 15:5)" (CCC, 2520).

relationships), but of "not looking" at what shouldn't be looked at, of keeping our heart clean, of fostering the recollection we need to stay close to God without doing anything odd. We need to keep our look pure not only to avoid what could lead to the sin of lust (which blinds a person to supernatural goods and also to authentic human values), but also in other areas where we can fall prey to the "concupiscence of the eyes": the desire for clothes and consumer goods, or cravings for food or drink. "The eye is the lamp of the body. So, if your eye is sound, your whole body will be full of light; but if your eye is not sound, your whole body will be full of darkness" (Mt 6:22–23).

Guarding the heart from becoming attached to people requires *maintaining a prudent distance* from those "with whom it is quite likely that this may happen" and "when God doesn't want it to happen." This is a matter of a spiritual and affective "distance," shown by avoiding undue confidences or the unburdening of sorrows and sufferings that weigh on one's heart. In certain circumstances, prudence may also dictate observing a physical distance from the person concerned. If one is truly seeking only to please God, a deep and sincere examination of conscience will bring to light any less than upright intention in keeping that person's company or opening one's heart.

We need to have big hearts, filled with the love God wants for us: a strong, clean love that defends our hearts from any affections displeasing to him.

A Big Heart

Guarding the heart also requires controlling the memory. We need to reject images of past scenes or dialogues that could enkindle the embers of old feelings and channel love in a misguided direction. Similarly, taking refuge in an uncontrolled imagination and unbridled fantasies makes it hard to focus on the daily reality around us. When one gives in with some frequency to this temptation—perhaps more acute in moments of fatigue and interior dryness, or as a compensation for the small annoyances of everyday life—a split opens up between one's interior world (where vanity always emerges triumphant) and the inhospitable real world, which is the only world where we can strive for sanctity. A person given to escaping into a private and unreal inner world will find it hard to be generous in confronting what needs to be done at each moment in order to grow in virtue. How can we struggle against our all-too-real defects when, instead of confronting them with humility and hope, we refuse to face them and defeat them only in our imagination?

It is also possible for our heart to become attached to people in a film or a novel, or to someone we have seen but with whom we don't have any personal contact. When the heart becomes attached (and perhaps stained) in this way, it is unable to rise up to God. As spiritual guides, we should teach people to examine where their hearts are placed throughout the day—who they think about and make the central figure of their interior world.

Interior purity, a prerequisite for all true love, is attained by a cheerful and constant struggle over the course of one's whole life. Through a daily examination of conscience, we fight against any complicity with thoughts and images that distance us both from God and from other men and women. Love for frequent confession, through which God purifies the soul and fills it with his grace, is also a great help here.

Interior purity strengthens the heart's capacity to love[45] and safeguards human dignity. The dignity of the human person is given great importance today, but unfortunately this dignity is

---

45. Guarding the heart has nothing to do with "constricting" it. On the contrary, it is the best guarantee of loving others even more. "Nothing is wider than Paul's heart," says St. John Chrysostom, "which embraced all the faithful with the vehemence of his love" (St. John Chrysostom, *Homily on the Second Epistle to the Corinthians*, 13).

often debased in new and very grave ways.[46] When one fails to guard one's heart, when it seeks "compensations," little by little love for God dries up and, unless one reacts, the interior life in the soul can die out completely.

CAUSES AND REMEDIES

Self-Knowledge

By corresponding to the graces we receive, we grow in self-knowledge. We begin to realize that everything good we have comes from God, and we see the need to give thanks and purify our hearts.[47] "With God enlightening our intellect, which seems to be inactive, we understand beyond any shadow of doubt that, since the Creator takes care of everyone, even his enemies, how much more will he take care of his friends! We become convinced that no evil or trouble can befall us that will not turn out to be for our good. And so, joy and peace become more firmly rooted in our spirit, and no merely human motive can tear them from us, because these 'visitations' always leave us with something of himself, something divine. We find ourselves praising the Lord our God, who has worked such great wonders in us

---

46. "The human heart continues today to feel the same impulses Jesus denounced as the cause and root of impurity: selfishness in all its forms, twisted intentions, the low motives that so often demean human behavior. But today's world also faces a new challenge that one could in some sense call 'new' because it is so widespread and serious: the debasement of human love and the wave of impurity and sensuality that has been unleashed in the world. This demeaning of man's dignity affects the very core of his being, the well-springs of his personality" (Jose Orlandis, *Las Bienaventuranzas*, EUNSA, Pamplona, 1982).

47. This self-knowledge, based on humility, is the first step in developing a real interior life. "In this school we seem to breathe wisdom and knowledge, and all this wisdom and knowledge is directed towards knowing God and knowing ourselves. That is the foundation of everything we are taught. Until this is well grasped by the soul it cannot make any progress. The Teacher suspends all his lessons, and until this fact is well rooted in the soul, he does not go ahead with his teaching" (Francisca Javiera del Valle, *About the Holy Spirit* [New York: Scepter, 2007], p. 44).

(see Job 5:9), and understanding that God has made us capable of possessing an infinite treasure" (see Wis 67:14).[48] The soul understands then with great clarity the immense gift it has received, and it strives to give thanks and to correspond in even the smallest things.[49]

Docility

Being docile to grace means striving, with God's help, to carry out what the Holy Spirit suggests to us in the intimacy of our heart. It means fulfilling our duties faithfully, first of all everything referring to our commitments with God, making a decisive effort in the goals he sets before us, accepting with simplicity and supernatural outlook the difficulties we face even when prolonged and hard to bear. God moves our soul interiorly, with gentleness, reminding us often of the advice received in spiritual direction, and the more faithful we are to these graces, the more prepared our soul is to receive others. We find it easier to carry out good deeds, and we experience a deeper joy. St. Augustine freely translated the words *abyssus abyssum vocat* from the Psalm: "grace calls out to grace" (Ps 41:8). Correspondence

---

48. St. Josemaría Escrivá, *Friends of God*, no. 305.

49. St. Teresa of Avila recounts the effect produced on her by some precious jewels she was shown in Toledo by her friend Luisa de la Cerda: "Once, when I was with that lady I mentioned, I was ill with heart sickness. . . . Since she was very charitable, she gave orders that I be shown some of her jewels of gold and precious stone that were very valuable, especially one of the diamonds that was appraised highly. She thought they would make me happy. Recalling what the Lord has kept for us, I was laughing to myself and feeling pity at the sight of what people esteem. And I thought of how impossible it would be for me, even if I tried, to esteem those things if the Lord didn't remove from my memory the things he had shown me. In this way the soul has great dominion, so great that I don't know whether anyone who doesn't possess this dominion will understand it. It is the detachment proper and natural to us because it comes without labor on our part. God does it all, for his Majesty shows these truths in such a way, and they are so imprinted on the soul, that it is seen clearly we couldn't acquire them by ourselves in this way and in so short a time" (*Book of Her Life*, 38:4, Institute of Carmelite Studies).

to a grace received draws down another grace and prepares us to better correspond to the following one.

Docility to the Holy Spirit's inspirations is necessary to preserve the life of grace and produce supernatural fruit. As our Lord teaches in the parable of the sower, the seed that the Holy Spirit sows in our heart has the strength to send out roots, to grow, and to yield fruit. But first we have to welcome it into our heart and never fail to nurture it.[50]

This path of docility to grace begins by refusing to allow into our life anything that could separate us from God, even slightly, and being faithful in little things:[51] small mortifications in our work or in family life, going to confession on the day we have set for this, making a careful examination of conscience to see where we have failed and where God wants us to struggle the next day, living the heroic minute when getting up in the morning, changing the topic (or at least keeping quiet) in conversations when an absent person is not spoken well of. In contrast, the daily resistance to grace in small points is as harmful as "hail on a tree in bloom which promised much fruit; the flowers are destroyed and the fruit will not form."[52] One's interior life becomes stunted and could even die out.

Correspondence in Little Things: "Grace Calls Out to Grace"

The closer the saints are to God, the more faithful they are to the graces they receive, and the more rapid is their progress towards

---

50. "God's opportunities do not wait; they come and they go. The word of life waits not—if it is not appropriated by you, the devil will appropriate it. He delays not, but has his eyes wide always and is ready to pounce down and carry off the gift which you delay to use" (J.H. Newman, *Sermon*, no. 3, "The Calls of Grace").

51. "Correspondence to grace is to be found also in the ordinary little things of each day, which seem unimportant and yet have the overriding importance of Love" (St. Josemaría Escrivá, *The Forge*, no. 686).

52. Garrigou-Lagrange, *The Three Ages of the Interior Life*, vol. I, p. 94.

him. "Modern physical science tells us that the velocity of a falling body increases uniformly. This is an image of the growth of charity in a soul which allows nothing to hold it back, and which moves faster towards God according as increasing nearness to Him increases His attraction."[53] Our Lord calls all Christians to holiness in the midst of their daily life. The spiritual director reminds each person that it is precisely amid the joys and sufferings of daily life that one must strive to reach God, corresponding to the graces we receive. The normal difficulties at work, the people we interact with every day, the small opportunities to serve others in our family all help us grow in our love for God each day.

The Holy Spirit grants us countless graces to avoid deliberate venial sins and also faults which, without being a sin, are displeasing to God. We also receive constant help to sanctify our ordinary life, to carry out our daily actions as perfectly as possible and with an upright intention, for noble human motives and for supernatural motives. A person who strives to be faithful to the graces received draws closer to God each day and is disposed to receive new helps. Each grace brings a new one along with it: "To him who has will more be given" (Mk 4:25). Everything is carried out through love and for love.[54]

But we can never forget that the interior life needs time; it grows and matures like grain sown in a field. Therefore, being faithful to grace also means not becoming discouraged over one's failings and unfulfilled resolutions. It means not becoming impatient when it continues being hard to uproot a defect, or to pray as one would like, or to remember God more often while working. And this is also true when many years have already been spent in the struggle for holiness. The farmer is patient; he doesn't dig up the seed or abandon the field when the fruit

---

53. Ibid., *The Mother of the Saviour* (Rockford, IL: Tan, 1993), p. 89.

54. "The summit? For a soul that has surrendered itself, everything becomes a summit to conquer. Every day it discovers new goals, because it does not know how, or want, to limit the love of God" (St. Josemaría Escrivá, *Furrow*, no. 17).

seems to be slow to arrive. He knows he needs to work and wait; he must allow for the days of frost and those of warm sun. He knows the seed is growing, without knowing how, and he is confident that the time for the harvest will come.

Spiritual directors encourage souls to be patient in the face of defects that refuse to disappear or the apparent lack of fruit—like the farmer who relies on the wisdom of centuries. Souls must be encouraged to "begin and begin again," with humility. "*Nunc coepi!*—now I begin! This is the cry of a soul in love which, at every moment, whether it has been faithful or lacking in generosity, renews its desire to serve—to love!—our God with a wholehearted loyalty."[55]

We teach people to fight with patient perseverance, convinced that the overcoming of a defect or the acquisition of a virtue normally does not depend on sudden and violent efforts, but on a humble and constant struggle, beginning over and over again, always relying on God's mercy. We should never allow impatience to prevent us from being faithful to grace—impatience that almost always is rooted in pride.

"RETARDED" SOULS

It is important to watch out for the danger of souls that get stuck at the beginning of the path, held back by laziness or negligence, when they were destined to have life and life in abundance. Some spiritual writers have used the term "retarded" for souls in this situation.[56]

---

55. Ibid., no. 161.

56. See Garrigou-Lagrange, *The Three Ages of the Interior Life*, part II, ch. 37. "Some souls, because of their negligence or spiritual sloth, do not pass from the age of beginners to that of proficients. These are retarded souls; in the spiritual life they are like abnormal children, who do not happily pass the crisis of adolescence and who, though they do not remain children, never reach the full development of maturity." Also see *Las Conversiones del Alma*, p. 67.

It is like a child who for some reason fails to mature properly and, as the years pass, is no longer a "child" but a person of deformed development. Something similar happens with a soul that has begun on the path of interior life but fails to advance owing to a lack of generosity and correspondence. These are the souls that St. Teresa says have remained in the outer court of the interior castle without daring to enter and enjoy the marvels within.[57] They have made a pact with spiritual mediocrity and are satisfied with being merely "good" instead of striving for sanctity, far removed from the rich life of prayer to which God is calling them. Perhaps they feel a positive sense of envy toward others who are advancing on the path, but they don't choose to really use the means that will bring them out of this situation. They are not truly convinced that they are called to be saints, with heroic virtues.

Properly speaking, a "retarded" or "underdeveloped" soul is not the same as a lukewarm soul, although they have much in common. The lukewarm person has experienced God's love and intimacy, but later the will has become trapped by material goods (compensations, excessive concern for one's health, a comfortable existence, and the desire not to "overdo things"). As a result, one's relationship with God becomes awkward; it is something "one has to do"—following rules and carrying out lifeless actions that provide little strength against temptations. But a "retarded" or "underdeveloped" soul has never known what it means to enjoy divine intimacy. These individuals have never gone beyond the first steps, where they have become stuck, struggling without really struggling, lacking in

---

57. There are many souls who remain in the outer court of the castle and "don't care at all about entering the castle, nor do they know what lies within that most precious place, nor who is within" (St. Teresa of Avila, *The Interior Castle*, ch. 1, 5). She adds that these souls seem to be "so used to dealing always with the insects and vermin that are in the wall surrounding the castle" (Ibid., ch. 1, 6), that they fail to enter within to converse with God.

the greatness of soul required to abandon oneself without limits to God's will.[58] They have failed to definitively burn their ships so as not to be able to turn back.[59] In some corner of their soul, a small door is still open.

The interior life requires continually nourishing one's love so that the initial fervor is not extinguished. With the passage of time, the Holy Spirit inspires in the faithful soul a more serene—but no less strong—eagerness for a complete and unconditional response. It is then that one has to be more vigilant (and the person giving spiritual advice especially so) so that an easygoing attitude doesn't develop that smothers one's eagerness for holiness, replacing it with the calculation of doing the "required minimum." What is at stake is an intimate friendship with God, the entrance into the "interior castle" St. Teresa speaks of. When the soul loses sight of God's call to holiness, it begins to confuse the golden mean with "not overdoing it." As a consequence, mediocrity sets in, along with a lack of virtue, giving in where, even in little things, heroism is required. One then tries in vain to combine the desire of not losing one's way with the maximum comfort possible, trying not to make waves (among friends, at work, with one's family), whereas Christians who seek to follow Christ closely of necessity must make their

---

58. "God is an infinite sea furrowed by countless sails. There are Christians who take in their sails when the divine wind increases. They are afraid to abandon the shore. Too many Christians fear God. Some, those who love him, entrust themselves to him. They don't know what he wants of them, but without knowing they trust. They don't ask for explanations but launch out into the deep. The one who fails to do so knows nothing of the bright blue of the water, or the cheerful lapping of the waves; they know nothing of the tranquil nights when the ship advances steadily and silently; they know nothing of the joy of finding oneself without any mooring, upheld only by God, more secure than the ocean itself" (*La vocacion*, Ed. Sigueme., p. 45).

59. When Hernan Cortes decided to go forward with his endeavor in Mexico no matter what the cost, he ordered that his ships be scuttled, so neither he nor anyone else would waver. As he explained in his message to the king of Spain, "Under the pretext that such ships were not navigable, I had them sunk; thus all hope of leaving was lost and I could act more securely" (*Hernán Cortés*, p. 205).

presence felt—for they are *ipse Christus:* Christ himself. They are called to do so by their joy and their Christian witness in so many situations in response to a world and its way of thinking that is becoming pagan. A soul that fails to reflect Christ doesn't grow. And if it had started growing at some point in the past, it now starts going backwards and becomes "deformed."

THE IMPORTANCE OF SINCERITY

Sincerity allows a person to be known with humility and clarity, without half-truths, without dissimulating or exaggerating, showing interior dispositions and the reality of one's life with simplicity, in order to receive all the help available in the struggle for holiness. Sincerity requires getting down to specifics, with details but always with refinement. It requires fleeing from anything complicated or entangled, calling things by their name, without trying to disguise weaknesses, defects, and defeats by adorning them with false justifications.[60]

Sincerity, when practiced well, leads to "calling things by their name" and fosters brevity: normally just a few words are required to get to the gist of the matter. A priest after visiting the Curé of Ars said, "In five minutes I poured my soul into his." The saint of Ars advised penitents: "Avoid useless accusations that don't achieve anything except to waste time, tire out those who are waiting to go to confession, and make devotion grow cold." As an example, he mentions a woman who, "after arguing with her husband and causing a scandal in her house, confesses to having omitted grace before meals or the thanksgiving afterwards;"[61] or the husband who tells of omitting his

---

60. "You understood what sincerity is when you wrote to me: 'I am trying to form the habit of calling things by their proper names and, above all, of not looking for words for what does not exist'" (St. Josemaría Escrivá, *Furrow*, no. 332).
61. See *Vida del Cura de Ars*, p. 152.

morning prayers, but fails to consider his injustices when paying his employees.

St. Jean Marie Vianney fostered clarity and concreteness in those who came to him by his vigilance and opportune questions. The spiritual guide has to practice and teach sincerity: by being brief in one's words of advice, asking for light in order to raise questions at the right time and in the right way, and helping souls to know themselves, showing them how to avoid being long-winded. It is possible to do so without wounding when one is truly striving to serve souls with an upright intention.

In opening one's soul in spiritual direction, one should avoid both inconsequential details and wordy generalizations, telling what has happened with simplicity, explaining the true state of one's soul, the suggestions of the enemy, the small victories and defeats, without beating around the bush. Complete sincerity is tarnished by generalities: "I wasn't humble," "I was lazy," "I wasn't very charitable." In what? How? When? Why? It is the circumstances that make deeds and situations personal and accurately express the state of one's soul.

A Right Intention

A right intention fosters sincerity, because one isn't trying to "look good" or protect one's image but only seeking to find the path that leads straight to God. This requires saying things briefly but fully. A person wouldn't tell the doctor, "Something hurts," or "I don't feel well," but rather, "I have a bad headache, in the front or in back, and it happens with this frequency, and this type of pain reliever seems to help, etc."[62]

---

62. We have to help people see how foolish it is to put on pretenses in spiritual direction: "Pretense is absurd, like going to a tailor and standing on tiptoe to appear taller. How odd that new suit will look and how badly that customer will have cheated himself" (Juan Luis Lorda, *The Virtues of Holiness: The Basics of Spiritual Struggle*, [New York: Scepter, 2010] p. 41).

The virtue of sincerity requires more than just "telling the truth." It requires revealing the wounds and bruises with contrition and the desire to be cured, with docility and the readiness to listen and put into practice the advice received. Someone isn't really being sincere if, after opening up his or her soul, that person isn't ready to rectify things, but instead makes excuses by saying: "That's the way I am," or "I can't do any more."

Winning a person's confidence little by little helps that person to make known those things that humanly might show him or her in a poor light, bringing about a full disclosure of his or her intimate thoughts and feelings.

We can help people to see the importance of this fundamental virtue by focusing on the rich fruit sincerity brings with it. There is nothing that cannot be fixed—including what might seem most disastrous—if one is humble and sincere and ready to begin again. A person with this attitude always ends up winning out in the end, even when apparently suffering a defeat. That is why this virtue is so essential for traveling the path of holiness. Sincerity also ensures that the inevitable suffering and setbacks one meets on the way don't lead to sorrow and discouragement. Rather, these experiences help to foster simplicity of heart, and above all they facilitate the action of the Holy Spirit in the soul.

Opposed to this virtue is any affectation in one's words or actions, the desire to attract attention, pedantry, an air of sufficiency, or boasting. These faults hinder union with Christ and create barriers—at times insurmountable ones—to helping those around us to draw closer to Jesus. A soul that is simple does not get entangled in useless complications, but rather makes steady progress towards God, taking advantage of all events, whether good or bad, that happen each day.[63]

---

63. Along with sincerity, naturalness, and simplicity are "marvelous human virtues that enable men to take in the message of Christ. On the other hand, all that is tangled and complicated, the twisting and turning about one's own problems, all this builds up a barrier which often prevents people from hearing Our Lord's voice" (St. Josemaría Escrivá, *Friends of God*, no. 90).

We also want to encourage people to live this virtue in all their dealings with those around them. In interacting with others, one's word should be enough; one's "yes" should mean *yes*, and one's "no," *no*. Our Lord stressed the value of the word of an upright person who stands by what he says (see Mt 5:37). Our words and deeds as trustworthy Christians should have great value in the sight of others, because we seek the truth in everything and flee from hypocrisy and double-dealing.[64] Truth is always a reflection of God and therefore commands great respect. If we cultivate the habit of always telling the truth, even in seemingly unimportant matters, our words will take on great power, "like the signature of a notary," and never be called into question. And thus we will be imitating our Lord.

Opposed to this Christian way of being is the "double-minded man, unstable in all his ways" (Jas 1:7–8), like an actor who presents a different face or outlook depending on the public in front of him. Today, it is especially urgent for a Christian to be a man or woman of a coherent, undivided life, shunning any masks or disguises in situations where it may be hard to uphold the truth, any undue concern for what "others might say," and especially all hypocrisy.

Facets of Sincerity

In Jesus' praise of Nathaniel, we see how Christ's heart is drawn to a person who is sincere: "Behold, an Israelite indeed, in

---

64. "Naturalness in behavior, behaving in accord with what one is and thinks, is another aspect of simplicity. At times charity may demand that one tone things down a bit; other times, courtesy may require some play acting (e.g., hiding boredom or impatience). But outside those obligations of charity or courtesy, we should behave naturally. Sin is the only thing we need to feel ashamed of—before God and at times before men. But nothing else. A man should not feel embarrassed, for example, that his father has a humble social position or a humble job. No one should feel ashamed of the color of his skin, his race, his ancestry, his physical defects, or those of family members or friends. Nor should our opinions, beliefs, customs, or work embarrass us if they are not an offense against God. It may not be necessary to proclaim them everywhere, but we have to avoid being ashamed" (Lorda, *The Virtues of Holiness*, pp. 41–42).

whom is no guile!" (Jn 1:47). The new disciple, comments St. Augustine, did not have "as it were, two hearts: one recess of his heart where he sees the truth, and another where he conceives falsehood."[65] It should be possible to say the same about every follower of Christ: undivided men and women who live the faith they profess with integrity. The liar, someone with a double mind, whose actions lack transparency, always ends up sounding like a cracked bell: "You were reading in that dictionary the synonyms for insincere: 'two-faced, surreptitious, evasive, disingenuous, sly.' As you closed the book, you asked the Lord that nobody should ever be able to apply those adjectives to you, and you resolved to improve much more in this supernatural and human virtue of sincerity."[66]

First and foremost, we must cultivate sincerity with God in prayer. We have to address him trustingly, as a child with its father, in our specific circumstances, never taking refuge in the group or the crowd.

Sincerity is needed to follow the inspirations of grace, even when they seem arduous. Being attentive to God's will requires a right intention in order to recognize what our own passions and whims may suggest and, if such is the case, what lies outside the path God intends for each of us.

We have to be sincere with God when difficulties arise and go trustingly to the One who can do all things. This requires acknowledging our sins and mistakes, without trying to disguise them. We also live sincerity with God when we ask for the virtues that counteract bad habits we find it hard to overcome. Our petition will always reach heaven if we have a true intention to change.

St. Augustine, in his *Confessions*, acknowledged the lack of sincerity that had marred his earlier life. "I had begged you for

---

65. St. Augustine, *Tractates on the Gospel of St. John*, 7, 18.
66. St. Josemaría Escrivá, *Furrow*, no. 337.

chastity and had said, 'Make me chaste and continent, but not yet.' I was afraid that you would hear me too soon and cure me too soon from the disease of a lust which I preferred to be satisfied rather than extinguished."[67] But afterwards he corresponded to grace and became one of the great saints in the Church.

Sincerity is also needed to prevent any disguised complicity with evil that requires a resolute reaction: "Agreed: there is a lot of pressure from outside and that excuses you in part. But there is also complicity within—take a good look—and there I see no excuse."[68] Recognizing this "complicity within" is often the first step towards overcoming the situation.

This virtue is equally necessary in the examination of conscience, in order to prevent the deceptions caused by the "mute devil," and to discover any signs of pride and lukewarmness. Sincerity will enable us to see the source of any sadness or bad humor, which perhaps stems from a lack of generosity or good use of time, and it will prevent us from becoming accustomed to what displeases God and enable us to rectify it quickly.[69]

Sincerity leads us to reveal ourselves as we are, without trying to present a false image or confusing what we are with what we would like to be. The doctor is only effective when he knows

---

67. Rex Warner, *The Confessions of St. Augustine* VIII, 7 (New York: New American Library, 1963) pp 173–74.

68. St. Josemaría Escrivá, *The Way*, no. 700.

69. "Apply a *savage* sincerity to your examination of conscience; that is to say, be courageous. It is the same as when you look at yourself in the mirror to know where you have hurt yourself or where the dirt is or where your blemishes are, so that you can get rid of them" (St. Josemaría Escrivá, *Furrow*, no. 148).

"Forgive me for insisting on these points, but I believe it is absolutely necessary for you to have deeply impressed on your minds the fact that humility, together with its immediate consequence, sincerity, is the thread which links the other means together. These two virtues act as a foundation on which a solid victory can be built. If the dumb devil gets inside a soul, he ruins everything. On the other hand, if he is cast out immediately, everything turns out well; we are happy and life goes forward properly. Let us always be *brutally sincere*, but in a good mannered way" (St. Josemaría Escrivá, *Friends of God*, no. 188).

the sickness well, in all its ramifications and possible complications. Spiritual direction is truly a powerful help when people let themselves be known as they are: with their mistakes as well as with their capacity for good. This sincerity must be even greater when the need is greater. "Do not let even the smallest focal point of corruption take root in your souls, no matter how tiny it may be. Speak out. When water flows, it stays clean; blocked up, it becomes a stagnant pool full of repugnant filth. What was once drinking water becomes a breeding ground for insects."[70] We can help ensure that the water never gets "blocked up" in those we are guiding by asking opportune questions in order to detect the first symptoms that the water is becoming muddied and undrinkable.

Sincerity is not only a question of speaking about one's mistakes and negative qualities. It is also important to mention virtues and good actions that, out of modesty, one might want to keep quiet about: how one's love for God is growing stronger, small details of affection with our Lady appropriate for a life of spiritual childhood, signs of greater refinement in one's relationship with God. If these good points are never mentioned in the conversation of spiritual guidance, they could over time become deformed or even lost.

Helping People to Be Sincere

In the old books used by catechists to help prepare children for their first confession and Communion, one often finds references to the ugly "toad": the biggest sin and often the hardest one to confess. A child with this interior "toad" must get rid of it quickly in order to receive the sacraments well. Adults too can have a "toad" inside, a failing they find it hard to mention. This can happen at the beginning of the path or after years

---

70. St. Josemaría Escrivá, *Friends of God*, no. 181.

spent struggling for holiness.[71] It could be something objectively important or even something quite small, but it's something one is reluctant to speak about because it causes shame or makes one look bad, humanly speaking.

In spiritual direction it is usually easy to "notice" when something is being kept inside that blocks complete trust and does damage to a soul. At times, one can observe an attempt to open up completely by a person of good will who finds it hard to do so. We assist such a person by our prayer, showing understanding, and making it easier for them to speak clearly through tactful questions.

We should advise people in spiritual direction to say first what they find most difficult.[72] When someone gets the "toad" out, an important step forward on the path to personal holiness has been taken.

Those who guide others spiritually should encourage them to be very sincere, with freedom and spontaneity, gaining their trust with affection, and showing them by deeds and words that one understands everything they are trying to say. While never requiring an account of someone's conscience, at times we will need to ask about deeper dispositions, probing the root of specific behavior and raising topics that go right to the heart

---

71. "If you have an ugly 'toad' inside you, my son, let it out! As I have always advised you, the first thing you must mention is what you wouldn't like anybody to know. Once the 'toad' has been let out in Confession—how well one feels" (St. Josemaría Escrivá, *The Forge*, no. 193).

72. "'What shall I say?' you asked when you began to open up your soul. And with a sure conscience, I answered: 'In the first place say what you would not like to be known'" (St. Josemaría Escrivá, *Furrow*, no. 327).

"Tell first what you would not like to be known. Down with the dumb devil! By turning some small matter over and over in your mind, you will make it snowball into something big, with you trapped inside. What's the point of doing that? Open up your soul! I promise that you will be happy, that is faithful to your Christian way, if you are sincere. Clarity and simplicity: they are absolutely necessary dispositions. We have to open up our souls completely, so that the sun of God and the charity of Love can enter in" (St. Josemaría Escrivá, *Friends of God*, no. 189).

of a person's life.[73] Carelessness in work or study, sadness or bad humor, can often stem from deeper causes than those that appear on the surface. A deep-seated selfishness may have taken root in the soul that leads one to see everything and everyone as a function of one's own interests. A persistent lethargy can creep into all one's actions: neglecting one's relationship with God, which little by little takes second place; giving little importance to small specific mortifications and apostolic plans; an undertow of sensuality that one seems incapable of escaping from.

We need to encourage people to be sincere at the first sign of symptoms that could hinder their union with God: the heart feels an attraction incompatible with commitments already taken on, or one begins to neglect one's family; someone fails to set aside the time needed to receive effective formation or gives excessive importance to work. With illnesses of the body, recognizing early symptoms and reacting quickly can often mean saving a person's life or at least can forestall the need for more traumatic and painful measures. The same happens with the life of the soul. If one speaks beforehand, with complete sincerity—explaining the whole truth, with humility and docility, asking for help—one always wins out.

Insincerity

However, sometimes it will be necessary to respectfully point out possible signs of insincerity: failing to get down to specifics, euphemisms or circumlocutions when sharing something that could be said in a few words, a superficial examination, or lack of real apostolic zeal that a life of prayer always entails. This

---

73. "You who have in your hands and in your heart the responsibility for other souls, the weight of other lives, never lose sight of the fact that trust cannot be imposed: it has to be won. And without the trust of the people around you, who collaborate with you and help you, how bitter your life would be, and how sterile your mission" (Salvador Canals, *Ascetica meditada*, p 72).

will also involve facilitating simplicity and trust, encouraging people to be clear and transparent.

Out of charity, one may at times need to confront head on, although also with refinement, symptoms of a possible habitual lack of sincerity, showing clearly the discordance between what the person says and the reality of his or her life. When one does so with supernatural prudence and first considers the matter in prayer, spiritual direction ends up being strengthened and goes forward on a firmer foundation, with a stronger mutual trust.[74]

This trust is fostered in a number of ways: by the interest shown by the person receiving spiritual direction, by facilitating punctuality, and by being refined in the questions one asks. We have to show true interest in the other person's concerns (at times quite small ones): worries about an examination, a financial problem, health concerns, etc. A spiritual director should never give the impression of being hurried or rushed, and must know how to be demanding with gentleness but also with strength. The one guiding others needs to show great understanding and never be surprised or scandalized by anything that is said. It is also very important to always be encouraging and optimistic, no matter how difficult the situation may be, using words that transmit peace and joy.

In striving to help people be sincere, one should not take things for granted. It would be foolish always to think that "everything is going fine" and avoid asking about certain sensitive topics: purity, chastity in marriage, generosity regarding

---

74. "In undertaking and advancing in the spiritual life . . . do not trust too much to yourselves, but with docile simplicity seek and accept the help of someone who, with wise moderation, can guide your soul, point out to you the dangers, suggest suitable remedies, and in every internal and external difficulty can guide you in the right way towards an ever greater perfection, according to the example of the saints and the teachings of Christian asceticism. Without these prudent guides for one's conscience, it is often very difficult to be duly responsive to the impulses of the Holy Spirit and of the grace of God" (Pope Pius XII, *Menti Nostrae*, no. 27).

the number of children, refinement in living this virtue when engaged, observing the demands of social justice and professional ethics, moderation in social relations—above all in environments where a Christian has to go against the current, etc.

Those just starting out on the spiritual path can be especially prone to mistakes absorbed from a non-Christian environment, and they might view how most people live as unobjectionable. Ignorance is the greatest enemy of the interior life.[75] The atmosphere of hostility to the faith that today has infiltrated all sectors of society can often result in a deformed conscience, which spiritual directors can help to rectify. When the family and school fail to carry out their educational role, the culture spreads through the means of communication which is frequently amoral, if not directly anti-religious.

---

75. "All the evils which poison men and nations and trouble so many hearts have a single cause and a single source: ignorance of the truth" (John XXIII, *Ad Petri Cathedram*, no. 6).

POSSIBLE TOPICS FOR SPIRITUAL DIRECTION

These conversations should be focused on deep dispositions, especially the main points of struggle in recent days and how one has followed through on resolutions and suggestions from the last session. It is good to habitually take up the thread of the last conversation: points of struggle, resolutions, concerns, etc.; in this way continuity is maintained from one session to the next.

Besides bringing up topics and major feasts tied to the Church's liturgical year, the following topics might also be addressed so that key points of Christian life are not neglected.

PRAYER

To follow our Lord closely, we need our daily life to be grounded in prayer. Our whole day should be lived for God, but some moments should be set aside especially for being with him, seeking the strength necessary to sanctify our work and life. Without these regular "pauses," it is very difficult to maintain the unity with God that gives meaning to all daily events. Just as in our natural life we need food at specific times and in specific amounts, so too in our spiritual life we need steady nutrition to grow normally.[1]

To ensure that each soul receives this nourishment, it is useful to suggest a *plan of life*, made up of specific spiritual practices spread throughout the day or week. These practices of piety serve as a channel for grace and provide the strength needed to make our entire day an offering pleasing to God. They enable us to live in God's presence, holding a simple and sincere conversation with him in the midst of daily occupations, much like the early Christians.[2] Our Lord comes to dwell in the center of our day, our family, and our work.

Practices of piety also serve as reference points to mark out the path, like signposts placed along mountain roads to indicate the route after heavy snow.[3]

For someone taking the first steps in the interior life, this "plan of life" will clearly differ from one suited to a person who has already spent many years in the struggle to be close to God.

---

1. "In recommending this unbroken union with God, am I not presenting an ideal so sublime that it is unattainable by the majority of Christians? Certainly the goal is high, but it is not unattainable. The path that leads to holiness is the path of prayer; and prayer ought to take root and grow in the soul little by little, like the tiny seed which later develops into a tree with many branches" (St. Josemaría Escrivá, *Friends of God*, no. 295).

2. "A woman busy in the kitchen or in sewing some fabric," writes St. John Chrysostom, "can always raise her thoughts to heaven and fervently invoke God. A person who goes to the market or travels alone, can easily pray with attention. Another who is in her shop, occupied in sewing wineskins, is free to raise her heart to the Master. The servant who cannot go to church because she has to go to the market to make purchases, or is busy in other occupations, or is in the kitchen, can always pray with attention and fervor. No place is indecorous for God" (*Homilies on the Prophetess Anna*, 6, 4).

3. In the interior life, "there are times of spring and summer, but there are also winters, days without sun and nights bereft of moonlight. We can't afford to let our friendship with Jesus depend on our moods, on our ups and downs. To do this would imply selfishness and laziness, and is certainly incompatible with love. Therefore, in times of wind and snow, a few solid practices of piety, which are not sentimental but firmly rooted and adjusted to one's special circumstances, will serve as the red posts always marking out the way for us " (*Friends of God*, no. 151).

But in both cases, care must be taken so that these practices don't become "rigid rules." Rather, they are meant to be flexible, designed for someone who lives "in the middle of the world, with a life of hard professional work . . . [the] plan of life ought to be like a rubber glove which fits the hand perfectly."[4] Equally uncomfortable and unsuitable would be a glove that was too big or one that was too small. When there is love, the plan of life adapts easily to days of intense work and to moments of relaxation, to times of sickness and to periods of good health.

Normally, with good will and the virtue of order, it is always possible to fulfill one's plan of life, although often this requires discerning difficulties that might arise (for example, a visit or a trip, or the time constraints professional work entails) and planning accordingly.

The goal we are striving for should always be kept clearly in mind: intimacy with God in the midst of our ordinary activities. Christian life consists in loving our Lord a little more each day, imitating him, following him closely, and being attracted by his life.[5] Holiness is not centered on the struggle against sin; it is not something negative. Rather, it is centered on Jesus Christ, the object of our love. We want to love and imitate the Master, who "went about doing good" (Acts 10:38). All the practices of piety in our plan of life are meant to lead us to grow in love for Christ, who dwells among us. From the first moment of each day, we need to "seek him, find him, get to know him, love him."[6]

---

4. See Ibid., no. 149.

5. In this point, vital for the soul's progress, we have to be attentive to what the Catechism calls *"failure in prayer*: discouragement during periods of dryness; sadness that, because we have 'great possessions,' (cf. *Mk* 10:22) we have not given all to the Lord; disappointment over not being heard according to our own will" (see CCC, 2728). We need to try to uncover the source of these "failures" in order to suggest the proper remedy and encourage these people to persevere in their friendship with our Lord.

6. "Seek him then, hungrily. If you act with determination, I am ready to guarantee that you have already found him, and have begun to get to know him and to love him, and to hold your conversation in heaven" (St. Josemaría Escrivá, *Friends of God*, no. 300).

LIFE OF FAITH

The whole Gospel is a call to live by faith. Our Lord asked two blind men who were beseeching him to cure them: "Do you believe that I am able to do this?" When they told him yes, he sent them on their way, healed: "According to your faith be it done to you" (Mt 9:28–29). He told another blind man in Jericho, whom he also cured: "Go your way; your faith has made you well," and that man, now able to see, "followed him on the way" (Mk 10:52). He assured the father of a dead child, "Do not fear; only believe, and she shall be well" (Lk 8:50). A few moments earlier he had cured a woman, sick for a long time, who demonstrated her faith by touching the fringe of his garment. "Daughter, your faith has made you well; go in peace" (Lk 8:48). He praised the Canaanite woman: "'O woman, great is your faith!' And he said to her: 'Be it done for you as you desire'" (Mt 15:28). "All things are possible to him who believes" (Mk 9:23), Jesus told the father of the boy possessed by a dumb spirit.

The apostles showed their true condition to our Lord in all simplicity. They knew their faith was often not as strong as it should be, so one day they asked Jesus: "Increase our faith!" Our Lord responded: "If you had faith as a grain of mustard seed, you could say to this sycamine tree, 'Be rooted up, and be planted in the sea,' and it would obey you" (Lk 17:5–6).

Faith should imbue every corner of our daily life: family, work, and social relations. It is not enough to give assent to the great truths of the Creed and have a solid doctrinal formation. We need to *live* the faith and *exercise* it, leading a *life of faith*—which is both the result and the manifestation of what we believe. "Our faith tells us who we really are—creatures made in the image of God, and his sons and daughters through grace—and what our true end is, which should preside over all our actions. It provides us with the light we need to learn to live as God's children, not only in isolated and sporadic moments when everything is gong well but amid the trials and difficulties of daily life."[7]

Therefore, a good topic for spiritual direction is how this supernatural virtue influences the events of one's daily life: how it affects the acceptance of sickness, the death of a loved one, a setback; how it fosters the optimistic vision of life proper to a child of God; how it affects one's behavior with colleagues at work, seeking above all the greatest good for them, bringing them closer to God.

Faith also helps us to see events that are less pleasant as part of the providential plan of our Father God, who "blesses with the Cross," to purify us and spur us to interior growth. It is important to teach those coming to us for spiritual direction to offer up these sufferings and annoyances, for they are a means—at times indispensable—for our sanctification.

We don't attain sanctity *in spite of* these painful events and circumstances but *through* them. Only thus can we grow in love for the Cross: an essential path for advancing in the supernatural life and learning to accept and love God's will, which does not always coincide with what we like.

The life of faith is shown in drawing close to our Lord in the Eucharist, asking him for what we need, going to our guardian angels, and trusting in God's help to go forward in difficult situations.

We have to ask God frequently to increase our faith. "Clearly," comments St. Augustine, "those who said, 'Lord, increase our faith,' already had faith. And while we are living in this world, that is the refrain of all who are making progress."[8] The virtue of faith can and should always increase.

When speaking about this virtue, it is good to bring up doctrinal topics that may be causing concern, especially nowadays

---

7. Ramon Garcia de Haro, *La Vida Cristiana*, p. 662.
8. St. Augustine, *Expositions on the Psalms*, 118, 17, 2.

when so much doctrinal confusion abounds. This can include asking for specific advice on studies, readings, etc. Since university students and those in the last years of high school are often told to read books undermining the Faith, it is important to speak about these matters and provide the opportune antidotes and remedies when necessary.

Moreover, television, radio, the press, the Internet, movies, and literature have a powerful influence on society, both for good and for evil. Along with positive messages, they spread many confusing ideas that contribute to a paganized atmosphere. Sometimes the message is diametrically opposed to the Christian faith. No one can consider himself or herself immune from the contamination from these widespread errors. In spiritual direction we need to provide solid formation, clarifying any doctrinal or moral deviations and suggesting useful readings and means of prudence when necessary. We must always remember that, in case of doubt (as in an epidemic), it would be foolish to drink from a source of water that could possibly cause the sickness—especially if there is no need to do so. Imprudence or rashness in these matters is often the origin of a crisis of faith, or at least indicative of a cooling off in one's relationship with our Lord.[9] The more adverse the environment, the stronger one's doctrinal formation has to be. And even greater should be the care put into choosing spiritual reading well suited to each person's situation.

Faith is the Christian's greatest treasure. We have to do everything possible to help each soul preserve and increase it.

---

9. In times of doctrinal confusion such as our own, special care is needed to ensure that no one yields in the content of the faith, not even in the smallest point. "If one cedes in any point of Catholic dogma, later it will be necessary to cede in another, and later in still another, until such abdications become something normal. And once one begins to reject dogma piece by piece, what is left in the end but to repudiate it in its totality?" (St. Vincent of Lerins, *Conmonitorio*, [Madrid: Palabra, 1976], no. 23).

PURITY, THE ENTRANCEWAY

It is good to habitually consider this virtue, always in a positive way—doing so with refinement but also with clarity, not taking anything for granted. Purity is a virtue intimately related to love for God, which is destined to grow continually in the soul through the action of the Holy Spirit. We need to confront the erroneous criteria found everywhere today and give each soul solid guidelines in this area. Although not first among the virtues, purity is nonetheless the "entranceway" to a deep interior life, and without it there can be no true apostolic zeal.

At times, circumstances in a person's past life may have left wounds that still cause problems. This shouldn't lead to trying to "forget about it," as though "nothing had happened," giving no importance to past and present experiences, or even seeing them as normal. The path to overcoming a situation that affects the soul in its depths is sincerity, a humble struggle, a desire for purification, reparation, and—when necessary—recourse to the sacrament of penance.

Conjugal Chastity

In matrimony, chastity teaches couples to respect each other mutually and to love one another with a firm, refined, enduring love. Moreover, conjugal love fails to attain its plenitude if it is not enriched, strengthened, and ordered by chastity.[10] In

---

10. "Love enables conjugal relations, without ceasing to be carnal, to be 'clothed,' so to speak, with the nobility of the spirit and to accord with human dignity. The thought that sexual union is destined to bring about new lives has a surprising power of transfiguration, but the physical union is only truly ennobled if it stems from love and is an expression of love. . . . When sex is completely separated from love and is sought for itself, then the person abandons his own dignity and also profanes the dignity of the other person. A strong love filled with tenderness is one of the greatest guaranties and, above all, one of the deepest causes of conjugal purity. But there is a still higher cause. Chastity, St. Paul tells us, is a 'fruit of the Spirit' (see Gal 5:23), that is, a consequence of divine love. To guard purity in marriage one needs not only a refined love that is respectful of the other person, but above all a great love for God. CONTINUED

this "ordered love," the acts proper to marriage, carried out in accord with God's will, are also a path to holiness. Therefore, the effort by the spouses to grow in affection is part of conjugal chastity, as well as a way to avoid any infidelity.

"To stop up the sources of life is a crime against the gifts that God has granted to mankind. It proves that a person is moved by selfishness, not love. Everything becomes clouded, because husband and wife begin to look at each other as accomplices, and the dissensions that are produced, if this state is allowed to continue, are almost always impossible to heal.

"When there is chastity in the love of married persons, their marital life is authentic; husband and wife are true to themselves, they understand each other, and develop the union between them. When the divine gift of sex is perverted, their intimacy is destroyed, and they can no longer look openly at each other."[11]

Celibacy and Virginity

When giving spiritual advice to married or single persons, it is important to stress the great value and fruitfulness of chastity.[12] This is especially relevant for those have dedicated themselves to God *indiviso corde*, with an undivided heart, renouncing a human love in order to give themselves entirely to God and to the spread

A person who strives to know and love Christ finds in this love a powerful stimulus for chastity. We know that purity draws one closer to Jesus in a special way and that being close to God, promised to those who keep their heart pure (see Mt 5:8), is the principal guaranty of purity" (J.M. Martinez Doral, "La Santidad de la Vida Conyugal," in *Scripta Theologica*, Pamplona. September-December 1989, pp. 880–881).

11. St. Josemaría Escrivá, *Christ Is Passing By*, no. 25.

12. "The more the faithful appreciate the value of chastity and its necessary role in their lives as men and women, the better they will understand, by a kind of spiritual instinct, its moral requirements and counsels. In the same way they will know better how to accept and carry out, in a spirit of docility to the Church's teaching, what an upright conscience dictates in concrete cases" (Congregation for the Doctrine of the Faith, "Persona Humana," *Declaration on Certain Questions Concerning Sexual Ethics*, no. 11).

of his kingdom.[13] Those who have given their whole heart to God, without human love in marriage intervening, have not done so "because of a supposed negative value of marriage, but in view of the particular value connected with this choice and which must be discovered and welcomed personally as one's own vocation. For that reason Christ said: 'He who is able to receive this, let him receive it' (Mt 19:12)."[14] The apostles, departing from the tradition of the Old Covenant where children in marriage were considered the greatest of all blessings, followed the example of Christ, convinced that thus they could be closer to him and better able to carry out the apostolic mission they had received. Little by little they came to understand, as Blessed John Paul II said, that this continence produces a particular "spiritual and supernatural fruitfulness which comes from the Holy Spirit."[15]

Perhaps in today's world chastity and, even more, apostolic celibacy and virginity may seem incomprehensible to many people. The early Christians also had to confront an environment hostile to this virtue. Therefore, an important part of spiritual guidance is stressing the value of chastity and its accompanying virtues. One has to make this virtue attractive by one's own exemplary conduct and by teaching the doctrine that the Church has always preserved regarding it. One should also take into account that our Lord asks those he calls to apostolic celibacy to live chastity with a special refinement of mind and heart: avoiding conversations inappropriate for someone close to our Lord; in the way one dresses; in guarding the eyes; and, above all, with the joyful example of their own lives. They have to show others the beauty of chastity by their own greater capacity to love, their generosity and cheerfulness, their refinement

---

13. Those who have dedicated themselves to God in virginity or celibacy *for the kingdom of heaven* know very well that "sex is not a shameful thing; it is a divine gift, ordained to life, to love, to fruitfulness" (St. Josemaría Escrivá, *Christ Is Passing By*, no. 24).

14. John Paul II, General Audience, March 10, 1982.

15. Ibid.

of soul. Thus they will proclaim with their lives that this virtue is always attainable, if one uses the means that our Mother the Church has recommended for centuries (discussed above).

VOCATION

An important part of spiritual direction is helping each person follow the path God has destined for him or her. Each one's vocation is a "precious pearl" (see Mt 13:45) and "treasure" (Mt 13:44)—whether already discovered or still to be found—and a sign of divine predilection. It is the greatest grace each person has received from God.[16]

Every believer has been called from all eternity to the highest divine vocation.[17] Our Father God expressly called us into life (no one has been born by chance); he directly created our unique and unrepeatable soul; and he has made us sharers in his intimate life through baptism. To each he has given a special task in life and has lovingly prepared a place in heaven, where he waits for us like a father awaiting his child after a long trip.

In addition to this radical vocation to holiness and apostolate addressed to all the faithful, God has given a particular call to each person. The majority he calls to live in the midst of the world so that they can transform it from within, direct it to him, and attain sanctity through earthly endeavors. Others (always few in relation to all the baptized) he asks to separate themselves from these realities, giving public witness—as consecrated souls—to their belonging to God.

A vocation is always a great gift, for which we have to give frequent thanks to God. It is the light that illumines our

---

16. See St. Josemaría Escrivá, *The Way*, no. 913.

17. "Even as he chose us in him before the foundation of the world, that we should be holy and blameless before him. He destined us in love to be his sons through Jesus Christ, according to the purpose of his will, to the praise of his glorious grace which he freely bestowed on us in the Beloved" (Eph 1:4–6).

daily life and work. If we were ignorant of this specific will of God that leads us directly to heaven, we would be traveling guided by the weak light of our own will, constantly in danger of stumbling. Our vocation gives us the light and grace we need to confront all the incidents of daily life. "A vocation provides a person, in a definitive way, with knowledge of himself, the world, and God. It is the reference point for judging accurately all the events of one's daily life."[18] God's will can be shown to us suddenly, as a bright light that illumines everything, like St. Paul on his way to Damascus, or little by little, through many small events.[19]

To help others discover their vocation is one of the noblest tasks God can entrust to us. In order to do so, lots of prudence is needed, along with the daring required for accepting every vocation. When the Holy Spirit gives sufficient signs of someone's call, it would be a great mistake to slow down or stop God's plans out of fear of family or social repercussions, etc. The plans of God always come with the graces needed to resolve any obstacles that arise in one's family, work, etc. Nevertheless, sometimes it is prudent to wait until difficulties are resolved that might endanger the development of one's vocation.[20]

---

18. Illanes, *Mundo y Santidad*, Rialp, Madrid 1984, p. 109.

19. "It is not a question of simply knowing what God wants from each of us in the various situations of life. The individual must do what God wants, as we are reminded in the words that Mary, the Mother of Jesus, addressed to the servants at Cana: 'Do whatever he tells you' (Jn 2:5). However, to act in fidelity to God's will requires a capability for acting and the developing of that capability . . . This, then, is the marvelous yet demanding task awaiting all the lay faithful and all Christians at every moment: to grow always in the knowledge of the richness of Baptism and faith as well as to live it more fully" (Bl. John Paul II. *Christifideles Laici*, no. 58). This is precisely one of the primary tasks of spiritual guidance.

20. "The fundamental objective of the formation of the lay faithful is an ever-clearer discovery of one's vocation and the ever-greater willingness to live it so as to fulfill one's mission. . . . This personal vocation and mission defines the dignity and the responsibility of each member of the lay faithful and makes up the focal point of the whole work of formation, whose work is the joyous and grateful recognition of this dignity and the faithful and generous living out of this responsibility" (Ibid. no. 58).

If, after giving one's life to God, temptations against being faithful arise, we should help that person to discover the causes, convinced that God never repents of his gifts, nor does a vocation disappear simply because one's first enthusiasm has cooled or one has failed to correspond fully. Often the solution is simply to remove a specific temptation and make an effort to draw closer to our Lord. And in every case, it is important to foster loyalty to the Church and to all souls, along with fidelity to one's word and to commitments freely taken on.

It is also important that one's vocation truly be a *shield*, a protective armor. It should be the "hinge" that supports all of one's actions and gives them meaning, as well as the "argument" always at hand to confront any temptation against perseverance. Whether just setting out on the path or after many years of dedication, the argument St. Josemaría gave when speaking about perseverance is always valid: "Because I have a vocation, in spite of my mistakes, God will give me the grace to go forward." Our Lord does not fail his friends, even though they sometimes fail to behave in a way worthy of him. We can always begin again.

We also need to make sure that people understand the moral ramifications of their freely-chosen commitments to God.

Every good Catholic should be eager to foster vocations to holiness among relatives and friends.[21] Parents, who want the

---

21. "One unmistakable sign of a priest's love for his mission is the need he feels to foster vocations to the priesthood. Although this is a duty of all the people of God, it falls particularly on the priest, who must yearn to give a continuous example of service, showing that he is happy in his own life; he must use every means, particularly the supernatural ones, to encourage people to feel the needs of the Church and the greatness of the priestly vocation and turn their lives into ministerial service of God and of men. A priest's heart must be in the seminary, knowing that the new priests will continue his mission and crown his life of self-surrender" (Alvaro del Portillo, *On Priesthood*, pp. 26–27).

Bl. John Paul II stressed that the maturity of the priest "contributes in a special way to the increase of vocations. He simply has to love his own vocation, has to be committed to it himself, so that in this way the truth about the ministerial priesthood becomes attractive to others. In the life of each of us should be read the mystery of Christ, from which the priest receives his role as another Christ" (Bl. John Paul II, *Letter to Priests on the Occasion of Holy Thursday*, March 10, 1991, no. 2).

best for their children, know to ask God to show each one their vocation, while doing what they can to foster it without trying to influence them directly. By their peace and joy, their humble and constant prayer, they will win from our Lord the light each child needs. The atmosphere of joy, piety, and human virtues that parents create in their home, their example of hard work, healthy freedom, good humor, temperance, and true concern for those in need, will help foster the vocations that the Church needs and that will be the greatest reward and honor for the parents themselves.

MORTIFICATION: AN ENCOUNTER WITH THE CROSS

To follow Christ, mortification is absolutely necessary: "To live you have to die."[22] "If any man would come after me, let him deny himself and take up his cross daily and follow me" (Lk 9:23). Without mortification neither virtue nor apostolic fruit nor intimacy with our Lord is possible.[23] As one begins to grow in interior life, "our Lord becomes more and more demanding with us. He asks us to make reparation, to do penance."[24] Being generous in reparation and penance prepares us to receive new graces and to attain a greater intimacy with God.

Given human nature's tendency to reject whatever causes inconvenience or pain, along with the hedonistic atmosphere that prevails today, it is important to emphasize the positive character of mortification—its close relationship to friendship

---

22. See St. Josemaría Escrivá, *The Way*, no 187.

23. "If at any time, my brother, someone, whether or not he is a prelate, tries to persuade you to a doctrine of ease and lightness, do not believe it nor embrace it, even though he confirm it with miracles . . . And never, if you want to possess Christ, seek him without the cross" (St. John of the Cross, "Carta al P. Juan de Santa Ana" *Vida y Obras* [Madrid: BAC, 1974], no. 23).

24. St. Josemaría Escrivá, *Friends of God*, no. 304.

with God and true joy, and its central role in the mystery of the Redemption. The pressure of an environment that sees self-denial and voluntary sacrifice as something dark and sad, from a bygone era and opposed to what is human, can have a strong negative influence, especially on those beginning on the path of interior life. Therefore, we need to stress that the spirit of Christian mortification is not something inhuman, a rejection of what is good and noble on earth. Rather, it is an expression of supernatural dominion over the body and created realities, over material objects and human relationships that, while being good, can easily drag down the soul due to the disorder introduced by original sin. Above all, it is a sign of love for Jesus Christ and for all souls.

Voluntary and Passive Mortification

Voluntary mortification (also mortification that comes without seeking it) is not merely a privation. It is an opportunity to love; it is the desire to draw closer to God, who chose to redeem us by the Cross. It is not just moderation, restraining our senses and the imbalance caused by disorder and excess, but a true self-sacrifice, union with Christ on the Cross. By it we make room in our soul for supernatural life, the foretaste of "the glory that is to be revealed to us" (Rom 8:18). Mortification is also "the drawbridge that enables us to enter the castle of prayer"[25] and the path to true spiritual progress.

Moreover, to grow in interior life and virtue, and above all in trusting surrender to God, we often need to confront obstacles and setbacks. St. Alphonse Liguori said that, just as a flame is strengthened on contact with air, so the soul is perfected by contact with tribulations.[26]

---

25. St. Josemaría Escrivá, *Furrow*, no. 467.
26. See St. Alphonse De Ligorio, *Sermones Abreviados*, in *Obras asceticas de . . .* , BAC, Madrid 1952, vol. II, p. 823.

From the beginning of the path to the end, anyone who wants to follow our Lord has to cultivate a spirit of sacrifice. This needs to be a stable, habitual attitude evident in one's whole life, although given clearer expression in specific moments.

Being a topic so vital for interior progress, it has to be present always, in one form or another, in spiritual direction. Without mortification progress is impossible; therefore, we must strive to ensure that those who are beginning the path of interior life, as well as those who have spent years in the ascetical struggle, and especially those who are younger, are convinced of its need. Our goal is to help those we direct to develop a strong and stable spirit of mortification suited to the ordinary life of Christians living in the midst of the world.[27]

A rich source of mortification is found in our daily work: laboring with intensity; not putting off unpleasant tasks; combating the laziness that seeks a thousand excuses; facilitating the work of those alongside us; joyfully offering our fatigue; punctuality; order; finishing our work well; putting care into little things. Another big area for mortification is our relationships, especially with those who are closest to us: small acts of service in our family, perhaps only noticed when they are lacking; overcoming moods that can make life unpleasant for others; a habitual smile. There are also mortifications related to guarding of the heart, the imagination, and the senses and opportunities for temperance in purchases, in food and drink, in sports. In addition, we need to take advantage of *passive* mortifications,

---

27. St. Josemaria wrote: "The easiest place for us to find mortifications is in ordinary, daily events: in intense, constant and ordered work, knowing that the best spirit of sacrifice is to persevere in finishing with perfection the task begun; in punctuality, filling the day with heroic minutes; in care for the objects we have and use; in a spirit of service, which leads us to fulfill carefully the smallest duties; in small expressions of charity, to make the path of sanctity in this world lovable for everyone: at times a smile can be the best sign of our spirit of penance. . . . A person who has a true spirit of penance overcomes himself every day, without fuss, offering God thousands of small things" (cited in the *Gran Enciclopedia Rialp*, vol. 16, p. 336, heading *Mortification*).

accepting with peace and joy, without complaining, whatever our Lord permits that goes against our own likes, plans, or interests[28]—sickness and suffering, in particular.[29]

Corporal mortification can also be recommended (with prudence but not necessarily as something exceptional), especially when the body is rebelling, or an apostolic work needs to go forward, or someone in a difficult situation requires special help. The spiritual director is the one who should advise or discourage these more extraordinary mortifications.

At times we might suggest certain mortifications in preference to others, always giving special importance to those related to better fulfilling one's duties towards God, a refined charity with one's neighbor, and diligence in one's work. To build up a habit of mortification and self-denial, it can be useful to recommend, in the beginning and also later on, a small list with mortifications on points of special struggle. The important thing is not the list; it's the habit that needs to take root and grow strong. These small renunciations throughout the day, foreseen and sought out, draw us much closer to our Lord and build up the habit of mortification, first in one area and then in another.

---

28. St. Francis de Sales suggests some examples of mortification: ". . . The headache, or toothache, or heavy cold; the tiresome peculiarities of husband or wife, the broken glass, the loss of a ring, a handkerchief, a glove; the sneer of a neighbor, the effort of going to bed early in order to rise early for prayer or Communion, the little shyness some people feel in openly performing religious duties; and be sure that all of these sufferings, small as they are, if accepted lovingly, are most pleasing to God's Goodness, who has promised a whole ocean of happiness to his children in return for one cup of cold water. And, moreover, inasmuch as these occasions are for ever arising, they give us a fertile field for gathering in spiritual riches, if only we will use them rightly" (*Introduction to the Devout Life*, III, 35).

29. The acceptance of pain and sickness can be a great means of purification and penance, and produce abundant fruit in the soul. "Suffering must serve for conversion, that is, for the rebuilding of goodness in the subject, who can recognize the divine mercy in this call to repentance. The purpose of penance is to overcome evil, which under different forms lies dormant in man. Its purpose is also to strengthen goodness both in man himself and in his relationships with others and especially with God" (Bl. John Paul II, *Salvifici Doloris*, no. 12).

Given our natural tendency to shirk and neglect whatever we find difficult, to set aside the Cross, this small human means is very advisable and often indispensable.

Interior Mortification

Interior mortification has special importance for the spiritual life. It helps us to control our imagination and memory and to reject useless thoughts that impede the habit of presence of God and bring so many temptations in their wake. When one is determined to purify one's heart, to keep it for God and for others out of love for him, the Holy Spirit, the soul's gentle Guest, gives even more graces. And there takes root an ever stronger joy, which is one of the fruits of the Paraclete, in those who choose him above all else and renounce pleasures that can leave a sediment of sadness and loneliness in the soul.

Those whom God has asked for their whole heart—not sharing it with another soul—have even stronger reasons to foster this interior mortification, which permits them to preserve their soul free of attachments. It would be very sad to allow oneself to become entangled in petty ties that can snuff out God's love.

SELF-KNOWLEDGE AND EXAMINATIONS OF CONSCIENCE

Spiritual accompaniment has as one of its main goals encouraging and guiding each soul's struggle. Carrying out this struggle requires knowing ourselves well, seeing clearly whatever separates us from God, and reacting in time. The lack of self-knowledge is a powerful ally of the enemy. A person who doesn't really know himself will attribute to himself gifts and qualities that belong to God. He will seek his own glory instead of God's, attributing to himself victories that, in reality, are the fruit of grace, and he will frequently project onto others his own defects and deficiencies.

Noverim te, noverim me: to know God and to know ourselves as we are known by him. That is how St. Augustine summed up the core of Christian wisdom.[30] St. John of the Cross said: "Knowledge of oneself: this is the first step a soul has to take to reach knowledge of God."[31] And St. Teresa, on seeing the great good that this knowledge achieves, wrote: "I consider it a greater mercy of God to have one day of humble self-knowledge, although it cost us great affliction and effort, than many of prayer."[32]

Self-knowledge is a prerequisite for humility, for fighting effectively against our own defects, and for having God bless that struggle. To attain this knowledge we need the help of grace, which shines a powerful spiritual "spotlight" on the soul. But we also have to *want* to see, not averting our gaze or closing our eyes, like those who "loved darkness rather than light, because their deeds were evil. For every one who does evil hates the light, and does not come to the light, lest his deeds should be exposed" (Jn 3:19–20). If one's intention is not truly upright, the heart becomes obscured and, since one is not aware of one's own weakness, it becomes hard to repent for faults committed, giving thanks to God for so many gifts and begging him for his help.

Knowing ourselves means seeing ourselves as God sees us. Then neither our victories nor the cooperation we provide in the apostolate will seem so important that they fill us with vanity, nor our failures so disastrous that they discourage us. We are in the hands of God, who knows us so well and is always ready to lift us up when we turn to him with humility. A sign that one

---

30. St. Augustine, *Soliloquies*, II, 1, 1.
31. St. John of the Cross, *Spiritual Canticle*, 4, 1.
32. St. Teresa of Avila, *Foundations*, 5, 16.

truly knows oneself is letting others see, in all simplicity, both one's weaknesses and the good that God's grace has produced. To a great extent, this is what being sincere means.

Self-knowledge enables us to see clearly, without false excuses, what is an occasion of sin or of distancing ourselves from God, and it gives us the ability to make use of the opportune remedies. It also leads us to distrust ourselves and to place our trust in God, to be unsatisfied with the goals already reached, and to marvel frequently at the disproportion between our personal condition and the wonders that our Lord works through us. Thus we are led to see, in an almost innate way, God's hand in everything. Self-knowledge helps us to return again and again to God, like the prodigal son.

Examination of Conscience

To truly know oneself, and therefore to carry out an effective struggle to draw closer to God, one must frequently examine one's conscience.[33]

Often we will need to teach people what it means to have "a spirit of examination" throughout the day, for as St. Augustine said, "Like good traders, we should know how much we have earned each day."[34] As we grow in love and refinement with God, we become more sensitive to whether a particular action is drawing us closer or leading us further away from him. Stopping for a few moments to consider this question is part of what it means to have an awareness of God. It would be good to find out from time to time how the examination of conscience is going (which is usually done at the end of the day).

Although the format for this is very personal, one can stress that every good examination of conscience should have a few

---

33. The examination of conscience "brings us to know ourselves fully, with all our misery and nobility" (Royo Marin, *Teologia de la perfeccion cristiana*, p. 700).

34. St. Augustine, *Sermon 20*, 1; *Sermon 32*, 3.

key elements: asking the Holy Spirit for light; briefly giving thanks to God for all his gifts that day; noting what has brought us closer to him; and asking pardon for those things, perhaps small ones, in which we have neglected to fulfill his will. The last point, contrition, is an essential part of any good examination of conscience, because the aim should not be to uncover superficial mistakes but sins (including the so-called hidden ones, omissions, etc.), and the lack of love for our Lord that we try to remedy by our compunction. And finally, we should formulate a specific resolution for the following day.

The General Examination

How best to examine one's day varies, depending on one's character and temperament. Some will find it useful to be quite specific and to carry out a closer accounting because of their tendency toward vague generalities, while for others this might lead to needless complications and problems. The examination also can be modified in accord with the different stages in a person's interior life: at the beginning perhaps one needs to go into greater detail, while later just a few questions might suffice: "Is it true that I pay more attention to trifles and trivialities—that bring me nothing and from which I expect nothing—than I do to my God? Who am I with when I am not with God?"[35] "Have I made any grimace of distaste, has there been anything in me that could have hurt you, my Lord, my Love?"[36] Or perhaps it will mean looking carefully at specific topics for that day: apostolic deeds, sanctifying work, self-denial, the effort to make life more pleasant for others, drawing close to our Lord in prayer throughout the day, a spirit of mortification. . . .

The general examination should help us to uncover the roots of our actions: the reason for bad humor and sadness, the

---

35. St. Josemaría Escrivá, *The Forge*, no. 511.
36. Ibid., no. 494.

lack of right intention in one's actions, the source of constant faults against charity with the same person, etc. Without this examination, the struggle becomes arduous, and one easily falls into lukewarmness. "There is an enemy of the interior life which is both little and silly. Unfortunately, it can be very effective. It is the neglect of effort in one's examination of conscience."[37]

St. Ignatius of Loyola distinguished two kinds of examinations of conscience, the general and the particular.[38] The first aims at growing in one's Christian life as a whole. The second looks more closely at a specific defect that one needs to root out or a virtue that one wants to acquire.

The Particular Examination

The particular examination helps us to carry out a more specific struggle. It is a brief but frequent examination on a well-specified point. "Your particular examination should be directed towards the acquisition of a definite virtue or the rooting out of your predominant defect."[39] At times the goal of the particular examination will be "to overthrow Goliath, the heart's dominant defect,"[40] shown in one's habitual way of thinking, judging, and reacting.[41] At other times, the particular examination will be aimed more directly at growing in a specific virtue.

We can find a great variety of possible topics for a particular examination: the presence of God in work or family life, or while out in society; being more aware of the nearest tabernacle

---

37. Ibid., no. 109.
38. See St. Ignatius of Loyola, *Spiritual Exercises* (New York: P.J. Kenedy & Sons, 1914), First week, Particular and General Examinations.
39. St. Josemaría Escrivá, *The Way*, no. 241.
40. Joseph Tissot, *The Interior Life* (London: Burns, Oates & Washbourne, 1912), p. 319.
41. "The enemy of souls seeks exactly this easily vulnerable point in each one, and he finds it without difficulty. Therefore, we must recognize it also" (Garrigou-Lagrange, *The Three Ages of the Interior Life*, vol. I, p. 367).

and addressing our Lord with a greeting or aspiration; striving to be more generous in serving others; growing in a spirit of mortification, in dealings with our guardian angels, in purity of heart. . . . Some authors even hold that this examination is more important than the general one, "because it enables us to run down, one by one, our defects and thus overcome them the more easily. Besides, if we examine ourselves thoroughly on some important virtue, we not only acquire that virtue, but all the others related thereto. Thus while we advance in the practice of obedience, we perform at the same time acts of humility, of mortification, and we exercise ourselves in the spirit of faith. Likewise, to acquire the virtue of humility means that we are perfecting ourselves in the practice of obedience, of the love of God, of charity, since pride is the chief obstacle to the exercise of these virtues."[42]

CHARITY AND APOSTOLATE

The interior life is readily manifested in how we treat others. "By this all men will know that you are my disciples, if you have love for one another" (Jn 13:35). Charity is a manifestation of love for God and also a path that leads directly to him; "it is the path to follow God more closely"[43] and "the measuring rod of the standard we set for our inner life, particularly our life of prayer."[44] Charity is a sure sign of progress in the spiritual life.

Charity has many practical manifestations. In first place, it makes the path leading to God easier for those who are closer to us—brothers and sisters, relatives, friends, colleagues at work, neighbors, people we see occasionally. Friendship, cordiality, and a positive and optimistic outlook on life provide a marvelous

---

42. Tanquerey, *The Spiritual Life*, no. 468.
43. St. Thomas Aquinas, *Commentaries on the Epistle to the Ephesians*, 5, 1.
44. Benedict Baur, *In Silence with God*, (New York: Scepter, 1997) p. 185.

path to help many people encounter God. An important topic for spiritual guidance is one's concern for the holiness of others, especially for those closest to us, the help we give them through fraternal correction, prayer for the one who needs it most, care for the sick, etc.

A person's growth in piety should be manifested in the family, for example, by a greater spirit of service, by a smile for someone who seems especially tired, by not raising disagreements in topics of little importance, by overcoming gloominess so as not to make life unpleasant for others, and by being attentive to birthdays and other special anniversaries and feast days.

The soul's growth in love for God is also shown by greater understanding for everyone, by speaking of others in a positive manner, by the practice of fraternal correction, by being generous with one's time and other goods, and by concern for the spiritual and human health of those around us. Truly, "actions speak louder than words."[45]

In spiritual direction, usually the best way to ascertain the true interior situation of a person is to ask about the virtue of charity and its specific apostolic manifestations. If someone's prayer life doesn't lead to a stronger charity and apostolic zeal shown in deeds, it's a sign that their prayer is not authentic. Perhaps they are seeking an arduous "self-perfection" that, sooner or later, will prove deceptive.

"People have often drawn attention to the danger of deeds performed without any interior life to inspire them; but we should also stress the danger of an interior life—if such a thing is possible—without deeds to show for it,"[46] wrote St. Josemaría. If activism is always sterile, passivity can be even worse, for it is easier to fool oneself by thinking that acts of piety are proof of one's love for God.

---

45. St. Augustine, *Commentary on the Letter of St. John*, 3, 8.
46. St. Josemaría Escrivá, *The Forge*, no. 734.

In spiritual guidance, it is important to make sure that these necessary manifestations of a growing interior life are in evidence. If this is not so, then with refined charity we have to open up apostolic horizons for that person. The apostolic concern to bring souls to Christ may very well be what renews a person's whole interior life. One should bring up this topic frequently, but with special force when someone seems to be content with "praying," yet fails to take advantage of specific opportunities to help others.

A sign of true love for God is apostolic initiative and determination, along with enthusiasm for the apostolic task. Apostolate is love turned into deeds with joy, with actions that perhaps are quiet but constant. The interior life is, above all, just that: life, creativity, determination, specific desires to draw others to the Master. As St. Augustine said, "Love always leads to actions."[47]

The conversations that take place in spiritual direction are also excellent opportunities to teach in a practical way, in accord with each one's circumstances, how to do apostolate with one's friends, colleagues at work or fellow students, relatives, acquaintances, etc., always putting the supernatural means in first place. If the fruit is slow in coming and the difficulties that are part and parcel of apostolate seem to increase, a word of encouragement may be needed, a reminder that when one works for God with a right intention, nothing is ever lost. Our Lord doesn't bless omissions, but he does bless apparent "failures." "When you work for God, *nothing* is unfruitful."[48]

It's a good practice to suggest specific apostolic goals, perhaps small ones, on which to fight in the upcoming days, and these can then be recalled in the next conversation. To foster an apostolic spirit, it is helpful to decide on a small plan of

---

47. St. Augustine, *Expositions on the Psalms*, 31, 2, 5.
48. St. Josemaría Escrivá, *The Forge*, no. 978.

apostolate for each day, with prayer and mortification for the souls one is trying to bring closer to God, along with some specific action, although it may be quite small. Helping a person to acquire a true apostolic zeal, with a real concern for the souls around them, will help prevent many other temptations. Apostolate is "a shield to withstand all the attacks of your enemies on this earth and in hell."[49]

This last point (making sure that souls have a true apostolic zeal) is essential in spiritual direction. Interior life cannot remain "closed up" in norms of piety, with no influence on the lives of others. Neither sickness nor isolation "dispenses" a person from living an apostolic life. St. Thérèse of Lisieux, despite never having left her convent, felt a burning eagerness for the salvation of all souls, even the most distant ones. She experienced in her heart Christ's words on the cross—"I thirst" —and her heart burned with the desire to reach the furthest corners of the earth. Once, when she was very sick, she took a short walk, and a sister, seeing her fatigue, recommended that she rest. But the saint responded: "You know what gives me strength? I offer each step for some missionary. I think that possibly, over there, far away, one of them is weary and tired in his apostolic labors, and to lessen his fatigue I offer mine to the Good God."[50] The prayer and sacrifice of the saints reach the farthest corners of the world.

Zeal for souls should always be present. Sickness, old age, or apparent isolation is no excuse. Through the communion of saints, we can reach very far—as far as our love for Christ reaches, and then our entire life, right up to our last breath here on earth, will help to lead souls to heaven. No prayer, no suffering offered with love, is ever lost. In a mysterious but real way,

---

49. St. Josemaría Escrivá, *The Way*, no. 923.
50. St. Therese of Lisieux, *The Story of a Soul* (London: Burns, Oates & Washbourne, 1912), XII, 9.

everything produces its fruit: "That of one person redounds to the benefit of others through love. This is what gives cohesion to the Church and makes all of its goods common."[51]

THE FAMILY

For those who have been called by God to marriage, the mutual love of spouses "can also be a marvelous divine way, a vocation, a path for a complete dedication to our God."[52] The spouses' love for each other should be shown in a real and effective desire to form the children who are the natural fruit of their married life, striving to ensure that they grow up as hardworking, temperate, well-mannered men and women—and as good Christians.

A person who, by vocation, seeks holiness in marriage is called to do everything possible to be an instrument of union among the various members of the family through joyful service and small daily sacrifices for them. Each spouse can help the other to improve in his or her relationship with God, without forcing them or imposing practices of piety. And each makes a real effort to help the other spouse understand one's own struggle for holiness, principally by providing a cheerful and cordial example of what it means to seek God in everything, making the path to God attractive and seeking a harmony centered on him. The struggle for holiness will lead each one to pray daily for the member of the family most in need, to give greater attention to the one who is weakest or seems discouraged, to show more affection towards the one who is sick or disabled. One's cheerful example has to be the starting point for apostolate with one's spouse and children, and with many other families—whether relatives or friends or families known through the shared effort in the education of the children. This cheerful example, in the

---

51. St. Thomas Aquinas, *On Charity.*
52. *Conversations*, no 121.

midst of the ordinary difficulties found in any family, stems from a life grounded in prayer and from an imaginative and creative response to the vocation of marriage received from God.

If the parents love each other with both human and supernatural love, if God is the center of their home, as in Nazareth, their children will turn to them for answers to all their doubts and questions, and their family will be united and firm in its Christian ideals. It will become a privileged place for fostering the new evangelization the world so greatly needs.

Parents whose love draws its strength from prayer are prepared to respect God's will regarding the number of children they will have. They are open to our Lord when he blesses them with a large family.[53] They are also ready to respect God's will if some of their children receive a vocation to full dedication to God, and they specifically ask him for this gift for their children. For they know that "giving up one's children to the service of God is not a sacrifice: it is an honor and a joy,"[54] the greatest honor and joy a family can receive.

True love for one's children also requires a diligent concern about the school where they are formed,[55] being zealous about

---

53. "A married couple should build their life together on the foundation of a sincere and pure affection for each other, and on the joy that comes from having brought into the world the children God has enabled them to have. They should be capable of renouncing their personal comfort; and they should put their trust in the providence of God. To have a large family—if such is the will of God—is a guarantee of happiness and of effectiveness, in spite of everything that the mistaken proponents of a life based on selfish pleasure may say to the contrary" (St. Josemaría Escrivá, *Christ Is Passing By*, no. 25).

54. St. Josemaría Escrivá, *Furrow*, no. 22.

55. Parents should never forget that "as those first responsible for the education of their children, parents have the right to choose a school for them which corresponds to their own convictions. This right is fundamental. As far as possible, parents have the duty of choosing schools that will best help them in their task as Christian educators" (see Vatican II, *Gravissimum Educationis*, no. 6). "Public authorities have the duty of guaranteeing this parental right and of ensuring the concrete conditions for its exercise" (CCC, 2229).

the quality of education they receive there, and especially about their religious instruction, because their very salvation may depend upon it.

A true love for their children should spur parents to seek a suitable place for vacations and times of relaxation—often giving up their own likes and interests. Parents need to be diligent in avoiding places that would make the practice of Christian life impossible or at least difficult to preserve. They should never forget that they are the stewards of a treasure received from God and that, as a Christian family (also teaching their children this truth), they form a family in which Christ is present, which imparts to it very specific and special characteristics.

Now more than ever, when attacks against the family seem to be growing, we need to help strengthen familial bonds through true human affection and therefore through self-sacrifice. We have to make God present in the home through specific Christian customs: the blessing at meals, saying prayers at night with the smaller children, reading with the older ones a passage from the Gospel, praying for the intentions of the pope, attending Mass together on Sundays . . . and, if possible, praying the rosary, the prayer that popes have so often recommended for families.

These practices of piety in the family shouldn't be overdone, but it would be strange if a home in which everyone (or almost everyone) is a believer didn't have at least some of them.[56]

Children should learn from their parents the human and supernatural virtues proper to God's sons and daughters: joy, optimism, cordiality, mutual respect, temperance, and

---

56. "Education in the faith by the parents should begin in the child's earliest years. This already happens when family members help one another to grow in faith by the witness of a Christian life in keeping with the Gospel. Family catechesis precedes, accompanies, and enriches other forms of instruction in the faith. Parents have the mission of teaching their children to pray and to discover their vocation as children of God (see *Lumen Gentium*, no. 11)" (CCC, 2226).

industriousness;[57] and they should come to see the fourth commandment as a "most sweet precept."[58] The fulfillment of this
commandment is so pleasing to God that he accompanied it
with the promise of many blessings: "Whoever honors his father
atones for sins, and whoever glorifies his mother is like one who
lays up treasure. Whoever honors his father will be gladdened by
his own children, and when he prays he will be heard. Whoever
glorifies his father will have long life" (Sir 3:3–6). This promise
of a "long life" to anyone who loves and honors his parents is
repeated again and again. "Honor your father and your mother,
that your days may be long in the land which the Lord your
God gives you" (Ex 20:12). St. Thomas Aquinas, commenting
on this passage, said that life is long when it is full, and that this
plenitude is measured not by time but by deeds. One lives a full
life when it is filled with virtues and fruit; then one has lived
richly, even if one dies young.[59] Those who honor their parents
are also promised a good reputation (despite suffering calum-
nies), riches, and numerous descendants. Regarding the latter,
St. Thomas says that "children of the flesh" are not the only
form of offspring. Various forms of spiritual paternity, deserv-
ing of equal respect and esteem, are also possible.[60]

The fourth commandment, which is part of the natural
law, requires all human beings, but especially those who want

---

57. "Father and mother receive from the sacrament of matrimony the grace and the
ministry of the Christian education of their children, before whom they bear witness
and to whom they transmit both human and religious values. While learning their
first words, children learn also the praise of God, whom they feel is near them as a
loving and providential Father; while learning the first acts of love, children also learn
to open themselves to others, and through the gift of self receive the sense of living
as a human being. The daily life itself of a truly Christian family makes up the first
'experience of Church'" (Bl. John Paul II, *Christifideles Laici*, no. 62).

58. This is how St. Josemaría used to refer to this commandment, seeing it as one of
the most pleasant obligations God has given to us.

59. See St. Thomas Aquinas, *On the Double Precept of Charity*, no. 1245.

60. See Ibid., no. 1247.

to be good Christians, to assist their parents with self-denying and affectionate concern, shown each day in a thousand small details.[61] This help is all the more important when parents are older or more in need.[62]

When we truly love God, who never asks us for anything contradictory, we will find the right way to care for our parents, even if we also have to fulfill other family, social, or religious obligations first. This is an important field of filial responsibility that children should frequently consider before God in their personal prayer, and it is a very fitting topic for spiritual direction. God repays with happiness, already here in this life, those who lovingly fulfill these duties towards their parents, even though sometimes arduous.

The precept of the fourth commandment is firmly rooted in the fatherhood of God, who "is the source of human fatherhood."[63] The only one who can rightly be called Father in all fullness is God, "of whom all paternity in heaven and earth is named" (Eph 3:15, Douay). Our parents, by engendering us, come to share in the paternity of God. In them we see a reflection, as it were, of the Creator, and in loving and honoring them we are honoring and loving in them God himself, our Father.

---

61. As long as a child lives at home with his parents, the child should obey his parents in all that they ask of him when it is for his good or that of the family. "Children, obey your parents in everything, for this pleases the Lord" (Col 3:20; see Eph 6:1). Children should also obey the reasonable directions of their teachers and all to whom their parents have entrusted them. But if a child is convinced in conscience that it would be morally wrong to obey a particular order, he must not do so.

"As they grow up, children should continue to respect their parents. They should anticipate their wishes, willingly seek their advice, and accept their just admonitions. Obedience toward parents ceases with the emancipation of the children; not so respect, which is always owed to them. This respect has its roots in the fear of God, one of the gifts of the Holy Spirit" (CCC, 2217).

62. "The fourth commandment reminds grown children of their responsibilities toward their parents. As much as they can, they must give them material and moral support in old age and in times of illness, loneliness, or distress. Jesus recalls this duty of gratitude" (see Mk 7:10–12) (Ibid., no. 2218).

63. See Ibid., no. 2214.

Joys and Sorrows

"Joys, sorrows, successes and failures, great ambitions, daily worries—even your weaknesses!"[64] Here we have important topics to speak with God about in prayer. Joy and sorrow, signs of what is going on in the depths of the soul, can also often provide the main topic for the conversation in spiritual guidance.

What causes us sorrow and joy reveals where our mind and heart really is—our true goal in life. It's true that sadness and discouragement can also sometimes stem from exhaustion or sickness, but it is important to distinguish this "physiological" sadness (which we also must try to find a remedy for, if possible[65]) from the sadness that results from distancing oneself from God. As might be expected, the remedies in these two cases are very different.

When someone is exhausted or sick, we need to show them great understanding and affection, encouraging them to rest, get enough sleep, engage in sports or take walks, and when necessary suggesting that they see a doctor. At the same time, we can teach them to offer up the situation and not feed their sadness with an excessive self-concern.[66]

Young people tend to speak sparingly about their joys, worries, and sorrows, instead talking mostly about recent events. It's hard for them to pinpoint the true causes for the states of their soul, since they don't really know themselves very well. We can assist them by asking pertinent questions to uncover the roots of their moodiness, sadness, and feelings of emptiness. From there we can help them decide on a very specific and positive particular examination: determining the best use

---

64. St. Josemaría Escrivá, *The Way*, no. 91.

65. St. Teresa of Avila warned: "I believe the devil takes melancholy as a means for trying to win over some persons. And if they do not walk with great care, he will do so" (*Foundations*, 7, 2; Collected Works, vol III, Carmelite Studies translation, p. 134).

66. "All those who love find that their life is a forge, a forging in the fire of sorrow. There, in that forge, our Lord teaches us that those who tread fearlessly where the Master treads, hard though the going is, find joy" (St. Josemaría Escrivá, *The Forge*, no. 816).

of their time, or becoming more generous, or guarding their senses with greater refinement. . . . [67]

Those who have spent more time attempting to draw close to God could face the opposite danger: speaking only about the topics that worry them, without getting down to specific points they are struggling with. Their sessions might be centered on their own weariness, difficulties in their professional work, anxiousness caused by lack of time, etc. We need to help them to put God first and offer up these problems, seeing them as a means to holiness. It would be a mistake to limit the conversation to only what is causing them concern. We should ask them about their personal prayer, about mortification, about how they show real interest in others, about their apostolate—even though they only want to talk about their own tiredness or the concern that is currently weighing them down. We can lessen a good part of their burden when we get them to see, amid these very difficulties, that they have close at hand a way to share in our Lord's cross and therefore a path of interior progress, of holiness.

We need to encourage souls to strive always to be cheerful, forgetting themselves and accepting any setbacks that may occur, since sadness is the source of many evils. It is like a diseased root that produces only bitter fruit. Sadness gives rise to many faults against charity; it makes a person eager to seek consolations and often results in a feeble struggle against temptations arising from sensuality.[68] The sad soul easily falls into sin,

---

67. Often it is the lack of self-giving that leads directly to sadness. "You wade into temptations, you put yourself in danger, you fool around with your sight and with your imagination, you chat about . . . stupidities. And then you are anxious that doubts, scruples, confusion, sadness and discouragement might assail you.

"—You must admit that you are not very consistent" (St. Josemaría Escrivá, *Furrow*, no. 132).

68. "Sadness leads to anger and resentment; thus when we are sad, we experience that we easily become angry and grow annoyed for any reason. What is more, it makes a person suspicious and malicious, and sometimes disturbs a soul so greatly that one seems to have lost one's senses, and to be beside oneself" (St. Gregory the Great, *Moralia*, 1, 31, 31).

at least into venial sin, and finds it hard to do good. "As a moth does a garment, and a worm the wood: so the sadness of a man consumes the heart" (Prov 25:20, Douay).

Spiritual guidance should help people to ventilate their souls and recover the peace and joy they may have lost. It is a mistake to wait for joy to "come by itself;" rather, one needs to foster it in a positive way, fighting against any sadness or pessimism. We should encourage people to consider God's love for us, the value of suffering united to the Cross, and teach them to ask for the joy the Holy Spirit infuses into the souls of those who are close to Christ.[69] The mere fact of the presence of sadness in the soul (although there can be exceptions due to exhaustion or sickness) means that something is not going well in one's relationship with God. This sadness may stem from a lack of generosity, laziness, or not accepting God's will—and often from a hidden pride.

When a soul is sad, it is easy prey for the temptation to seek false satisfactions that fill the void left by the departure of joy. No one can remain for a long time mired in sadness. Such a person ends up like "those who, unable to enjoy spiritual delights, turn to those of the body."[70] Many temptations to impurity have their origin in sadness, in interior emptiness. When someone is not truly happy, that person becomes prone to seeking a fictitious joy in external goods.

We have to be on the alert when someone seems overcome by pessimism. That person could easily come to see

---

69. "The attainment of such an outlook is not just a matter of psychology. It is also a fruit of the Holy Spirit. This Spirit, who dwells fully in the person of Jesus, made him during his earthly life so alert to the joys of daily life, so tactful and persuasive for putting sinners back on the road to a new youth of heart and mind! It is this same Spirit who animated the Blessed Virgin and each of the saints. It is this same Spirit who still today gives to so many Christians the joy of living day by day their particular vocation, in the peace and hope which surpass setbacks and sufferings" (Pope Paul VI, *Gaudete in Domino*, no. 75).

70. St. Thomas Aquinas, *Summa Theologica*, II–II, 1. 35, a. 4 ad 2.

everything—and first of all a life of dedication—in a negative light which, if not fought against energetically, could even end up distancing the soul from God. There may also be an inordinate concern about the future, since trust in God is replaced by the futile effort to ensure by one's own effort that the years of life that remain are secure. To the extent that a human outlook prevails, less importance is given to the interior struggle and to practices of piety, and lukewarmness and discouragement can easily creep in. And not infrequently a critical spirit may take hold, at times quite strongly, leading to faults against charity and distancing oneself from others, evaluating everything with the bitterness of someone who isn't happy. Truly, "sorrow has destroyed many, and there is no profit in it" (Sir 30:23).

We are never sad—even amid suffering, poverty, or sickness—when we truly walk with our sights set on God and respond generously to what he asks of us in that situation, even when arduous. With St. Paul, we will always be able to say: "I am filled with comfort. With all our affliction, I am overjoyed" (2 Cor 7:4). If we are truly seeking God, nothing can take away our peace and joy. Suffering purifies the soul, and sorrow itself is transformed into joy.

Often the best signs of true union with God is joy and good humor in fulfilling one's duties, interacting with others, and accepting setbacks and suffering. The apostolate itself is, in good part, a superabundance of supernatural and human happiness, transmitting the joy of being close to God.

LOVE FOR THE CHURCH AND THE COMMUNION OF SAINTS

A spiritual guide has to always keep in mind this truth: No one can be a good child of God if he or she is not also a good child of the Church, because "no one can have God as Father who does not have the Church as Mother."[71] A great love for Christ is inconceivable without a great love for his Mystical Body.[72]

Growing in one's interior life means growing in union with and love for the Church. This love leads us to look at her with eyes of faith, to see her as she is: holy, most pure, without stain or wrinkle; and we won't allow anyone to treat her as an outmoded human society, forgetting the profound mystery she encloses.[73] We can never be indifferent when someone criticizes the pope, bishops, priests, and religious. And if ever we were to see mistakes and defects in those who should be most exemplary, we must teach people to forgive—to emphasize other positive aspects in those persons, pray more for them, and, if possible and prudent, to help them by a friendly and positive fraternal correction. We can never blame the Church for the mistakes and weaknesses of any of its members.[74]

Right up to the end of time, the Church will encompass both saints and sinners, the latter having left their Father's house

---

71. St. Augustine, *On the Unity of the Catholic Church*, 6.

72. "To have a Catholic spirit means that we should feel on our shoulders the weight of our concern for the entire Church—not just of this or that particular part of it. It means that our prayer should spread out north and south, east and west, in a generous act of petition. If you do this you will understand the cry—the aspiration—of that friend of ours, when he considered how unloving so many people are towards our Holy Mother: 'The Church: it hurts me to see her treated so!'" (St. Josemaría Escrivá, *The Forge*, no. 583).

73. "Just as in Christ there are two natures, both a human and a divine one, so by analogy we can refer to the presence in the Church of human and divine elements. No one can fail to see the human part. The Church, in this world, is for men, who are its raw material. And when we speak of men we speak of freedom, which permits the co-existence of grandeur and meanness, of heroism and failure. If we were to focus only on the human side of the Church, we would never understand her. We would still be distant from the threshold of her central mystery" (St. Josemaría Escrivá, *In Love with the Church* [London: Scepter Ltd., 1989], no. 20).

74. "May you never fall into the error of identifying the Mystical Body of Christ with a particular personal or public attitude of any of its members. And may you never let other people with less formation fall into that error. Now you realize the importance of your integrity, of your loyalty!" (St. Josemaría Escrivá, *Furrow*, no. 356).

and wasted the inheritance they received in baptism.[75] Sinners belong to the Church, not because of their sins, but because of the indelible character they received at baptism and confirmation, the faith and hope (although "lifeless") that remain in the soul, and the help that reaches them from the rest of the faithful who are struggling to be holy. They are joined to those who are striving each day to love God more, just as a sick or paralytic member receives the influence of the entire body.[76] The Church never loses sight of her role as Mother. She prays unceasingly for the children of hers who have fallen sick; she hopes with infinite patience and tries to help them with a limitless charity, since sinners can always return to the Father's house, even at the last moment in life. By baptism, they bear within a hope of reconciliation that not even the gravest sins can erase.

The sin the Church finds in her bosom is not part of her. Rather, it is the enemy that has to be fought against until the very end, especially through the sacrament of confession. While it is true that her children stained by sin form part of her, this is not true of their stains. It would be very sad if we, her children, allowed the Church to be judged by what she can never be.

When people talk about the Church's defects in the past or present, or say that the Church should purify her faults,

---

75. "Christ, 'holy, innocent and undefiled' (Heb 7:26) knew nothing of sin (see 2 Cor 5:21), but came only to expiate the sins of the people (see Heb 2:17). The Church, however, grasping sinners to her bosom, at once holy and always in need of purification, follows constantly the path of penance and renewal" (Vatican II, *Lumen Christi*, no. 8).

76. "The Church continues to live even in her children who are no longer in grace. She wages war in them against the evil that destroys them; she strives to keep them in her bosom and to rally them continually in the rhythm of her love. The Church guards them as a treasure with which one parts only by force. It is not that she desires to take care of dead weight; but she hopes that by the power of patience, meekness, and pardon, the sinner who is not completely separated from her will convert some day in order to live with fullness. She hopes that the lethargic branch will not (thanks to the little sap that is left in it) be cut off and thrown into the eternal fire, but that it will flourish." (Charles Journet, *Theology of the Church* [San Francisco: Ignatius, 2004], pp. 209–210).

they forget that those faults and mistakes are due precisely to persons who, with personal responsibility, are not living their Christian vocation or following the teaching that Christ left to his Church.[77]

It's possible that some who come for spiritual guidance hold prejudices against the Church—perhaps coming from "afar" or having been influenced by negative remarks about ecclesiastical figures. We must help them to distinguish between the holiness of the Church and the sins that her members commit. In 2000, Blessed John Paul II, while giving thanks to God for "a wonderful harvest of holiness, missionary zeal, total dedication to Christ and neighbor," also said that we cannot "fail to recognize the infidelities to the Gospel committed by some of our brethren, especially during the second millennium." And he expressly asked forgiveness "for the violence some have used in the service of the truth."[78]

The Church is holy and the font of holiness for the world. She offers us unceasingly the means to come in contact with God, and over the centuries she has given birth to so many saints. First, the martyrs who gave their lives in witness to the faith they professed. Later came the example of many men and women throughout history who dedicated themselves out of love for God to assisting their brothers and sisters in every possible situation of poverty and want. There is scarcely any human need that has not awakened in the Church a vocation

---

77. "If we love the Church, there will never arise in us a morbid interest in airing, as the faults of the Mother, the weaknesses of some of her children. The Church, the spouse of Christ, does not have to intone any *mea culpa*. But we do: *mea culpa, mea culpa, mea maxima culpa*. The only true *mea culpa* is a personal one, not the one which attacks the Church, pointing out and exaggerating the human defects which, in this holy mother, result from the presence in her of men whose actions can go far astray, but which can never destroy—nor even touch—that which we call the original and constitutive holiness of the Church" (St. Josemaría Escrivá, *In Love with the Church*, no. 7).

78. Bl. John Paul II, *Day of Forgiveness*, no. 4, Rome, March 12, 2000.

for men and women determined to solve it, even to the point of heroism. And today there are so many fathers and mothers who quietly and heroically spend their lives for their families, fulfilling the vocation they have received from God; and also men and women who, in the middle of the world, have dedicated themselves entirely to God in celibacy, giving a special glory and joy to God, sanctifying themselves in their respective professions, and carrying out an effective apostolate among their companions.

The Church is also holy because all of her members are called to sanctity. However, the holiness of the Church is a permanent reality and does not depend on the number of Christians who live their faith to its fullest potential. She is holy through the constant action of the Holy Spirit, not because of any human behavior. Therefore, even in the gravest moments, "If human failings were to outnumber acts of valor, the clear undeniable mystical reality of the Church, though unperceived by the senses, would still remain. The Church would still be the Body of Christ, our Lord himself, the action of the Holy Spirit and the loving presence of the Father."[79]

This love for the Church, along with a firm theological foundation, will lead to specific daily deeds of prayer and mortification for her: offering a mystery of the Rosary, hours of study or work, daily sufferings and setbacks, praying for the Church at Mass. . . . Thus we will always have in our heart the love of a good son or daughter.

Love for the Pope and the Hierarchy

The Pope takes Christ's place on earth: he is his *Vicar*. As St. Catherine of Siena said, the Holy Father is the "sweet Christ on earth," the tangible presence of Jesus. Therefore we have to teach

---

79. St. Josemaría Escrivá, *In Love with the Church*, no. 22.

people to love him—with deeds of prayer and mortification. This love is shown in a special way at particular moments: when the Roman Pontiff is carrying out an apostolic trip, when he is sick, when the attacks of the Church's enemies grow more fierce, when for any reason we find ourselves physically closer to him.

Our love for the Church is also shown in appreciation and prayer for bishops and priests, on whom our Lord relies so greatly and on whom the holiness of the faithful entrusted to them largely depends.[80] The bishops, in union with the Pope, have been given by Christ himself the mission of ruling and guiding the Church.[81] So much depends on their union with the Good Shepherd.

The Communion of Saints

It is good to remember often the wide repercussions of our personal ascetical struggle. When we fight we help others, and we

---

80. "Scarcely is he born before the priest baptizing him, brings him by a new birth to a more noble and precious life, a supernatural life, and makes him a son of God and of the Church of Jesus Christ. To strengthen him to fight bravely in spiritual combats, a priest invested with special dignity makes him a soldier of Christ by holy chrism. Then, as soon as he is able to recognize and value the Bread of Angels, the priest gives it to him, the living and life-giving Food come down from heaven. If he falls, the priest raises him up again in the name of God, and reconciles him to God with the Sacrament of Penance. Again, if he is called by God to found a family and to collaborate with Him in the transmission of human life throughout the world, thus increasing the number of the faithful on earth and, thereafter, the ranks of the elect in Heaven, the priest is there to bless his espousals and unblemished love; and when, finally, arrived at the portals of eternity, the Christian feels the need of strength and courage before presenting himself at the tribunal of the Divine Judge, the priest with the holy oils anoints the failing members of the sick or dying Christian, and reconsecrates and comforts him.

"Thus the priest accompanies the Christian throughout the pilgrimage of this life to the gates of heaven. He accompanies the body to its resting place in the grave with rites and prayers of immortal hope. And even beyond the threshold of eternity he follows the soul to aid it with Christian suffrages, if need there be of further purification and alleviation. Thus, from the cradle to the grave the priest is ever beside the faithful, a guide, a solace, a minister of salvation and dispenser of grace and blessing" (Pope Pius XI, *Ad Catholici Sacerdotii*, nos. 18–19).

81. See Vatican II, *Christus Dominus*, no. 16.

harm them when we let ourselves be overcome by lukewarmness and indifference. The doctrine of the communion of saints is a great encouragement to continue fighting, especially when the path becomes more arduous. "If one member suffers, all suffer together; if one member is honored, all rejoice together" (1 Cor 12:26). We need to teach souls the value that difficulties take on when they are offered for others. Offering up the aridity we may experience in our norms of piety, the effort and tiredness that work and study entail, and the small discomforts of each day can be a great help to our brothers and sisters in the faith all over the world—and to others who perhaps are far from God but who could return to him through our supernatural help.[82] This truth often spurs people to begin again or strive to live a particular virtue with greater refinement, so as not to be a hindrance to others.

Each of the faithful, through good works and the effort to come closer to our Lord, enriches the whole Church, while also drawing on her common riches. "This is the 'Communion of Saints' which we profess in the Creed. The good of all becomes the good of each one and the good of each one becomes the good of all."[83] In a mysterious but real way, by our personal holiness we contribute to the supernatural life of all the Church's members. Every day we give and receive much. Our life is a continuous interchange in human and supernatural goods.

Those providing spiritual guidance can infuse in souls the joyful awareness of belonging to the Church with a *universal* Christian vision (even if one lives in a small village or is lying in a hospital bed). For apart from the fact that this is God's will for them (which is what really matters), without that universal vision one's Christian vocation is in danger of being constricted

---

82. "You will find it easier to do your duty if you think of how your brothers are helping you, and of the help you fail to give them if you are not faithful" (St. Josemaría Escrivá, *The Way*, no. 549).

83. Bl. John Paul II, *Christifideles Laici*, no. 28.

and narrowed down, centered on oneself and one's own concerns, instead of on God and others. Even when we find ourselves alone and separated from others, we can always send supernatural life to the whole Church and especially to those most in need.

We can also trust in the help of those who have preceded us in reaching God's kingdom (see Heb 12:1), especially those the Church recognizes as saints. With the testimony of their lives and the transmission of their writings, they take part in the Church's living tradition of prayer. The saints contemplate God and praise him, and they never stop caring for those they have left here on earth. On entering "into the joy" of the Lord, they have been "set over much" (see Mt 25:21). Their constant intercession is the highest service they render to God's plan. We can and should ask them to intercede for us and for the whole world.[84]

LUKEWARMNESS AND COMFORT-SEEKING

"As a deer longs for flowing streams, so longs my soul for thee, O God. My soul thirsts for God, for the living God" (Ps 42:1–2). The saints were men and women who wanted to fill themselves with God's life—while always recognizing their own defects and confronting the difficulties present in everyone's life.[85]

We need to ask those who come for spiritual guidance, "Do you truly want to be a saint? Do you want to have a growing friendship with our Lord? Do you want to get closer to him

---

84. See CCC, 2683.

85. "We have run 'like the deer, longing for flowing streams' (Ps 42:1); thirsting, our lips parched and dry. We want to drink at this source of living water. All day long, without doing anything strange, we move in this abundant, clear spring of fresh waters that leap up to eternal life (see Jn 4:14). . . . I am not talking about extraordinary situations. These are, they may very well be, ordinary happenings within our soul: a loving craziness which, without any fuss or extravagance, teaches us how to suffer and how to live, because God grants us his wisdom" (St. Josemaría Escrivá, *Friends of God*, no. 307).

through your professional, family, and social duties?" These are questions that we have to raise in one way or another so as to ensure that those who come in search of advice have firm aspirations and foster them more deeply in their hearts.

The decision to make Christ the goal of our life, the desire to be a saint, has to be frequently and firmly renewed. The greater the adversity and darkness we confront, the stronger must be our determination to reach the goal.[86] A Christian is a man or woman who is passionately in love, and this love must grow in the face of difficulties, since we know that by overcoming them we are drawing ever closer to the object of our love.

The Big Enemy: Lukewarmness

The desire for holiness is shown in the eagerness to fulfill God's will, even in the smallest things, the zeal expressed in actions designed to bring others to God, and the consistent effort to advance in one's interior struggle, especially through the examination of conscience. It is shown in the loving care

---

86. "'I will arise and go through the city; through its streets and squares I will seek my love' (Song 3:2). And not only through the city; I will run from one end of the world to the other—through all nations and peoples, through highways and byways—to find peace of soul. And I discover this peace in my daily occupations, which are no hindrance to me; quite the contrary, they are my path, my reason to love more and more, and to be more and more united to my God.

"And if we are waylaid, assaulted by the temptation of discouragement, opposition, struggle, tribulation, a new dark night of the soul, the psalmist places on our lips and in our minds these words: 'I am with him in the time of trial' (Ps 91:15). Jesus, compared to your cross, of what value is mine? Alongside your wounds, what are my little scratches? Compared with your Love, so immense and pure and infinite, of what value is this tiny little sorrow, which you have placed upon my shoulders? And your hearts, and mine, become filled with a holy hunger and we confess to him—with deeds—that 'we die of love' (Song 5:8).

"A thirst for God is born in us, a longing to understand his tears, to see his smile, his face . . . The best way to express this, I would say, is to repeat with Scripture: 'Like the deer that seeks for running waters, so my heart yearns for thee, my God!' (Ps 42:1). The soul goes forward immersed in God, divinized: the Christian becomes a thirsty traveler who opens his mouth to the waters of the fountain" (St. Josemaría Escrivá, *Friends of God*, no. 310).

of little things to please God and in the small victories—along with defeats—in the particular examination, relying on prayer to attain these goals, convinced that sanctity is the work of the Holy Spirit.

The desire for sanctity is the unifying theme of all spiritual direction. Therefore, it is easy to understand the importance of detecting immediately the first symptoms of lukewarmness, when the eagerness for holiness begins to slacken and earthly aspirations and satisfactions start to take first place.

Lukewarmness, a sickness of the soul that affects both the intellect and the will, can appear at any stage of the interior life. It is a sickness that leaves the soul sad and impoverished, with little apostolic drive. Frequent failures to respond to grace and culpable neglect weaken the will and, if one does not react, the intellect can no longer discern Christ clearly. Our Lord becomes a vague and distant figure after so much carelessness in small points of love.

For a person in this state, Jesus is no longer at the center of the soul, the goal of everything one does. Practices of piety begin to seem empty; they are done not with eagerness and love, but out of habit. There is little desire to struggle, per-haps due to discouragement upon seeing the apparent failure of so many attempts to uproot one's defects. Fear of anything unpleasant grows, and sacrifice ceases to be actively sought out. An entrance way is opened to venial sin, which is no longer given much importance. Little by little one begins to accept a habitual way of thinking, willing, and acting that is unhealthy and lethargic, colored by an earthbound outlook.[87]

---

87. Here are some other clear symptoms of this sickness of soul: "You are lukewarm if you carry out lazily and reluctantly those things that have to do with our Lord; if deliberately or 'shrewdly' you look for some way of cutting down your duties; if you think only of yourself and of your comfort; if your conversations are idle and vain; if you do not abhor venial sin; if you act from human motives" (St. Josemaría Escrivá, *The Way*, no. 331).

Lukewarmness can arise in the early stages of the struggle, when taking the first steps on the path of holiness. Human consolations may fade, and the soul begins to experience dryness and aridity in its spiritual practices. Perhaps having falsely felt itself already close to sanctity, it now realizes how distant the goal still is.[88] We have to be especially vigilant for souls in this situation, which, paradoxically, is also very propitious for laying the foundations for a true interior life. Timely advice is essential here. It is the moment to remind people that they need "to seek Jesus for Jesus himself," and not for the consolations this may bring. With the help of grace, the will can and should hold more firmly to our Lord, and this first encounter with the Cross—finding it hard to pray, receiving no sensible consolation in practices of piety—can in itself be a very important step forward. But if the soul becomes discouraged by this first obstacle (which perhaps it did not expect), it could be a sign that deep down it was seeking itself more than our Lord. It is very important to help someone experiencing these circumstances (which are quite normal on the path of sanctity) and to encourage them to purify their intention and seek our Lord, and only him, through these very difficulties.

A person beginning the interior life is like a mountain climber who starts scaling a mountain only to discover, at some point, that one has no choice but to abandon the broad and easy path and follow a steeper and narrower one. Since the only important thing is to reach the top, the twists and turns along the path don't really matter; it would be a mistake to abandon the climb just because the trail becomes more rugged.

---

88. "Interior dryness is not lukewarmness. When a person is lukewarm the waters of grace slide over him without being soaked in. In contrast, there are dry lands which seem arid but which, with a few drops of rain at the right time, yield abundant flowers and delicious fruit. That is why I ask: When are we going to be convinced? How important it is to be docile to the divine calls which come at each moment of the day, because it is precisely there that God is awaiting us!" (St. Josemaría Escrivá, *The Forge*, no. 224).

In spiritual guidance it is very important to confront these ordinary difficulties, which in some sense are even necessary in order to make progress and purify one's intention. More than a few people begin the path of holiness with enthusiasm, only to become disconcerted when, after a while—or after years of dedication—the support provided by these sensible consolations disappears, and they think they have lost everything. This is a critical moment in the interior life. A word of encouragement, a brief explanation of what is truly necessary, can be decisive for that person.

For those who have spent a longer time in the struggle, lukewarmness usually doesn't come about all at once, or even after a big fall. Rather, it begins little by little, along a downward inclined plane, through habitual neglect in small mortifications; disorder and routine in the plan of life, perhaps due to excessive attention given to professional work; unfulfilled resolutions; scant effort in the apostolate; and coolness in one's dealings with God and in charity towards others.

One begins to seek small compensations, and the heart is burdened by little attachments. One tries, perhaps in a surreptitious way, to combine holiness with a worldly life. We should never forget that the struggle in little things is what strengthens the soul and prepares it to hear the continuous inspirations of the Holy Spirit. And it is also there, in the neglect of what seems of little importance (punctuality, dedicating the best time to prayer, small mortifications at meals, guarding the senses), where the enemy becomes dangerous and difficult to defeat.

It could also be the case that no special difficulties are present when lukewarmness makes its entrance, but the firm determination to love God above all things is absent. Any difficulties that do exist are often attributed to external circumstances (lack of time, the climate, the environment), naively thinking that a change in circumstances will alter everything. The real source is overlooked: that one is praying little, with little reliance on supernatural means—in short, that one's life is no longer centered on our Lord. Other concerns have taken his place.

Sometimes when this sickness of the soul appears, a person will plunge into hectic external activity in professional or social life in an effort to escape the interior emptiness. We have to help someone in this situation to ask themselves this question: "Whom am I really seeking in all this activity? God or myself?" And they will usually see clearly that something has taken the place that our Lord previously held.

It's Worthwhile

We may need to remind this person that God is always "worth the effort," and that nothing matters if it is not done for him. This is the moment to pray more for that person, encouraging him or her to be humble, begin again, and make a contrite confession. We can encourage them to recover their personal dialogue with our Lord, to give importance once again to small mortifications, and to ask for light from the Holy Spirit. And this is the moment to bring up the importance of having a right intention, which is not measured by subjective criteria, but above all by the docility with which one receives and puts into practice the opportune suggestions.

Finally, it is important not to confuse lukewarmness with weariness or sickness, or with a real struggle without visible fruit. The person who is simply tired should have the humility to trust the doctor, as well as the advice given in spiritual direction, and continue the effort to stay close to our Lord, even though everything is more difficult. The same is true if it is a matter of a deep exhaustion and one hardly seems to have the strength needed to put into practice the advice given.

In spite of everything, a person in this situation has the certainty of having found the Cross and, if faithful, will emerge purified and with the unshakable peace of those who place all their hope in God.

HUMILITY AND FORGETFULNESS OF SELF

The virtue of humility is the foundation of the supernatural life. Without it, growth in holiness is impossible: "Humility is a prerequisite for every true virtue, every perfection. . . . The soul is never more ready for grace than when it is humble."[89] This is one of the pillars on which all spiritual direction rests.

Humility is based on the awareness of our true place before God and others and on the moderation of our excessive desire for self-glory. Nevertheless, this virtue is not only a matter of rejecting the insinuations of pride, selfishness, and vanity. Neither Jesus nor his mother Mary ever experienced the slightest reaction of pride, but they were humble in the highest degree. And, as in everything, Christ is our Model for living this virtue as well: "Learn from me; for I am gentle and humble of heart" (Mt 11:29).

In trying to help those who receive spiritual advice to acquire this virtue, we should not forget that humility, like all the other virtues, is a positive quality, far removed from timidity, pusillanimity, or mediocrity. Humility is quite compatible with being aware of the talents we have received and making use of them with an upright heart. It doesn't constrict but rather enlarges the soul. By it we recognize that every good thing we have, both in the order of grace and of nature, is God's gift, and that "from his fullness we have all received" (Jn 1:16). Humility "is born of knowing God and knowing oneself."[90]

The saints experienced a deep joy in acknowledging that all human achievement, if not seen as a reflection of God's goodness, is a lie. Therefore, they relied firmly on divine grace to carry out all their endeavors: apostolic plans, service to those in need, resolutions to improve . . . They were magnanimous

---

89. Benedict Baur, *In Silence with God* (New York: Scepter, 1997), p. 117.
90. St. Josemaría Escrivá, *The Forge*, no. 184.

men and women, filled with daring, ready to place their life at the service of great enterprises for the glory of God.[91] A humble person is daring because he or she relies on God, who can do everything, and turns frequently to prayer, convinced of the absolute need for God's grace. Moreover, the one who is humble has a special facility for friendship and therefore for apostolate.

We also should consider briefly *what humility is not*, since this virtue has not infrequently taken on negative connotations in colloquial language.[92] One is not being humble, for example, when one hides behind his or her "many defects" as an excuse for not being more generous with our Lord, or when one speaks constantly about one's own "misfortunes" and many sins. Nor is someone humble who is not apostolic, using the excuse that he or she doesn't know enough or is of little worth in comparison to others; neither is the person who "wallows" in discouragement on seeing his or her own defects or those of others. St. Teresa of Avila herself came to see as one of her greatest temptations that of giving up prayer for a time because she thought that by doing so she was being more humble.[93]

Humility: The Cornerstone

The spiritual edifice built up in a soul without basing it on humility is "like a great pile of straw which, at the first gust of

---

91. It may be useful to stress once again, even at the risk of being repetitive, that one can "give one's life to a great enterprise," in the service of God's glory, amidst a life of ordinary work. The spiritual guide's task is to ensure that the person being guided is truly "living in Christ." It is this self-giving of one's entire being to Christ that leads to a true humility and a big heart. *Pusillanimity*, in contrast, is the result of selfishness, of thinking only about oneself, and of lukewarmness.

92. The dictionary gives several meanings for the word "humble" that are very far removed from the real meaning of this virtue. For example, we find the following synonyms given for "humble": "low in importance, rank or dignity," "submissive," "meek," "plain," "common," "poor," "insignificant," "timid."

93. St. Teresa of Avila, *Life* 7, 1 and 11. Further on (19, 4), the saint wrote: "The devil carried out a great assault upon me in this matter . . . making me think it was a lack of humility to practice prayer" (*Collected Works*, Carmelite Studies, vol. I, p. 166).

wind, is scattered all over the ground. The devil has little fear of devotions not based on humility, for he knows perfectly well that he can demolish them whenever he pleases."[94] Growth in virtue and true apostolic zeal are impossible without a parallel growth in this virtue.

This is especially true of charity, since "the dwelling place of charity is humility,"[95] which fosters a true appreciation for others. In contrast, many faults against charity are preceded by sins of vanity, pride, envy, and the selfish desire to excel over others. "Charity spurs us to make progress on the spiritual path," St. Augustine says, "while pride leads us to fall."[96]

Some points to consider with regard to this virtue are the following: whether the person being guided is growing in self-knowledge; whether one's defects and errors are the source of an optimistic and hopeful struggle, or instead lead to discouragement and carelessness; whether one has true sorrow and contrition for failures and falls, and goes trustingly to sacramental confession. Other aspects of humility to consider are: whether the person being guided has a real trust in God and the supernatural means, and is not relying simply on one's own strength; whether lack of trust in oneself is accompanied by a strong trust in God, so as not to become discouraged; how the person receives corrections, indications, suggestions, etc.

We have to always keep very much in mind that pride is the devil's main ally in trying to undermine the work the Holy Spirit carries out in souls. Pride is the greatest hindrance to fidelity in corresponding to grace, to family life, to friendship. It is the "root and mother" of all sins, including the most serious ones.[97]

---

94. St. John Vianney, *Sermon on Humility*.
95. St. Augustine, *On Virginity*, no. 51.
96. St. Augustine, *Expositions on the Psalms*, 120, 5.
97. See St. Thomas Aquinias, *Summa Theologica*, II–II, q. 162, a. 7–8.

Pride is the false valuation of one's own qualities and a disordered desire for self-glory. Along with the selfishness to which it is so closely tied (seeing everything in terms of what is of benefit to oneself), pride lies at the origin of every sin and failure to make progress on the path.

Selfishness is frequently reflected in an interior monologue, centered on one's own interests and aspirations; there conflicts arise or fester, objectivity is lost, and one always comes out exalted. A selfish person shows an excessive concern for personal interests—one's health, profession, rest, future, external image—along with an obvious lack of abandonment and trust in God. How many personal problems, angry conflicts and useless worries are caused by pride and selfishness![98]

More difficult to uproot is pride disguised as humility. True humility has certain unmistakable qualities. Those who are truly humble are loath to make negative judgments about others; they are grateful persons, quick to excuse the possible failures of others and slow to justify themselves. In their work, they don't seek the praise of others, and if praise comes, they direct it immediately to God. All their hope is placed in God, who is the true source of their happiness: it is he who gives meaning to everything they do.

Humility is shown not so much in contempt for oneself as in forgetting oneself, recognizing with joy that everything we have has been received from God. Humility leads us to realize and sense deeply that we are small children of God who find all their strength in the strong arms of their Father.[99]

---

98. "How many through their pride and imagination, enter upon Calvaries that have nothing to do with Christ's!" (St. Josemaría Escrivá, *The Way of the Cross* [London: Scepter, 1982], Third Station, Point 5).

99. "You told me, in confidence, that in your prayer you would open your heart to God with these words: 'I think of my wretchedness, which seems to be on the increase despite the graces you give me. It must be due to my failure to correspond. I know that I am completely unprepared for the enterprise you are asking of me. And when I read in the newspapers of so very many highly qualified and respected men, with formidable talents, and no lack of financial resources, speaking, writing, organizing CONTINUED

The saints advise us to contemplate the great good humility works in the soul and its absolute necessity for the interior life. They advise us to desire it zealously and beseech God for it; to bear small daily humiliations joyfully and to rectify frequently our intention, seeking God's glory in everything; to forget ourselves and serve others, striving to make life more pleasant for them. Above all, we learn to be humble by meditating on Christ's passion and death, his acceptance of such great humiliation, letting himself be led "like a lamb that is led to the slaughter" (Is 53:7), and also by contemplating his humility in the Holy Eucharist, where he waits for us to visit him and speak to him.

The royal path to humility is centered on imitating Jesus in his self-giving and constant availability for others. Our holiness consists not in an external imitation of Jesus, but in allowing our entire being to be transformed by Christ. "Put off the old nature with its practices and put on the new nature," St. Paul urges the Colossians (Col 3:9–10). This renewal of our entire being means striving to uproot defects and anything not in conformity with Christ's life,[100] but above all it means striving to ensure that the way we react towards others, the way we evaluate created realities, and the way we accept tribulation become each day closer to that of Christ in similar circumstances. Our entire life becomes then in a certain sense a prolongation of his, for God has "predestined

---

in defense of your kingdom . . . I look at myself, and see that I'm a nobody: ignorant, poor: in a word, so little. This would fill me with shame if I did not know that you want me to be so. But Lord Jesus, you know how gladly I have put my ambition at your feet. . . . To have faith and love, to be loving, believing, suffering. In these things I *do* want to be rich and learned: but no more rich or learned than you, in your limitless Mercy, have wanted me to be. I desire to put all my prestige and honor into fulfilling your most just and most lovable will'" (St. Josemaría Escrivá, *The Forge*, no. 822).

100. This struggle has to be very concrete and realistic, because one often finds "a soul that has just made a resolution of being *humble of heart* or *to accept with joy any kind of humiliation*, and a few moments later cries to heaven if anyone has had the imprudence of causing them a small bother, or an involuntary and insignificant humiliation" (Antonio Royo Marín, *Teologia de la perfeccion cristiana*, p. 573).

[us] to be conformed to the image of his Son" (Rom 8:29). Divine grace, the more we correspond to the action of the Holy Spirit, makes us ever more similar to the Master.

Trying to help people to "forget themselves," an attitude so closely linked to humility, requires confronting the deep roots of disordered self-love that often lie hidden within, in order to apply the required remedies. In first place is the remedy of interior mortification—rejecting thoughts, memories, or images that center attention on oneself and lead to self-complacency. Interior mortification is also required when one's thoughts are centered on bitter or painful experiences, an attitude that betrays a spirit more humiliated than humble and that sows disquiet and sadness in the soul. Often this self-centeredness is the sign of a disguised concupiscence that is difficult to uproot. The disordered "thinking about oneself" is the source of a lack of love for God and many omissions in charity and the apostolate.

Sometimes this concern about oneself can take on the semblance of virtue, when thoughts such as the following arise: Am I truly effective? Am I really going forward in my interior life? Do others appreciate my efforts? Do I have this or that defect? The spiritual counselor will know if these thoughts are helpful to the extent that they lead that person to struggle to improve. That is, do they lead to contrition, to effective and optimistic resolutions, and to a deeper humility, with the realization that our Lord, in spite of everything, is counting on us? Self-forgetfulness leads to giving oneself to others with a readiness to serve them.

POVERTY AND DETACHMENT

Poverty is a Christian virtue that our Lord asks of everyone— religious, priests, parents, lawyers, students. . . . But many books of spirituality fail to highlight the fact that Christians in the midst of the world also need to live this virtue. Hence the paradoxical situation that its practice is often considered not in reference to lay men and women who live in the world, but rather in regard to religious who, by their proper vocation, are called to give public and official witness to their *contemptus mundi*—their separation from the world. Something similar happens with other Christian virtues such as temperance, obedience, humility, and industriousness, which everyone who aspires to follow Christ needs to live.

The Christian virtue of poverty is essential to follow our Lord, with the detachment from created goods that it entails: "Whoever of you does not renounce all that he has cannot be my disciple" (Lk 14:33). We have to teach those living in the world how to live it well, especially with so much external pressure from a consumer society and its superfluous expenses, luxury items, expensive travel plans, and mindless pastimes. Without real detachment, growth in holiness is impossible. Love for poverty purifies our heart, annulling a baser love that is trying to drag us down: "the concupiscence of the eyes" (1 Jn 2:16), the disordered desire for earthly goods. And "any lessening of concupiscence," St. Augustine says, "means an increase in charity."[101]

Poverty is a sign of trust in God; it keeps our eyes fixed on our true goods. For the ordinary Christian it is shown in "detachment, trust in God, temperance, and a readiness to share with others."[102] In spiritual direction we have to teach people how to harmonize two aspects "that may at first seem contradictory. There is on the one hand, *true poverty*, which is obvious and tangible and made up of definite things. This poverty should be an expression of faith in God and a sign that the heart is not satisfied with created things and aspires to the Creator; that it wants to be filled with love of God so as to be able to give

---

101. St. Augustine, *On 83 Diverse Questions*, q. 36.
102. Congregation for the Doctrine of the Faith, *Instruction on Christian Freedom and Liberation*, March 22, 1989, no. 66.

this same love to everyone."[103] At the same time, we need to stress that secularity, living in the middle of the world, requires that each Christian "be *one more amongst his fellow men*, sharing their way of life, their joys and happiness; working with them, loving the world and all the good things that exist in it; using all created things to solve the problems of human life and to establish a spiritual and material environment which will foster personal and social development."[104]

In spiritual guidance, then, we help people to live this virtue in specific and real ways, teaching them to love and practice it in the context of one's daily life. Those who have begun traveling the path towards holiness need to be fully convinced that without it they cannot follow Christ. Each should be able to say: "I am truly poor as our Lord asked." And this should be true also when they possess abundant goods, which they have to administer and make bear fruit, and of which they will have to render an account to God.

Our Lord's words continue to resound throughout the ages: "You cannot serve both God and mammon" (Lk 16:13). It is impossible to please God and bring him to others if we are not ready to make sacrifices—at times costly ones—in the possession and use of material goods. Christ's warning is of particular importance in our day and age when it might strike many people as strange, with an unbridled desire for material goods daily feeding people's greed. So many aspire to have more, to spend more, to enjoy as much pleasure as possible, as if that were our aim here on earth or what brings us real happiness.

In sacred Scripture, poverty expresses the readiness to place ourselves completely in God's hands, abandoning the control of our life to him and not seeking any other security. *Poverty shows the spiritual rectitude of a person who doesn't want to find the foundation of*

---

103. *Conversations*, no. 111.
104. Ibid.

his life in the goods of this world, even when he may in fact possess them. It is the firm resolution to have only one Lord, since no one can serve two masters (see Mt 6:24). When one's heart is set on riches and earthly goods of whatever form, these become an idol—the idolatry, the covetousness that St. Paul told the first Christians should not even be mentioned among them (see Eph 5:3–5).

REAL POVERTY

Real poverty has many practical manifestations. It requires being detached from material possessions, making use of them as good things created by God, but never considering anything that, with a bit of good will, we could do without.[105] "If we are truly happy with possessing only what is necessary," St. Augustine says, "we will realize how many of the things we have are superfluous; but if we seek what is superfluous, we will never have enough."[106] The human heart can be filled only by God, and it will never be satisfied by earthly goods.

The same holy doctor advised Christians of his time: "Seek what is sufficient, seek what is enough. The rest is a burden, not a balm; it drags us down, rather than elevates us."[107] This reality is seen clearly in spiritual guidance. True Christian poverty is incompatible not only with superfluous goods, but also with an anxious concern over necessary ones. When we find someone with this disordered anxiousness, it is a sign that their spiritual life is becoming lukewarm and their love starting to cool.

---

105. "We have to make demands on ourselves in our daily lives. In this way we will not go about inventing false problems and ingenious needs which, in the last analysis, are prompted by conceit, capriciousness and a comfort-loving and lazy approach to life. We ought to be striding towards God at a fast pace, carrying no dead weights or impediments which might hinder our progress" (St. Josemaría Escrivá, *Friends of God*, no. 125).

106. St. Augustine, *Expositions on the Psalms*, 148, 4.

107. Ibid, *Sermon* 85, 6.

Especially among laypeople, poverty should also be shown in *the positive aspect of making good use of one's talents*. In the context of work, this entails making them bear fruit for the benefit of the whole of society—not only for one's own support. Poverty is shown by diligently fulfilling our professional duties—by caring for work instruments, whether or not they are one's own, so they are not ruined, and by avoiding excessive expenses, even when paid for by one's business.

Poverty means "genuinely not considering anything as one's own;"[108] choosing the worst for ourselves (above all when at home) if the choice isn't noticeable;[109] accepting with peace and joy scarcity, the lack of even what is necessary; avoiding personal expenses motivated by caprice, vanity, the desire for luxury, or laziness; being austere with oneself—for example, in regard to frivolous publications, food, and drink—and always being generous with others.

Christian detachment refers not only to financial concerns and their consequences; it also means being detached from our health, from the good plans we have made, etc. This in turn requires "a long-term preparation, by practicing daily a holy detachment from self, so that we are prepared to bear sickness or misfortune gracefully if our Lord permits them. Begin now to make use of everyday opportunities: something you may have to do without, small recurring pains, voluntary mortifications, and also put into practice the Christian virtues."[110]

---

108. St. Josemaría Escrivá, *The Forge*, no. 524.

109. See St. Josemaría Escrivá, *The Way*, no. 635.

110. St. Josemaría Escrivá, *Friends of God*, no. 124.

St. Teresa wrote this advice to her nuns, which is relevant for everyone: "The first thing we must strive for is to rid ourselves of our love for our bodies, for some of us are by nature such lovers of comfort that there is no small amount of work in this area" (*The Way of Perfection*, 10, 5; Carmelite Studies translation, vol. II, p. 77). In another place she wrote: "What is the purpose of life and health, save that they be lost for so great a King and Lord? Believe me, sisters, you will never go astray in following this path" (*Foundations*, 28, 18; Carmelite Studies translation, vol. III, p. 257).

In spiritual guidance, we should remind people from time to time of the spiritual fruits of poverty and detachment. By this virtue, the soul readies itself to receive supernatural goods and the heart expands, making room for a sincere concern for others. God grants a special joy to a detached soul, even amid the privation of what seems most necessary.

WORK

In giving us the example of his life, Jesus spent most of his time working as a carpenter and (toward the end of his life) as a teacher. Therefore, imitating Christ means working a lot and working well. Work is closely tied to many aspects of the interior life and unity of life. It is a very important topic to bring up when guiding others, insofar as it is related to the interior life and apostolate (although naturally one will not discuss other aspects of work about which the person seeking spiritual advice has a duty to maintain silence of office). Normally, the focus should be on the *way* one works: whether work helps the person to draw closer to God or not; how one is striving to sanctify it; how charity is being lived with those one works with; whether one is fulfilling in an exemplary way, at times with heroism, the ethical obligations that work brings with it; how one is striving to truly be a contemplative in the midst of one's work.

Spiritual guidance does not get involved in the content of a person's work or professional decisions. However, frequently people ask for advice in important decisions that affect their interior life, family life, etc. This advice, which the person concerned can make prudent use of, obviously refers to the moral aspect involved—that is, how it affects their struggle for sanctity or other people, not the *technical* content of their work.

The spiritual guide should remind people that we have been created by God *ut operaretur* (see Gen 2:5, 15), to work, to dominate the earth, and lead it to its completion, making God's perfections shine forth here on earth. We thereby achieve our own perfection, and we also draw closer to God.[111] Work is a great good, not a punishment. It is as natural to us as walking or breathing. Love for our work, for our professional vocation, is an essential part of the call to holiness and to attaining human maturity. A person unable to work seriously would find it difficult, perhaps impossible, to go forward in the interior life. It is important to strive for professional prestige, to trade with all our talents (see Mt 25:15ff), to make the most of the qualities we have been endowed with. A saint living in the midst of the world serves society by working well, being exemplary and competent in one's activities, and living justice and the other moral virtues well.

The struggle for sanctity in the middle of the world also entails the duty to strive to Christianize culture, politics, science, art, and social relationships.[112] Jesus, in his years of hidden life, was known among his neighbors as "the carpenter, the son of Mary" (Mk 6:3); he was known by his work, to which he dedicated most of his life. And in those years of hidden life, he was redeeming humanity. Work done with human perfection is a path of sanctity.[113] At the same time, it is a natural channel for apostolate, because it is one of the most important places of human interaction.

---

111. "We have reminded Christians of the wonderful words of Genesis which tell us that God created man so that he might work, and we have concentrated on the example of Christ, who spent most of his life on earth working as a craftsman in a village. We love human work, which he chose as his state in life, which he cultivated and sanctified. We see in work, in men's noble creative toil not only one of the highest human values, an indispensable means to social progress and to greater justice in the relations between men, but also a sign of God's Love for his creatures, and of men's love for each other and for God: we see in work a means of perfection, a way to sanctity" (*Conversations*, no. 10).

112. See Bl. John Paul II, *Christifideles Laici*, nos. 42–43.

113. Some of the human characteristics of well-done work are: intensity, order, punctuality, good use of time, eagerness to improve, initiatives, care for little things. Our Lord *omnia bene fecit*, he did everything well (Mk 7:37), including material things.

FINDING OUR LORD

It is in the midst of our daily work that we have to *find our Lord* (asking for his help, offering him our work, realizing we are helping to complete his creation, even if in seemingly small ways that are of little importance). And it is there that we have to *exercise charity* (cultivating the virtues that make life pleasant for others, providing small services to those around us, praying for our colleagues and their families, helping them to resolve their problems). Our struggle for sanctity is not carried on *in spite of* our work, but rather *through* it—taking advantage of our work to unite ourselves to Christ's redemptive sacrifice on the Cross, made present at Mass. All the varied incidents of our daily work, some pleasant and others less so, are where we find our Lord, making our work a daily offering to God.

Nor should we forget that our professional vocation is part of our divine vocation; it is where we have to strive to attain sanctity and carry out apostolate, living a *unity of life* with Christ at the center. The need to acquire professional prestige can never be a cover for selfish goals—for vanity and self-affirmation, for the desire to stand out. Since we all have the disordered tendency to seek our own glory rather than God's, it is important to frequently examine *why* we are working intensely.

Professional success, for a Christian, does not mean simply obtaining a good position or developing a brilliant career; rather, it means fulfilling God's will, even in the context of our professional duties. True prestige is not a question of "rising high on the ladder" (and even less so, at any price). If ever the danger should arise of overvaluing one's professional work, disconnected from its sanctifying value, we should remind the person involved of the supernatural sterility of working in that way, losing sight of the one thing that really matters:

holiness.[114] Interior life is otherwise reduced to a few stale norms, and one's unity of life disrupted, with God set aside in an out-of-the-way corner. We should also remind people of the duty to provide a good example and to know and live very well the demands of personal and professional ethics in their work, even when others fail to do so.

Signs of a right intention in one's work are, among others: carrying out an effective apostolate among one's colleagues, dedicating sufficient time to one's family, fulfilling one's daily obligations towards God, seeing one's work as a service to God's glory and to society, and finding the time needed for one's own spiritual and human formation.[115]

It's a warning sign when the person being guided brings up many complaints about work, viewing it with a negative outlook. Work should be the opportunity for a continual exercise of the human and supernatural virtues. A mother working in her home should offer to God the care of her children and husband, in the thousand small details that make a house into a true home; while a doctor, working with professional competence, offers the kind and friendly treatment of each patient; and a nurse, hours filled with continual service, offers treating each sick person as if he or she were Christ himself.[116]

---

114. "You must be careful: don't let your professional success or failure—which will certainly come—make you forget, even for a moment, what the true aim of your work is: the glory of God!" (St. Josemaría Escrivá, *The Forge*, no. 704).

115. This rectitude should be found when beginning our work, in carrying it out, and when the work is finished. It is present at every moment: it is not like a label that one adds at the end. In spiritual guidance we should teach people to frequently examine the interior dispositions with which they work.

116. "This Christian spirituality of work should be a heritage shared by all. Especially in the modern age, the spirituality of work should show the maturity called for by the tensions and restlessness of mind and heart" (Bl. John Paul II, *Laborem Exercens*, no. 25).

Health, Sickness, Rest

Christians should see life as God's gift, as an immense good—a gift that doesn't belong to us, and one we must care for. We are meant to live as long as God wants, having carried out the task he entrusted to us. And therefore, out of love for God and others, we need to observe the norms of prudence in caring for our own health.

Those who are sick or who find themselves exhausted require special attention. And this is especially true if those in this situation have dedicated a good part of their lives to God's service. In these circumstances, the will of that person could find itself weaker, with less energy for the struggle, and discouragement could creep in, or old problems resurface. We have to help anyone in this situation realize that these difficult moments are not mean to be sterile, but rather are wanted or permitted by God as an opportunity to grow in virtue.

No matter what the circumstances were that led to this condition, it can be a means of sanctity and apostolate, as can everything in our life. Our Lord himself experienced fatigue, and he taught us how to react in such moments. He often ended the day exhausted by intense work. Mark recounts that, during a storm on the lake, Jesus was sleeping on the boat after spending the whole day preaching (see Mk 4:38). He was so exhausted that not even the storm-tossed waves could awaken him. He wasn't pretending to be asleep to test his disciples; he truly was exhausted.

We also see Christ sitting by a well, tired out after a long journey. Sometimes he would leave the crowds behind and go with his disciples to a quiet place, so they could rest for a while.[117] Even in those moments of real physical exhaustion,

---

117. "The Lord made his disciples rest to teach those who govern that we cannot work without interruption" (St. Jerome, *Commentary on the Gospel of St. Mark*).

Jesus is redeeming mankind. His example shows us how to accept sickness and tiredness and draw fruit from them.

We should encourage people in this situation to offer up their suffering, whether short-lived or lasting for many months or years, to obey and keep trying to serve others, even if it seems they have no strength for anything.[118] When sickness comes, our first thought should be: "From now on I have to be a holy sick person."

When we suffer from an illness, we come to understand better how our Lord sometimes blesses with the Cross, especially when he wants to grant great graces. If he lets us experience his Cross with greater intensity, it is a sign that he considers us especially beloved children. Physical pain, humiliations, failures, or family setbacks can and will arise. But rather than becoming sad, we have to run to God's fatherly love and seek his consolation. His help is never lacking to turn those apparent evils into a great good, both for our own souls and for the entire Church.

Sickness can be a marvelous teacher of humility. Realizing that we can't do everything on our own and that we need others, accepting that situation while it lasts, obeying and letting oneself be helped, are all a royal road to humility. Sickness can also help us live detachment and foster the virtue of fortitude, since often one has to learn how to work without the physical strength needed to do so without a special effort.

An Apostolic Means as Well

Sickness can also be a marvelous apostolic means, not only by offering our suffering to God (which is already a lot), but also

---

118. The saints too experienced moments of weakness and fatigue. "There come days," wrote St. Teresa of Avila, "when a single word distresses me and I long to leave the world altogether, for everything in it seems to weary me. And I am not the only person to be like this, for I have noticed the same thing in many people better than myself, so I know it can happen" (*The Way of Perfection*, 38, 6). On the sick person's struggle for holiness, see Miguel Ángel Monge, *Medicina Pastoral* (Pamplona: Eunsa, 2010).

because those who are sick can greatly help others by their behavior and words to come closer to God. Sometimes it can even be one's illness that provides the opportunity to speak about God. St. Paul told the Galatians that it was a "bodily ailment" that had offered him the chance to preach to them and help them convert to Christ (see Gal 4:13). In giving spiritual direction to people who are sick, we have to insist—in new ways—that no circumstance should separate us from love for God and for all men and women.

Suffering is a privileged way to share in Christ's redemptive Cross[119] and a means God makes use of to purify us of our faults and imperfections and unite us more closely to him.[120]

Spiritual directors can encourage people in this situation to fight against centering their thoughts on themselves, to obey, and to give themselves to others, insofar as possible, in small services. Their first concern should be to seek our Lord, even if

---

119. The most ardent desire of our Lord "is to enkindle in our hearts the flame of love and sacrifice that consumes his own; and if we correspond at least a bit to this desire, our heart will soon become a fire of love that will consume little by little the dross built up by our faults and convert us into victims of expiation, happy to attain, at the cost of a little suffering, a greater purity, a closer union with our Beloved; happy also to complete the passion of our Saviour for the good of the Church and of souls (*Col* 1:24) . . . At the feet of the Crucified One, we will come to understand that in the present world it is impossible to love without sacrifice, and that sacrifice is sweet for the one who loves" (Tanquerey, *La divinización del sufrimiento* [Madrid: Rialp, 1960], pp. 203–204).

120. "Down through the centuries and generations it has been seen that in suffering there is concealed a particular power that draws a person interiorly close to Christ, a special grace. To this grace many saints, such as St. Francis of Assisi, St. Ignatius of Loyola, and others, owe their profound conversion. A result of such a conversion is not only that the individual discovers the salvific meaning of suffering but above all that he becomes a completely new person. He discovers a new dimension, as it were, of his entire life and vocation. This discovery is a particular confirmation of the spiritual greatness which in man surpasses the body in a way that is completely beyond compare. When this body is gravely ill, totally incapacitated, and the person is almost incapable of living and acting, all the more do interior maturity and spiritual greatness become evident, constituting a touching lesson to those who are healthy and normal" (Bl. John Paul II, *Salvifici Doloris*, no. 26).

they don't "feel anything." Every moment is a good moment to love. It is important to foster a greater piety in them, a greater closeness to the Master: "Come to me, all who labor and are heavy laden, and I will give you rest" (Mt 11:28).

We should also encourage them to bear their sickness with human refinement, trying not to complain, obeying the doctor, and doing everything possible to recover their health. For "when we are sick we can get very tiresome: 'they aren't looking after me properly, nobody cares about me, I'm not getting the attention I deserve, nobody understands me . . .' The devil, who is always on the lookout, can attack from any angle. When people are ill his tactics consist in stirring up a kind of psychosis in them so as to draw them away from God and fill the atmosphere with bitterness, or destroy that treasure of merits earned (on behalf of souls everywhere) by pain—that is, when it is borne with supernatural optimism, when it is loved! Therefore, if God wills that we be struck down by some affliction, take it as a sign that he considers us mature enough to be associated even more closely with his redeeming Cross."[121]

Teaching People to Rest and Sanctify Rest

In fulfilling our duties, in giving ourselves in apostolic service to others, it is natural that we sometimes become tired. Therefore, we should teach people how to rest, staying close to God, because rest is another human reality that we need to sanctify.

By uniting our fatigue to the tiredness Christ experienced, offering it for the redemption of souls, we find our own burden easier to bear. Finding ways to rest that enable us to practice charity with others greatly helps to alleviate our own tiredness, although it may require a bit more effort to do so. The moments spent restoring our depleted energies can never be

---

121. St. Josemaría Escrivá, *Friends of God*, no. 124.

isolated from the rest of our spiritual struggle, as though permitting us to seek selfish compensations, to seek ourselves in the end. Love never takes a rest.

It is also good at times to consider how Jesus himself made use of the moments he spent restoring his strength, so as to be able to go out again in search of souls. While he was resting by Jacob's well, a woman came to fill her water jug. Our Lord took advantage of that opportunity to spur the Samaritan woman to radically change her life (see Jn 4:8ff). Great fruit can be drawn from moments of special tiredness. We should encourage souls to offer up even their exhaustion or apparent uselessness. At times it will not be possible to take a few days of rest, and we will have to joyfully offer God the necessity of carrying out the same job with less strength. St. Teresa of Avila recounts how our Lord once told her that "now was not the time for rest, but that I should hurry to establish these houses; that he found his rest with the souls living in them."[122]

In spiritual guidance we need to remind people of their duty to rest, so as to be able to serve God and others with more strength and joy. But we should also remind them that "to rest is not to do nothing: it is to relax in activities which demand less effort."[123] Rest is an opportunity for interior enrichment and frequently for doing more apostolate, strengthening a friendship, etc. One should not confuse rest with laziness. It should not become an escape, for in every circumstance of life we are called to be *alter Christus*, another Christ. A person who needs "to escape," to turn aside from intimacy with the Master or concern for one's family, lacks unity of life. We have to learn for ourselves and teach others how to rest in God: "Oh Jesus! I rest in you,"[124] St. Josemaría

---

122. St. Teresa of Avila, *Spiritual Testimonies*, no. 6 (Carmelite Studies translation, vol. III), p. 387.
123. St. Josemaría Escrivá, *The Way*, no. 357.
124. Ibid., no. 732.

Escrivá used to say. "I have always seen rest as time set aside from daily tasks, never as days of idleness. Rest means recuperation: to gain strength, form ideals and make plans. In other words, it means a change of occupation, so that you can come back later with a new impetus to your daily job."[125]

Sometimes it can be prudent to advise an especially tired person to see a doctor. Most of the time, however, it is a matter of using the ordinary means: following a schedule, dedicating enough time to sleep, taking regular walks, or making a simple excursion. Failing to live order in one's daily life could often be a sign of laziness and lack of struggle, more dangerous to the extent that it leads to a weakening in one's interior life and a falling into activism. A person who lives with a bit of order will habitually find ways to rest prudently, amid demanding and self-sacrificing activity.

More than a few people dedicate time spent resting from work to activities that fail to facilitate or even hinder an encounter with Christ. Far from letting oneself be dragged along by a paganized environment, it is important to be careful in choosing the place for a vacation, planning for a trip, or engaging in the weekend activity that helps us rest for a while. Our rest should be ruled by the same norm as our work: love for God and neighbor. We always have to guard against giving in to our whims, creating an artificial need for special trips or expenses, and frequenting frivolous surroundings. At every moment we must seek union with God and be concerned about others, listening to them and trying to help them. It is always a good time to love. Love does not allow any blank spaces. Jesus rested out of obedience to the Law of Moses, because of the demands of friendship, or due to his own fatigue—never because he had become tired of serving others. Likewise, we should never say: "Now it's my turn!" The moments we spend recovering lost

---

125. St. Josemaría Escrivá, *Furrow*, no. 514.

strength can never be a pagan "escape," or a hindrance to interior life, poverty, and detachment.

BY WAY OF A CONCLUSION

I asked a priest who is a good friend of mine, with experience in giving spiritual guidance, to write down what he said to me in a conversation about this book. I think his words can serve as a conclusion to the book, since they provide a sound framework for personal spiritual direction.

Those called to provide spiritual assistance face a great challenge. Theirs is a particularly delicate service, since the only two protagonists in this "business" are God and the person seeking guidance. The spiritual guide has to shun any hint of self-affirmation; in some way, he has to learn to contemplate the interior world of the other person with the reserve, skill, and humility of the professional whose success consists in helping another person to improve while his own role is scarcely noticed.[126]

We might compare the work of spiritual direction with that of an expert asked to give a discreet evaluation of the value of a family chest of jewels acquired over a long period of time, with objects of varying values and conditions.

In requesting that service, the owner is not trying to hand over the responsibility for its care and much less its ownership. Rather, he is seeking someone who can advise him on the value of what he owns and how to protect it, providing supervision on a regular basis to help maintain it and conserve its value.

The owner of the chest goes to the expert because he wants to. No one has obliged him to do so, especially not the expert himself since he has no power whatsoever to oblige anyone to make use of his services. The owner asks for this

---

126. The need for someone to gently "shake us" out of our self-complacency is not restricted to the strictly religious sphere, but is a demand of our human condition itself.

evaluation because he himself does not have the information or discernment needed to sort out all the technical questions involved. He expects the person he has sought out to provide advice, support, and guidance, but never to adopt an attitude of dominion or control.

When the owner brings him the chest, the expert waits for him to open it. If because of its age or other factors, it proves difficult to open, he does not take the initiative to open it himself as if it were his own; he intervenes only if asked to. His knowledge and experience, shown with a serene attitude, are what enable him to win over the owner's trust, convincing him that if he is allowed to open it, there is less danger of damaging the lock. In contrast, if he were to assume a role that doesn't belong to him, he would generate a lack of trust that would in all likelihood end up undoing all his work.

Once the chest is opened, the owner takes out—in the order and the way he wishes—the objects contained inside. It would be out of place for the expert to begin handling the various objects out of curiosity or caprice, and even less to claim ownership over any of them.

If the owner hides some objects from the examination of the expert, it would certainly be inconsistent with the advice being sought; but this still wouldn't give the expert the right to demand that the owner show him everything. If he were to sense any lack of transparency in the responses to his questions, he would try to present them better, making clear that he has no interest in entering into what is not his business, since his mission is to help, not to meddle.

In spite of everything, if he is not given the information needed for his work, he should try to gain his client's confidence, making him see that the help he has requested is only possible if the expert has access to everything inside. And no matter what happens, he should always maintain a calm and professional attitude; it would make no sense to try to resolve that lack of transparency by adopting a cynical or wounding tone, being angry because he has not been fully informed. The owner, who is in charge of making decisions about the chest, has contracted with him. If in the end he is not provided with what he needs to carry out his work, he either has to abandon it, or perhaps wait a while, using all the means at his disposal to bring things to light.

When he finds that an object requires a more detailed look because of its singular or poor condition, the expert will explain this clearly to the owner so that he knows the situation and can decide what he wants to do. He will try to give the owner opportune reasons for doing what he thinks necessary to ensure that the treasure is given its true value—perhaps even going to another specialist—but always making it clear that the ultimate decision is up to the owner alone.

If he judges it necessary to set an object aside because it could damage the other objects owing to its deteriorated condition, he frames this advice in a positive context, reminding the owner of the great value of the chest and its contents. And in doing so, he makes it clear that the removal of the harmful item is the owner's decision, not his. If for whatever reason the owner doesn't see himself as capable of getting rid of it, the expert can offer to provide that service, since his training enables him to know how to do it properly. But he will never act on his own, as though in giving advice he can do whatever he likes.

When the moment comes for formulating his recommendations, he will present them in a positive light. Although he may suggest some changes in how the possessions are cared for or advise getting rid of some of them, he will stress that the material as a whole is valuable. Even if the content is nothing special, it always has the value of a family heirloom. Besides, one shouldn't lose sight of the fact that not only is the content valuable, but the chest itself is also of great value.

Finally, since it is a confidential consultation, the expert knows that his knowledge of the chest doesn't give him any right of ownership, or even the right to reveal that he knows its value or has been entrusted with that task. The only person he can discuss this work with is the owner. If anyone has to decide what should be made known and to whom, it is the owner, not the one consulted, since his role his simply to give advice.

In short, if a faithful friend should be seen as a treasure,[127] how much more so is this true of a guide, someone who can advise us what means to use, someone we can talk with about our ideas and plans, and someone who can assure us that the route we are taking is suited to the goal we seek and that we are truly making progress in the right direction.

---

127. "A faithful friend is a sturdy shelter: he that has found one has found a treasure. There is nothing so precious as a faithful friend, and no scales can measure his excellence. A faithful friend is an elixir of life; and those who fear the Lord will find him" (Sir 6:14–16).